A Blueprint for Teacher Retention

In this practical and inspiring guide, educational leaders are invited to tackle the teacher retention challenge head-on by creating intentional systems to keep passionate, motivated educators in classrooms.

Grounded in a research-based Teacher Retention Model, this book equips school leaders with actionable strategies to combat teacher burnout and turnover. It delves into the complex nature of today's educational demands and their impact on teacher well-being, providing leaders with tools to build environments where educators can thrive. Step-by-step exercises and real-world examples illustrate how leaders can transform their schools into places where teachers feel valued, supported, and energized. Finally, the book offers a broader perspective on how school districts can align policies and practices to bolster teacher retention at the local level.

Whether you're a principal or district administrator, this book is a vital blueprint for reversing the tide of teacher turnover and building schools that teachers, and students, deserve.

James A. Bailey is a former teacher, principal, principal consultant, and superintendent. He is Co-founder and Managing Partner of Brass Tacks Innovations, a firm specializing in teacher retention, and serves as Academic Program Coordinator and Core Faculty Member in Educational Administration and Leadership at Walden University, USA.

Also Available from Routledge Eye on Education
(www.routledge.com/eyeoneducation)

The International Education Leadership Companion: Lessons and Best Practices from Expert Leaders
Lindsay Prendergast, Catarina Song Chen, Colin Brown

Leadership Teams in America's Best Schools: Improving the Lives of All Students
Joseph F. Johnson, Jr., Cynthia L. Uline, Stanley J. Munro, Jr., Francisco Escobedo

Making Community Schools a Reality: Harnessing Your Power as a School Leader through Collaboration
Emily L. Woods

Wholehearted School Leadership: Rewiring our Schools for Courage, Justice, Learning, and Connection
Kathryn Fishman-Weaver

Data Analysis for Continuous School Improvement, 5th Edition
Victoria L. Bernhardt

Culturally Conscious Decision-Making for School Leaders: A Toolkit for Creating a More Equitable School Culture
Shauna McGee

Teacher Leadership Practice in High-Performing Schools: A Blueprint for Excellence
Jeremy D. Visone

A Blueprint for Teacher Retention: Leading Schools that Teachers Don't Want to Leave
James A. Bailey

A Blueprint for Teacher Retention

Leading Schools that Teachers Don't Want to Leave

James A. Bailey

Designed cover image: © Getty Images

First published 2026
by Routledge
605 Third Avenue, New York, NY 10158

and by Routledge
4 Park Square, Milton Park, Abingdon, Oxon, OX14 4RN

Routledge is an imprint of the Taylor & Francis Group, an informa business

© 2026 James A. Bailey

The right of James A. Bailey to be identified as author of this work has been asserted in accordance with sections 77 and 78 of the Copyright, Designs and Patents Act 1988.

All rights reserved. No part of this book may be reprinted or reproduced or utilised in any form or by any electronic, mechanical, or other means, now known or hereafter invented, including photocopying and recording, or in any information storage or retrieval system, without permission in writing from the publishers.

Trademark notice: Product or corporate names may be trademarks or registered trademarks, and are used only for identification and explanation without intent to infringe.

ISBN: 978-1-041-04551-9 (hbk)
ISBN: 978-1-041-04550-2 (pbk)
ISBN: 978-1-003-62876-7 (ebk)

DOI: 10.4324/9781003628767

Typeset in Optima
by SPi Technologies India Pvt Ltd (Straive)

Access the Support Material: www.routledge.com/9781041045502

This book is dedicated to the thousands of teachers who have chosen to surrender their passion to restore their well-being and to the thousands of principals searching for a way to regenerate passion in those who remain.

Contents

Support Material — ix
Acknowledgements — x
Meet the Author — xii
Preface — xiii

1. The Growing Challenge for Leaders — 1
2. The Teacher Retention Model — 14
3. The Role of Adult Social-Emotional Skills in Retention — 33
4. Developing the Adult Social-Emotional Path as a Retention Strategy — 53
5. Reducing Demands as a Retention Strategy — 85
6. Increasing Resources as a Retention Strategy — 118
7. The District's Role in Improving Teacher Retention — 155
8. Solving the Retention and Attrition Crisis — 179

Appendix A   Your Blueprint for Teacher Retention — 194
Appendix B   Well-being Diagnostic — 197
Appendix C   Personal Level Diagnostic — 201
Appendix D   Interpersonal Level Diagnostic — 205
Appendix E   Collective Level Diagnostic — 210
Appendix F   The Habit Formation Guide — 217
Appendix G   Habit Development Plan — 219

Contents

Appendix H Social-Emotional Walk-Through Protocol 221
*Appendix I   The Job Demands and Resources Diagnostic
              for Schools* 224
Appendix J   PDSA Planning Template 232
*Appendix K Developing a Theory of Action for
              District Support* 235

# Support Material

The appendices in this book are also available on the book product page online, so you can easily print them for use. To access these downloads, go to www.routledge.com/9781041045502 and click on the "Support Material" link.

Acknowledgements

I am deeply grateful to the many individuals who contributed to making this book possible. The origin of this book began in a casual conversation one day around the use of data and analytics in baseball with my business partner, Randy Weiner. We were discussing how, in baseball, the amount of physical stress placed on a pitcher's arm can now be measured using sensors. Right after we had finished a meeting with a group of principals on how to develop adult social-emotional skills in their schools, we both remarked how interesting it would be to use simple metrics or sensors to measure teacher stress. This idea sparked the thought of what a more intentional system for teacher retention using data could look like. Thanks to Randy for the good conversations that helped move this project forward.

I also thank the many students I have had the privilege of working with at Walden University, who focused on this issue for their dissertations and trusted me enough to apply the Job Demands-Resources Theory in their studies. Exploring this theory together and hearing about the various issues surrounding teacher retention from around the country gave me a deeper insight and perspective on this issue.

Additionally, I would like to thank my editors, Heather Jarrow and Sean Daly, at Routledge, who helped shepherd a series of ideas into a polished final idea aimed at solving a major issue in our educational system today. Your trust in the ideas is greatly appreciated.

Last, I would like to thank my family for providing me with a solid foundation of love and support. To my sons, Charlie, Connor, and Reed, I am thankful to be your dad. To Letty, I am thankful to have you as my daughter-in-law. To the newest member of our family and our first grandson, Walter,

Acknowledgements

I wish for you the best teachers in the world and a system that can support who you were born to be in the world. And finally, to the best partner in the world, Sharon, who indulges my habit of sticking my nose in a book or staring at my computer screen at all hours of the day. I couldn't have asked for a better person to go through life with.

Meet the Author

Dr. James Bailey is a dedicated educational leader, entrepreneur, and scholar committed to transforming schools and educational systems into environments where educators and students thrive. With a career spanning teaching, school and district leadership, consulting, and higher education, Dr. Bailey brings a wealth of practical experience and research-backed insights to the critical issue of teacher retention among other issues. He is the Co-founder and Managing Partner of Brass Tacks Innovations, a firm specializing in teacher retention, leadership development, and adult social-emotional learning. Currently, he also serves as an Academic Program Coordinator and Core Faculty Member in Educational Administration and Leadership at Walden University, guiding doctoral students in research related to educational leadership.

Dr. Bailey's work is characterized by a focus on continuous and measurable improvements, systems thinking, and the practical application of theory to challenging problems in education and organizations. His hands-on experience as a superintendent and principal has provided him with a deep understanding of the challenges and opportunities within educational systems. This background informs his latest work, *A Teacher Retention Blueprint: Creating Schools Teachers Don't Want to Leave*. He is also the author of *Building Learning Capacity in a Time of Uncertainty* (Routledge, 2021) and co-author (with Randy Weiner) of *The Daily SEL Leader: A Guided Journal* as well as numerous academic articles on social-emotional learning and school leadership. Through his writing and professional practice, Dr. Bailey aims to equip leaders with the strategies to build truly supportive and engaging schools.

Preface

For over 30 years, I have worked as a teacher, principal, superintendent, or college professor. In these various roles, I have evaluated teachers, led professional development for teachers, interviewed and hired numerous teachers, and worked with many teachers who were undecided about staying in the profession. Having grown up in a family of educators, I am a teacher at heart, as were my grandmother, mother, and father. Through all my experiences in both rural and urban settings, I have found that the majority of teachers are passionate and dedicated to their students and their profession. And yet, throughout the decades, I've witnessed an alarming trend of educators leaving the profession.

Even before the era of accountability, I began to take note of the literature on teacher turnover, attrition, and shortages in the late 1990s, as I was working on my doctoral degree. Then, throughout the early 2000s, I saw more shortages in critical areas. In the decade preceding COVID, I observed a striking difference in the districts I led: fewer teachers to interview, more teachers leaving for other employment, increased pushback against extra duties, and a higher number of teachers with serious health issues than ever before. I had always known teaching was a difficult job, but it dawned on me that this felt different than before: more serious, more challenging, more permanent.

I left K-12 education in 2018 to work at the college level, and when the COVID-19 pandemic hit in 2020, my interest in this issue accelerated. Throughout this ordeal, I began to wonder how teachers were being supported, and I delved into the research on adult social-emotional learning, teacher attrition, occupational health, teacher stress, and teacher emotions as more demographic reports emerged about the increasing numbers of teachers and principals leaving the profession. I began to understand that while COVID-19 was one serious cause of stress, burnout, and attrition, the alienation of teachers did not begin in 2020. It began much earlier. I had heard it but did not realize the seriousness of the issue until much too late.

Many well-intentioned politicians, leaders, and researchers have offered solutions, focused primarily on raising salaries and increasing benefits and inquiring about what it would take to attract more people into the teaching profession. While we know that teachers pay a salary tax, with starting salaries around 19% lower than those in other comparable professions (Economic Policy Institute, 2019), many young, passionate individuals enter the profession anyway, only to leave within five years, disillusioned by the current working conditions they encounter. The current attrition rate for teachers within the first five years of entering is close to 44%. The salary solution addresses the rational and economic aspect of a teacher's decision to enter or stay in the profession but is only one facet of the larger problem.

Organization of the Book

Salary and compensation are only one part of the equation, alongside workplace conditions, teachers' emotions, and overall well-being. So, how can we better understand the dynamic and systemic problem of teacher turnover and attrition? What follows in this book is my attempt to help district and school leaders, state leaders, and policymakers understand this issue more deeply, without placing blame but rather offering a new and different way to comprehend and solve the problem. Serious problems, such as increased teacher turnover and attrition, require that the education field examine the issue from as many new perspectives as possible until new solutions become apparent. This book aims to analyze this problem through a synthesis of fields as diverse as occupational health, stress psychology, organizational design, organizational behavior and psychology, emotional leadership, and affective science. I argue that by combining findings from these diverse fields, we may discover new solutions and begin to stem the tide of promising educators who prematurely leave their students.

The book examines the significant issue of teacher turnover and retention in eight chapters. Chapter 1 orients the reader to the problem of teacher turnover and attrition, supported by evidence from the increase in teacher stress, changes in the mental health of teachers, the impact of COVID-19 on teacher stress, rising teacher attrition, and growing teacher shortages. Chapter 2 introduces the Teacher Retention Model (TRM), which will be used to create a more intentional teacher retention system throughout the rest of the book. The chapter begins by exploring the eight key ideas that the TRM is based on, and then explains the TRM and how it helps define the working conditions within a school. The chapter next discusses the three primary strategies based on the model that school leaders can use to create an intentional retention system: developing adult social-emotional skills, including emotional leadership, reducing demands, and increasing resources.

Chapters 3–6 focus on the three primary strategies needed to create an intentional teacher retention system. Chapter 3 introduces the adult social-emotional climate as a path of influence and a critical resource for teacher retention, highlighting how supportive emotional leadership in schools can be a primary asset for reducing teacher turnover. The chapter argues that by developing better adult social-emotional and leadership skills, leaders can better lead the adult social-emotional climate for their educators as a primary strategy for creating an intentional retention system. Chapter 4 extends the discussion of the adult social-emotional path and explores the primary skills that school leaders and other educators can practice and develop at the personal, interpersonal, and organizational levels. Chapter 5 focuses on examining the three primary categories of demands placed on teachers, which carry a heavier burden than they should, potentially leading to excessive stress and burnout. The central argument presented in this chapter is that the cumulative impact of demands on teachers can have a profound and detrimental effect on teacher well-being. Next, the chapter helps leaders understand how to reduce demands by utilizing a continuous improvement protocol to make the work more problem-specific and user-centered. Chapter 6 examines the physical, emotional, and social resources that have been found to lessen demands, stress, and burnout, which can assist in teacher retention. Specific resources that can be developed to offset demands will be explored in concert with the three categories of demands, as school leaders often overlook the need to develop and attend to these resources as a buffering force to improve the working conditions of teachers. Next, the chapter guides leaders to increase resources using a simple protocol based on continuous improvement.

Preface

Chapter 7 examines the role of the district or charter management organization in supporting school leaders in establishing an intentional teacher retention system. This involves adopting a capacity-building approach for schools, based on three key strategies, and fostering the development of principals as retention leaders. Finally, Chapter 8 reviews the TRM and examines the paradox of increasing complexity in our society with how our schools and teachers are being led by the wrong drivers to incentivize and retain them. Therefore, new ideas are needed regarding the purpose of schools, the role of teachers in our society, and how we can make education a more manageable and attractive field.

Each chapter opens with a vignette about a principal facing the challenge of teacher turnover in his building, along with the issues that cause the turnover. Each chapter also starts with an exercise to help school leaders dissect the issues in their building. Chapters and appendices include helpful tools, diagnostics, and forms that school leaders can use to understand the teacher turnover problem and develop a blueprint for retaining more teachers. All the appendices can also be found online, allowing leaders to access multiple copies as needed.

The 2001 federal legislation promised to leave no child behind, but in the intervening years, many teachers have been forced to ask if they should leave their children behind to salvage their physical, emotional, and mental well-being. Many of our teachers have chosen to leave the profession and not return until it becomes a more viable choice for their well-being and life. Now is the time to rethink teacher retention and craft a blueprint that turns schools into places where educators truly want to stay.

> COVID had many devastating impacts, but this time offered the education field an opportunity for needed changes and to reevaluate things such as state assessments, teacher workload, and flexibility that could have helped maintain and attract teachers. But this did not occur.
> Source: Teacher interview Chalkbeat, 2022

The Growing Challenge for Leaders

Principal Bridges sat at his desk, staring out the window. He had just received another resignation letter from one of his special education teachers, who had been at the school for only two years. In her letter, she cited the number of students she had to serve, a perceived lack of support for student behavior, a lack of materials, and the lack of time and support from her fellow teachers as primary reasons for her resignation. As Mr. Bridges watched the clouds grow in the distance out his window, he wondered where he could find another special education teacher or if he would have to find someone willing to work on an emergency license. He also began to wonder what it would take to stop the constant turnover of teachers in his building. He had tried many things, from assigning mentors to new and struggling teachers to hiring a family liaison and implementing a new student behavior system, which all his teachers were trained in. He wondered, however, if these solutions had been successful or if they had been the right solutions for the right problems. As he rose from his chair to go home for the night, he contemplated what he was missing and whether his way of thinking about problems was still the right approach. Before he shut off his desk lamp, he gathered the resignation letter and put it in his briefcase to read again after dinner was over that night.

A blueprint is a step between the spark of an idea and the actual product you create. Architects, designers, engineers, and planners all create some form of a blueprint to move ideas into action. When Michelangelo painted the ceiling for the Sistine Chapel, he had a blueprint. Dwight Eisenhower spent several years developing the blueprint for the D-Day invasion of Normandy. All NFL coaches script the first 15 offensive plays as a blueprint for the game. No construction crew shows up at a building site with a set of materials and asks, 'What should we create today?' Instead, they refer to a blueprint.

While people may have a spark of an idea about a problem they are facing, it is difficult to move to action without a blueprint in place. That is the purpose of this book. To help you, as a school leader, design a blueprint (see Appendix A) to solve the growing problem of teacher turnover in your school.

Introduction

In a country marked by technological advancements and wealth, we are still witnessing a concerning number of educators leaving their profession. This problem poses a critical question for educational leaders: Why are so many teachers leaving, and what can be done to prevent it? This is not just a problem for schools – it threatens the future of our students.

Teacher turnover (moving to a different school) and attrition (leaving the profession entirely) have been issues for decades. However, rapid changes in our society and the design of work in schools have exacerbated the situation, leading to an increase in teacher departures and a decline in the number of people entering the profession over the past decade. While higher salaries and benefits are necessary, they may not be enough to keep teachers in the profession. To that end, this book will reframe many of the reasons that teachers leave, using a different model called the Teacher Retention Model (TRM), and explore the role of stress and well-being in a teacher's decision to leave. This book proposes an alternative explanation for teacher turnover and attrition and explores actionable strategies you can use to mitigate the impact of attrition and turnover in your school. My hope is that school leaders who feel like Principal Bridges every year can begin to feel a sense of relief as they begin to create a more intentional retention system.

The well-being of teachers has declined sharply, especially since the COVID-19 pandemic. Even before the pandemic, the teacher turnover rate was already a troubling 16% (Sutcher et al., 2016). Now, that rate has jumped to 18%–19%, meaning that about 760,000 teachers need to be replaced yearly. Some states are seeing an even bigger increase (Bleiberg & Kraft, 2022). This rising turnover rate highlights the need for better support, including a balance of work demands and resources, as well as increased social-emotional support. The need for action is urgent if students are to be prepared for their futures.

In this chapter, we begin by examining the size of the growing crisis of turnover and attrition by having you explore the costs of turnover and attrition in your school or district and compare that with recent data on attrition, turnover, and shortage rates facing US schools. We will explore the complex causal chain of turnover and attrition, specifically tracing how ongoing changes in our schools can lead to chronic stress, burnout, and ultimately the decision to leave the school or the profession entirely. We conclude by discussing the book's organization.

The Size of the Problem

Teacher turnover and attrition come with significant costs, in terms of not only dollars but also time, energy, and student learning loss. When teachers leave, school leaders must invest time and resources in recruiting, hiring, and training new staff. Students often lose out due to instability, and the school culture suffers as a result. Take a few minutes to reflect on the costs of turnover in your school or district using the **Costs of Attrition Exercise** (Table 1.1 below). Compare your estimates with national data on teacher attrition and shortages. This exercise will provide you with a clearer understanding of how turnover impacts your school.

Now, compare your estimates with national averages from recent studies on teacher attrition and shortages.

Teacher Attrition and Turnover
- A study conducted by McKinsey and Company (Bryant et al., 2023) revealed that 2020 marked the highest teacher attrition rate in this decade thus far and that attrition increased by 20% from the previous year. This study also found that attrition increased by 17% between

A Blueprint for Teacher Retention

Table 1.1 Costs-of-Attrition Exercise

Question	Number	Multiplier	Answer
1. How many teachers have you had to replace over the previous two years?		$11,860 (small)–$24,930 (large) cost of replacing a teacher (LPI, 2024)	=
2. What is your two-year turnover/attrition rate?	# of teachers replaced	/ by total number of staff employed year 1 and year 2	=
3. How much time do you spend replacing teachers?	# of teachers replaced	Estimated 20–25 hours of personnel time to replace teachers	=
4. How many unfilled positions have you had?		Estimated teaching load that had to be reassigned	= number of students
5. Of the teachers you have had to replace, how many were in their first five years of teaching?		$10,000–$25,000 estimated costs of training new teachers	= $ cost
6. How many beginning teachers have you had to hire in the last two years or who were not fully certified?		X - 3–4 months less learning gains for new teachers X number of students served	= total months in learning loss
7. Of your current staff, how many show ongoing signs of stress or burnout?		X $23,000 estimated costs of burnout per person (Pfeffer, 2019)	= burnout costs $

2021 and 2022, and quitting the profession accounted for 64% of overall separations (Bryant et al., 2023).

- Over 40% of respondents in districts with high percentages of students receiving free or reduced lunch planned to leave, compared with 25% in districts with fewer students on free or reduced lunch.
- Seventy-five percent of respondents who planned to leave stated they had too much work and insufficient staff to help meet expectations.

- The attrition rate is most severe among teachers in their first five years of service. Ingersoll et al.'s (2018) findings on changes in the teaching profession in the US, however, showed that the attrition rate of teachers within their first five years was 44%.

Teacher Shortages

- Sutcher et al.'s (2016) study also showed that most teachers who left teaching worked in high-poverty schools had less than five years of experience, and only 59.3% of the teachers had a background in the main subject they taught.
- These data are overwhelming across the board but even worse for teachers in high-poverty areas and in certain disciplines (Sutcher et al., 2016). This study found that, in 2015–2016, across the US, only 91.2% of teachers were fully certified, and only 68.5% had a background in the subject they taught. In addition, certain fields of study tend to show more shortages, including special education, math, science, and English as a second language.
- In a review of national data (Garcia & Weiss, 2019), 79.8% of schools reported at least one teacher vacancy, 9.4% were unable to fill a vacancy in at least one subject area, and 36.2% found it very difficult to fill a vacancy in at least one subject area.
- The review by Garcia and Weiss (2019) also found that 37.8% of newly hired teachers were in their first year of teaching and that a larger number of these teachers were in high-poverty schools.
- A similar report by the Annenberg Institute (Nguyen et al., 2022) found that, at the start of the 2021–2022 school year, 36,000 open positions remained, along with at least 163,000 positions being held by underqualified teachers across the US.
- Sutcher et al. (2016) projected an increase in the teacher shortage to over 200,000 teachers by 2025.

While many view teacher shortages as a policy issue, stemming from supply and demand in the teaching workforce, the reasons for high turnover run deeper. As we will explore in the next section, turnover is related to the growing complexity of teaching, leadership, and school working conditions.

The Systemic Complexity of Teacher Turnover and Attrition

Teacher stress, burnout, and eventual turnover do not happen because of a single event, perception, or thought of the teacher. Instead, they result from a complex system of interconnected factors that build up over time, influencing teacher well-being. These factors link the demands placed on teachers, the lack of resources, and the emotional toll of the job, all of which affect teachers' well-being. Our research and experience working with schools suggest that the increasing complexity of today's world has made teaching more challenging, leading to increased burnout and a decline in teacher well-being.

First, one of the most significant changes in the 21st century is the rapid increase in complexity and uncertainty in education, for which we do not yet have ready-made solutions. There are two main reasons for this:

1. The sheer amount of information available today.
2. The interconnectedness brought on by technology makes problems spread faster and harder to solve (Schwab & Malleret, 2022).

The speed at which information comes at school leaders and teachers is overwhelming. The velocity of information makes it hard to absorb and make sense of it all. Velocity is everywhere: in our crises, in our focus on change, and in our impatience with learning gains, all of which add new pressures. Digital tools make it easier to accelerate concerns, while new technologies, such as artificial intelligence (AI), also bring new challenges. All of this contributes to the complexity of the teaching job.

Second, as the complexity of education has increased, so have the demands placed on teachers. Teachers now have more tasks to do, often with fewer resources and less time to do them. This phenomenon is called work intensification (Lawrence et al., 2019). This concept implies that teachers are expected to accomplish more, juggle multiple responsibilities, and make swift decisions, all while navigating the emotional toll of their work (Beck, 2018). Said another way, more must be achieved in less time with fewer resources, which causes almost permanent stress and little time to relieve that stress (Ballet & Kelchterman, 2008).

The accountability measures introduced over the past two decades have only exacerbated the situation, increasing teachers' workloads without improving their working conditions. COVID-19 also created an enormous sense of intensification due to the sudden shift to remote teaching and the increased social-emotional needs of students (and teachers) throughout and following the pandemic.

Third, teaching is not just hard work; it is emotional work (Ye & Chen, 2015). Teachers constantly manage their emotions to create a positive learning environment for students. This phenomenon is known as emotional labor and occurs when teachers must regulate their emotions to meet the job's expectations (Kwok, 2011). For example, a teacher might suppress frustration when dealing with a difficult student or a demanding parent. Over time, managing these emotions takes a toll and requires extra energy. The demands of emotional labor become much heavier when teachers are asked to manage their responses to dealing with poverty, trauma, abuse, and other understandably upsetting situations. Teachers often feel overwhelmed by these situations, and a constant emotional burden can lead to burnout.

Fourth, if complexity has led to work intensification and increased emotional labor, then decreases in job satisfaction due to these issues over time help us understand why teachers lose commitment to the profession. Job satisfaction is a "a state of mind determined by the extent to which the individual perceives his/her job-related needs to be met" (Evans, 1997). Job satisfaction is highly related to teacher retention, as more satisfied teachers are less susceptible to stress and burnout, offer better instruction and support to students, and demonstrate a greater commitment to the profession (Toropova et al., 2021). In contrast, low job satisfaction leads to teacher turnover, which affects faculty collegiality, staff trust, and overall school performance, as well as incurring significant financial costs for recruiting, hiring, and training new teachers (Ronfeldt et al., 2013). One critical factor contributing to high levels of dissatisfaction is the perception that school leaders lack support for their teachers (Urick, 2016; Price, 2021; Player et al., 2017; Merrimack College, 2024).

Unfortunately, teacher satisfaction has been declining for years, even before the pandemic (Steiner & Woo, 2021), beginning with the era of accountability. The Merrimack College Teacher Survey (2024) found that teacher satisfaction dropped from 62% in 2008 to just 18% in 2024. Even more concerning, 48% of teachers said their mental health was affecting their ability to teach, an increase from 42% the year before.

The Impact of Teacher Turnover on Schools and Students

When teachers leave, it affects not only them but also their students, fellow teachers, and the school as a whole. For instance, Sorenson and Ladd's (2020) findings show that turnover increased schools' share of math and English Language Arts (ELA) teachers with low levels of experience, and the number of teachers without full licensure or certification in these fields increased, which directly impacts student learning. Ronfeldt et al.'s (2013) study of students over eight years also showed that in grade levels with higher teacher turnover, students scored lower on ELA and math, especially in schools with more low-performing and diverse student populations.

Hanushek et al. (2016) found similar decreases in the quality of instruction due to turnover, especially in lower-achieving schools. Similarly, Kirksey (2024) found that with increasing numbers of uncertified teachers being hired in Texas due to staffing shortages, students with uncertified teachers lose four months of learning in reading and three months in math. Relative to other teachers and schools, Ronfeldt et al. (2013) describe the disruptive factor of teacher turnover on staff cohesion, community, instructional coherence, and the challenges faced by stayers who must now mentor others, all of which can impact student achievement. Last, Holme et al. (2024) found that teacher turnover "disrupted schools' abilities to create and sustain the organizational conditions that matter for school improvement" (p. 1).

The problem of teacher turnover is part of a larger, complex system that has been growing over time. A complex set of demands has been placed upon schools and educators without any changes to relieve teachers' default working conditions. As demands on teachers increase and resources fail to keep up, educators' well-being suffers. Burnout, health issues, and eventually leaving the profession are natural outcomes.

That is why simply increasing teacher pay, while necessary, isn't enough to solve this problem. As I like to ask: even if we paid every teacher $100,000 per year, would that change the working conditions that cause them to leave? The answer is currently no, and many of the current proposed solutions to this problem fail to consider the complexity of the issue. What we need is a deeper understanding of the problem and solutions that address the root causes.

Conclusion

The growing crisis of teacher turnover and attrition demands urgent attention because teachers are among the most important factors in shaping students' success and future. Without healthy, flourishing teachers, achieving deep learning with students becomes difficult. Unfortunately, many teachers have experienced the complex system we discussed in this chapter and left the profession, taking their skills and passion with them. They leave because they cannot continue working under conditions that make them question the role of education today.

In the following chapters, we will look at how to begin solving this problem:

- **Chapter 2** introduces the **Teacher Retention Model** as the foundation for improving teacher retention by establishing a more intentional retention system.
- **Chapter 3** will focus on the critical role of the **adult social-emotional climate** in schools.
- **Chapter 4** will examine how school leaders can provide essential **emotional support** and help teachers develop **social-emotional skills** at different organizational levels.
- **Chapter 5** examines the **demands** placed on educators and offers strategies for analyzing and mitigating these demands through a straightforward process.
- **Chapter 6** will explore the **resources** that teachers need and provide strategies for identifying and adding those resources to better support educators.
- **Chapter 7** examines the critical role of the **district** and how leaders at that level can also support schools and school leaders to reduce turnover.
- Last, **Chapter 8** will demonstrate how school leaders can integrate these concepts to address the **turnover crisis**, utilizing continuous improvement and a rethinking of important drivers to establish a long-term, intentional retention system.

Each of these chapters will help leaders move beyond the knowing–doing gap with specific actions that school leaders or leadership teams can take to create a healthier and more supportive environment for their teachers. I close this chapter with a further call to prevent the attrition of our teaching force. Sutcher et al. (2016) suggest:

> High levels of attrition, estimated to be nearly 8% of the workforce annually, are responsible for the largest share of annual demand. The teaching workforce continues to be a leaky bucket, losing hundreds of thousands of teachers each year—the majority of them before retirement age. Changing attrition would reduce the projected shortages more than any other single factor.

Let's turn next to how to start changing retention levels, focused on understanding the evidence-based TRM.

Leadership Considerations

- What did your cost estimate show you?
- Are you facing teacher shortages in only critical areas, or are you starting to see shortages in other areas too?
- Do you have a regular method for assessing the level of stress and burnout among your teachers?
- Do you know why teachers leave your district or school? How do you know?
- What processes have you used to try new ideas to retain teachers? How do you know they worked or not?

References

Ballet, K. & Kelchterman, G. (2008). Workload and willingness to change: Disentangling the experience of intensification. *Journal of Curriculum Studies*, 40(1), 47–67. DOI: 10.1080/00220270701516463

Beck, J. L. (2018). The weight of a heavy hour: Understanding teacher experiences of work intensification. *McGill Journal of Education*, 52, 3), 617–635.

Bleiberg, J. & Kraft, M. (2022). What happened to the K-12 education labor market during COVID? The acute need for better data systems. (EdWorkingPaper: 22–544). Annenberg Institute at Brown University. DOI: 10.26300/2xw0-v642

Bryant, J., Ram, S., Scott, D. & Williams, C. (2023, March). K-12 teachers are quitting. *What would make them stay?* McKinsey & Company. https://www.mckinsey.com/industries/education/our-insights/k-12-teachers-are-quitting-what-would-make-them-stay?

Evans, L. (1997). Understanding teacher morale and job satisfaction. *Teaching and Teacher Education*, 13(8), 831–845. DOI: 10.1016/S0742-051X(97)00027-9

Garcia, E. & Weiss, E. (2019). The teacher shortage is real, large, and growing, and worse than we thought. *Economic Policy Institute*. https://www.epi.org/publication/the-teacher-shortage-is-real-large-and-growing-and-worse-than-we-thought-the-first-report-in-the-perfect-storm-in-the-teacher-labor-market-series/

Hanushek, E. A., Rivkin, S. G. & Schiman, J. C. (2016). Dynamic effects of teacher turnover on the quality of instruction. *Economics of Education Review*, 55, 132–148. DOI: 10.1016/j.econedurev.2016.08.004

Holme, J., Jabbar, H., Trautman, K. & Solis-Rodriquez, J. (2024). *How teacher turnover disrupts school improvement efforts*. The University of Texas at Austin and the University of Southern California. https://sites.edb.utexas.edu/wp-content/uploads/sites/170/2024/10/USCRossierUniversityofTexas_Report1_FINAL2-1.pdf

Ingersoll, R. M., Merrill, E., Stuckey, D. & Collins, G. (2018). *Seven trends: The transformation of the teaching force*. CPRE Research Reports. https://repository.upenn.edu/cpre_researchreports/108

Kirksey, J. J. (2024). *Amid rising number of uncertified teachers, previous classroom experience proves vital in Texas* (No. 1). Center for Innovative Research, Texas Tech University College of Education. https://ttu-ir.tdl.org/items/e8d785a0-2be3-4942-bb43-d71705fb2d4f

Kwok, K. T. (2011). Emotional labor of teaching. *Educational Research*, 2(8), 1312–1316.

Lawrence, D. F., Loi, N. M. & Gudex, B. W. (2019). Understanding the relationship between work intensification and burnout in secondary teachers. *Teachers and Teaching*, 25:2, 189–199. DOI: 10.1080/13540602.2018.1544551

Learning Policy Institute (2024). 2024 Update: What's the Cost of Teacher Turnover? https://learningpolicyinstitute.org/product/2024-whats-cost-teacher-turnover

Merrimack College (2024). The teachers are not all right: Improving the mental well-being of teachers and their students. https://www-edweek-org.proxy2.library.illinois.edu/research-center/reports/the-teachers-are-not-all-right-improving-the-mental-well-being-of-teachers-and-their-students/2024/08

Nguyen, T. D., Lam, C. B. & Bruno, P. (2022). Is there a national teacher shortage? A systematic examination of reports of teacher shortages in the United States. (EdWorkingPaper: 22-631). Annenberg Institute at Brown University. DOI: 10.26300/76eq-hj32

Pfeffer, J. (2019 April-June). Solving the workplace health crisis. *Workforce Solutions Review*. https://peopleserv.com/userfiles/Jeffrey%20Pfeffer%20-%20WSR_June_19vweb-2.pdf

Player, D., Youngs, P., Perrone, F. & Grogan, E. (2017). How principal leadership and person-job fit are associated with teacher mobility and attrition. *Teaching and Teacher Education*, 67, 330–339. DOI: 10.1016/j.tate.2017.06.017

Price, H. (2021). Weathering fluctuations in teacher commitment: leaders relational failures, with improvement prospects. *Journal of Educational Administration*, 59(4), 493–513. DOI: 10.1108/JEA-07-2020-0157

Ronfeldt, M., Loeb, S., & Wyckoff, J. (2013). How teacher turnover harms student achievement. *American Educational Research Journal*, 50(1), 4–36. DOI: 10.3102/0002831212463813

Schwab, K. & Malleret, T. (2022). *The great narrative*. Forum Publishing.

Sorenson, L. C. & Ladd, H. F. (2020). The hidden costs of teacher turnover. *AERA Open*, 6(1), 1–24. DOI: 10.1177/2332858420905812

Steiner, E. D. & Woo, A. (2021). Job-related stress threatens the teacher supply: Key findings from the 2021 state of the US teacher survey. *Rand Corporation*. https://www.rand.org/pubs/research_reports/RRA1108-1.html

Sutcher, L., Darling-Hammond, L., & Carver-Thomas, D. (2016). *A coming crisis in teaching? Teacher supply, demand, and shortages in the U.S.* Palo Alto, CA: Learning Policy Institute. https://learningpolicyinstitute.org/product/coming-crisis-teaching

Toropova, A., Myrberg, E. & Johansson, S. (2021). Teacher job satisfaction: the importance of school working conditions and teacher characteristics, *Educational Review*, 73(1), 71–97, DOI: 10.1080/00131911.2019.1705247

Urick, A. (2016). The influence of typologies of school leaders on teacher retention: a multilevel latent class analysis. *Journal of Educational Administration*, 54(4), 434–468. DOI 10.1108/JEA-08-2014-0090

Ye, M. & Chen, Y. (2015). A literature review of teachers' emotional labor. *Creative Education*, 6(20), 2232–2240. DOI: 10.4236/ce.2015.620230

# The Teacher Retention Model

> Principal Paul Bridges, weary from the day chasing down various issues, walked by a young teacher's room one day in late October and saw her sitting at her desk, head in hand. He saw the weariness in her eyes—a look that someone her age shouldn't have. When he stopped and asked how she was doing, she looked up and broke down in tears, sobbing that nobody had told her it would be this hard, that her students weren't learning like they should, how she didn't know how to help her students who didn't understand English very well, how unsupportive her colleagues were to new ideas, and how she had tried to talk to her team lead, but he just kept saying things would be ok and asking her to take on more new things. In that short window of five minutes, Principal Bridges listened to her pour out her frustrations about herself, her classroom, and the working conditions she was living through, all the concerns he had been trying to figure out a way through over the past few years in his school. It seemed to him that some force was at play that he couldn't quite grasp. She survived the year but left for a different profession at the end. He still feels pangs of remorse a year later for her and others who chose to leave the teaching field. He often wondered on his drive home: How can I be more intentional about keeping teachers in place?

Let us start with a simple choice: As school leaders, you can unknowingly keep running an unintentional turnover system behind the scenes in your schools, or you can develop a more visible and intentional retention system that helps retain teachers. The book is designed to help you, as a school leader, achieve the latter: creating an intentional retention system that keeps more of your teachers in the classroom. Every system is perfectly designed to get the results it achieves, whether we realize it or not. Unfortunately, many schools have developed systems that unintentionally push teachers out, and these systems are working well but in the wrong direction. Each school has its own version of this turnover system, and without intentional intervention, it will continue to function effectively, leading to teacher attrition.

Take the latest findings from the Pew Research Center's 2024 Teacher Survey. The results show that 77% of teachers frequently find their job stressful, 68% feel overwhelmed, and 70% report that their school is understaffed. Additionally, teachers are less satisfied with their jobs than most other workers in the United States. Every year, 20%–22% of teachers have to be replaced compared with much lower turnover rates in fields like the information industry (6.5%), finance (8.3%), or sales (10%). The only sector worse off than education is healthcare, which had a 27.1% turnover rate in 2023 (Mercer, 2024). To address this issue, we must shift our perspective from viewing teacher turnover as an individual problem to recognizing it as a systemic issue.

Systems Thinking for Retention

Most school leaders have been exposed to systems thinking, yet traditional linear thinking remains the default mode for solving complex problems, such as teacher retention (Allen et al., 2009). A system is an interconnected set of elements that organize to achieve something that is typically beyond our awareness until a significant event occurs. For example, a tornado is a system, as is the human body or even a school district's transportation system.

So, what are the interconnected elements driving teacher turnover in schools?

- First, every job has **demands** that drain our energy and create stress (Collie et al., 2020; McCarthy et al., 2016). For schools and teachers, we can identify these demands as personal, classroom, and workplace demands. The more demands there are, the less energy teachers have for their primary role of instruction. The unprecedented demands

- placed on teachers over the past few decades, combined with the COVID-19 era and its aftermath, have significantly increased these risk factors for teachers.
- Second, every job also has **resources** that can help reduce demands. Like demands, job resources can be personal, classroom-related, and workplace-related and can be defined by their ability to increase energy (Quinn et al., 2012). Beyond the free gym memberships and dress-down Fridays, fluctuating budgets and leadership turnover in many places have prevented the development or sustained implementation of new job resources.
- The third element is adult **social-emotional skills**, crucial for managing stress and demands, serving as a powerful stress-mitigating resource. Teachers with resilience, emotional regulation, and positive communication skills, among others, are better equipped to handle the demands of the job. These skills are especially important for school leaders as school leaders' social-emotional competencies, skills, and demonstrated support for teachers emerge as *the most salient resource for teachers and are highly associated with teachers' decision to stay in a school or leave* (Ford et al., 2019; Gui, 2019; Tran, 2022).
- Fourth is the influence that the first three elements have on the people in a school and their overall **well-being**. Well-being extends beyond physical health to encompass psychological well-being, a sense of purpose and meaning in life, positive relationships, self-determination, and optimism (Zhou et al., 2024). Unfortunately, teacher well-being is declining. For example, the Merrimack College Teacher Survey (2024) revealed that 48% of teachers reported that their mental health affected their teaching, up from 42% in 2023.

Over the past 20 years, we have seen a significant increase in demands (workload, student behavior, and technology) and a corresponding decrease in resources (time, leadership support, and safety). At the same time, we have neglected the emotional environment for adults. As a result, we have unintentionally created a system that causes stress, burnout, and decreased well-being, leading to teacher turnover. Systems are perfectly designed to get the results they achieve, often outside our awareness, and our turnover system is alive and working well because we have not understood the system at play.

Focusing solely on increased salaries or promoting self-care that teachers need to undertake on their own is a linear approach that is frequently promoted for addressing problems like teacher turnover, yet it may not be suited to address a complex, chronic issue like this. These solutions, while necessary, assume a simple linear cause-and-effect relationship. Pay teachers more, and they will stay. Give teachers a free gym membership, and they will relieve their own stress. Instead, systems thinking is required to see how the parts interact to achieve your turnover results.

Intentional vs. Unintentional Exercise

Here is a simple exercise to help you identify the hidden factors contributing to teacher stress in your school.

1. Use the table below and start by asking yourself: What is the one thing causing teachers the most stress in my school?
2. Then ask: Why is that happening? Write down your answer.
3. Repeat the process four more times, asking, "Why is that?" of the previous answer.
4. Try this exercise again with two additional issues that cause teachers stress.

At the end of this exercise, review your answers. Which reasons are caused by something intentional happening in the school? Which ones are unintentional? This exercise can help you identify differences between intentional and unintentional causes of stress in your school that, over time, may contribute to excess stress, burnout, and eventual turnover.

Building an Intentional Teacher Retention System

Instead of allowing an unintentional teacher turnover system to operate in the background, we need to intentionally develop a teacher retention system based on the insights from research. This system should improve your school's working conditions and emotional climate and provide the necessary support to mitigate stress and burnout. A teacher retention system

Table 2.1 Intentional vs. Unintentional

What is one thing causing your teachers the most stress?	Example 1:	Example 2:	Example 3:
Why is that?			
Why is that?			
Why is that?			
Why is that?			
Why is that?			
How many of these reasons are intentional vs. being unintentional			

focuses on the same elements as the turnover system (demands, resources, and adult social-emotional skills) but aims to increase teacher well-being and keep them in the classroom. However, the teacher retention system is more intentional about utilizing these elements to serve a different purpose. Here is what an intentional retention system includes:

- **A clear model for understanding teacher well-being**: You need a simple way to think about what is happening in your school. The model should focus on three key areas: demands on teachers, the resources they have to manage those demands, and the social-emotional skills they need to navigate their work and feel supported.

- **Tools to collect useful data**: You need accurate and reliable data to improve teacher retention. Simple tools can help you gather information on stress and energy levels (leading indicators) and track how demands, resources, and social-emotional skills affect your teachers (lagging indicators). The data will indicate where problems exist and where intervention is needed.

- **Processes for small-scale changes**: You do not need to overhaul everything completely. Instead, start with small, manageable changes that shift your school's system in the right direction using Plan-Do-Study-Act cycles. Over time, you can learn what best improves teacher well-being and adjust your approach accordingly.

Every year, US schools face the challenge of replacing a significant number of teachers. Growing shortages are making replacements harder to find.

These replacements have become increasingly difficult to find, and 52% of current teachers (Pew Research Center, 2024) say they would not recommend teaching as a profession. That is why we need to create intentional retention systems that can dramatically reduce the number of teachers who turn over yearly. Let us examine the eight key ideas that support the evidence-based Teacher Retention Model (TRM).

Eight Key Ideas of the Teacher Retention Model

To develop a more effective approach to retaining teachers, we examined research from various fields, including occupational health, organizational psychology, stress and energy management, organizational turnover, social-emotional learning, emotional leadership, and teacher attrition and turnover. From this research, we identified eight key ideas central to reducing teacher turnover. These eight key ideas are categorized into stress and energy, job demands and resources, and adult social-emotional skills.

Stress and Energy

Key Idea #1: Teaching Is Energy-Intensive

Teaching and leading schools require multiple types of energy, including physical, cognitive, and emotional energy, as well as energetic activation, which helps to initiate action (Baker, 2019). Invested wisely, this resource can lead to an optimal state, enabling educators to experience motivation and vitality rather than exhaustion. However, stress represents a significant factor that can intensify demands on educators' energy resources, especially their emotional energy. The more energy that teachers expend in dealing with stress, the more likely they will burn out and consider leaving their jobs.

Key Idea #2: Stress Is a Biopsychosocial Process

Stress is not just a mental state; it is a biopsychosocial process (Hase et al., 2020) combining physical, psychological, and social factors. Biopsychosocial processes suggest that, in many social situations, individuals see these as either a challenge or threat defined by conscious or subconscious evaluations, which then trigger stress, hormonal, and cardiovascular responses. When teachers face stressful situations, such as students not responding to a lesson, their minds perceive this as a threat, and their bodies react with physical stress that lowers their energy.

Teacher Emotions and Adult Social-Emotional Skills

Key Idea #3: Emotions Impact Energy

Teachers' emotions and emotional energy play a major role in their daily work (Baker, 2019; McCarthy et al., 2016). Teaching requires emotional energy, and the relationships that teachers have with students and colleagues can drain or replenish that energy. Teachers want the best for their students and colleagues, which often requires a vast repertoire of emotional skills; however, too much or the wrong emotions can drain resources. Emotional skills and support are essential for maintaining teacher motivation and preventing stress from escalating into burnout.

At the organizational level, Leithwood et al. (n.d.) argue that school leaders can support teachers' social and emotional well-being through the *Emotional Path*, a form of influence that directs teachers' attention, cognition, and perceptions of the school. The conditions on the Emotional Path encompass "distinct feelings, dispositions, and affective states of individual and collectives of teachers about school-related matters" (Leithwood et al., 2017). The model identifies common affective states or emotions, such as collective efficacy, trust, and organizational citizenship behavior (utilizing discretionary energy to benefit the organization) (Leithwood et al., 2017). Many studies have focused on this path, and others highlight the critical importance of paying attention to teacher emotions, as they "seep across paths" to help improve other areas.

Key Idea #4: Leaders' Social-Emotional Leadership Skills Matter for Teacher Retention

Research indicates that school leaders' social-emotional skills and support for teachers are the most crucial resources for teachers, and they are highly correlated with teachers' decisions to stay in or leave a school (Price, 2021). These social-emotional leadership skills help build individual and team support, as well as the Emotional Path, within a school, which teachers can experience and utilize as a powerful stress-mitigating resource. Related to other key ideas and energy, Seppala and Cameron (2022) find that leaders who develop as positive energizers produce higher levels of engagement, lower turnover, and enhanced employee well-being. A significant aspect of this key idea is acknowledging the role that school leaders play in fostering and sustaining teacher commitment, cultivating feelings of individual and collective efficacy among teachers, and offering emotional support along the way (Price, 2021).

Job Demands and Resources

Key Idea #5: Job Demands Drain Energy

The job demands-resources (JDR) model (Bakker & Demerouti, 2007; Bakker et al., 2023; Demerouti & Bakker, 2023) explains that every job has specific risk factors, or job demands, that deplete energy. Job demands are "physical, psychological, social, or organizational aspects of a job that require sustained physical and psychological (cognitive and emotional) effort or skill, and are therefore associated with certain physiological or psychological costs" (Bakker & Demerouti, 2007). Teaching and leading schools present specific energy depletion demands that differ from other occupations. Managing a classroom of 25 students can be very demanding, as can serving on school committees or working on a team, depending on the circumstances. According to the JDR model, if demands become too extreme, they can impede performance (Collie et al., 2020). The more demands placed on the educator, the more energy is required to meet those demands, leading to increased stress and further decreases in energy.

Key Idea #6: Excess Demands Can Impair Health through Stress and Burnout

In the JDR model, the health impairment process begins when excess demands consume available resources and deplete energy, eventually leading to burnout and potential health problems. High or increasing job demands sustained over time can uniquely predict burnout (Granziera et al., 2021) due to the increased energy requirements. For instance, if a teacher lacks support for handling classroom behavior, the constant emotional strain can wear them down, pushing them closer to exhaustion and burnout.

Key Idea #7: Job Resources Replenish Energy

In contrast to job demands, job resources such as supportive colleagues, a good working environment, supportive leadership, and personal resilience help increase energy. Job resources are "the physical, psychological, social, or organizational elements of the job that either help to achieve work goals, reduce the demands associated with the physiological or psychological costs from demands, or stimulate personal growth, learning and development" (Granziera et al., 2021). Resources act as buffers, reducing the negative effects of demands. When teachers have these resources, they feel more capable and energized.

Key Idea #8: Resources Foster a Motivational Process and Promote Thriving

When teachers have access to supporting resources, the resulting motivational process leads to enhanced engagement with their work, resulting in job satisfaction even when demands are high (Granziera et al., 2021). Job resources can act to buffer and lower demands over time (Bakker & Albrecht, 2018). For instance, if a teacher perceives high social connections with other teachers or works with a designated specialist to improve classroom behavior, the job demands may be lessened, and less energy will be depleted. With high resources, demands are shared, lessening their impact on the individual.

The TRM is built on these eight key ideas. When woven together and used intentionally, they can become a transformative force that changes the landscape of teacher retention. When school leaders pay attention to their interactions, they can create an intentional retention system. Since these key ideas already exist in every school worldwide, learning how to make them interact to retain teachers is in the best interest of leaders, teachers, and all of our students. Now, based on these key ideas, let us turn to the actual model.

The Teacher Retention Model

Many attempts have been made to address teacher turnover, but most focus on increasing incentives to bring new teachers into the field to increase

The Teacher Retention Model

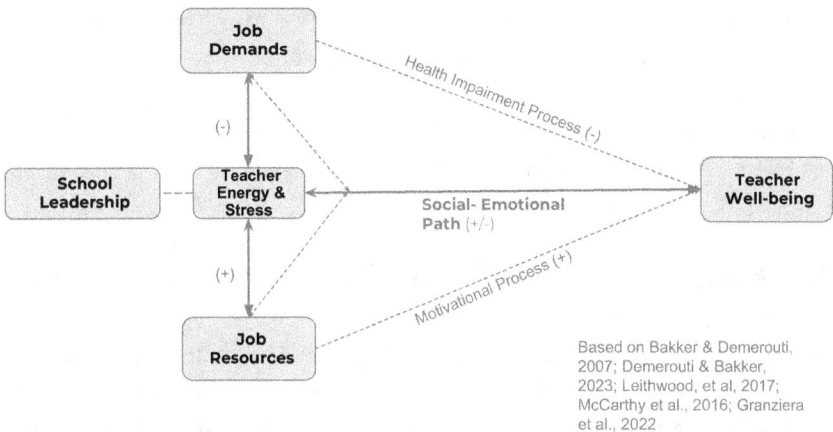

Figure 2.1 The Teacher Retention Model.

the supply of teachers, not paying attention to why they leave in the first place. While these efforts are necessary, they miss a crucial part of the puzzle: what happens once a teacher is hired? How do we keep them happy, healthy, and productive in the classroom? How might we support them and create conducive working conditions to keep them in your school? With around 44% of new teachers leaving the field within five years (Ingersoll et al., 2018), we clearly need a new approach.

The TRM provides a comprehensive approach to developing an intentional retention system essential for all teachers. Based on the eight Key Ideas discussed above, the TRM (Figure 2.1) employs a system-oriented framework comprising four key elements: teacher well-being, job demands, job resources, and the adult social-emotional climate. By focusing on these areas, school leaders can create a supportive environment that helps teachers want to stay.

Teacher Well-Being

Teacher well-being is at the heart of the TRM (Key Ideas #1 & #2). If our educators are healthy and flourishing and have a positive sense of well-being, they have more energy to focus on the needs of their students and each other. Similarly, our schools can become either healthy places where people flourish or toxic environments where people burn out. Therefore, while policy may increase teacher incentives, we also need a system that prioritizes the well-being of educators in our schools. Research indicates that workplace conditions have a greater impact on teacher well-being than individual factors (Ainsworth & Oldfield, 2019), suggesting that leaders must ensure their schools' conditions promote health and well-being.

The Emotional Path and Adult Social-Emotional Climate

The emotional path and adult social-emotional climate, influenced by the school leader, are other key elements in teacher retention (Key Ideas #3 & #4). The Emotional Path (Leithwood et al., n.d.) suggests that emotions shape cognitive processes, including perceptions, attention, memory, and judgment, and underscores the importance of teacher emotions in responding to their environment and engaging in effective classroom practices. For example, a teacher who struggles with emotional regulation and stress after a conflict-laden professional learning community (PLC) meeting, lacking the skills to reframe the issues from this meeting, may not be as effective when they return to classroom instruction. Likewise, school leaders who fail to develop the skills to support teachers' emotions and the social-emotional skills of others are minimizing a primary resource for teacher support. In a review of the emotional leadership of school leaders, Gomez-Leal et al. (2022) find that the degree to which school leaders build trusting and supportive relationships with their teachers can highly influence the development of teachers' satisfaction and performance. Simply stated, "Principals' social-emotional competencies... form the foundation that influences the school climate, teachers' commitment, and well-being" (Mahfouz et al., 2019).

Job Demands

Every school has job demands (personal, classroom, and workplace) that contribute to teacher stress and decreased energy (Key Ideas #5 & #6). To create an intentional retention system, a school leader must be able to diagnose and understand the multitude of demands placed on teachers and work through a process to remove any excessive demands – which prevent students or teachers from thriving – rather than simply letting them accumulate and diminish energy over time. The TRM includes tools such as a weekly or every two weeks flash survey that collects data on teacher stress and energy levels. These data help school leaders pinpoint when stress is rising, allowing for quick adjustments or interventions to be employed. For example, we know parent–teacher conference weeks are stressful, but we often do not track or address other high-stress periods. These data allow leaders to gather real-time data and respond accordingly. Similarly, the JDR Diagnostic enables a more in-depth review of demands that can be reduced or eliminated over time.

Job Resources

Job resources, including personal, classroom, and workplace factors, are the elements that help teachers perform their jobs more effectively (Key Ideas #7 & #8). These resources, such as helpful feedback, time for planning, or support with classroom management, are crucial for balancing demands and reducing stress. For example, coaching can be a valuable resource, but it may be considered an additional burden if it focuses only on instructional content and does not address teachers' emotional needs. Similarly, perceptions of resources such as helpful feedback, input in decision-making, collaboration, and discipline support have also been found to reduce teachers' demands and increase job commitment (Collie, 2021). School leaders must regularly assess the available resources and develop new ones as needed. The TRM also utilizes diagnostics and flash surveys to monitor the effectiveness of resources and make prompt adjustments as needed. The goal is to develop resources that help teachers manage demands and maintain motivation.

The TRM focuses on the common factors that can lead to increased stress and burnout, which lower teachers' well-being and increase the likelihood of their leaving your school or the profession entirely. Teacher well-being is at risk when school leaders fail to address job demands, resources, and the adult social-emotional climate. If, however, school leaders intentionally work to balance demands and resources while developing their own and others' adult social-emotional skills, a greater likelihood exists that the common stressors of teaching will not lead to turnover. Strategies to help achieve this will be explored in the next chapter and subsequent chapters.

Strategies for Creating a More Intentional Retention System

The TRM employs three core strategies to enhance teacher retention. To increase the health and well-being of our teachers, school leaders need to focus on (1) developing adults' social-emotional skills, (2) reducing demands, and (3) increasing resources. These three strategies work together to improve teachers' working conditions and well-being. We explore each strategy in more detail below.

Developing Adult Social-Emotional Climate

One of the most important factors in teacher retention is the adult social-emotional climate in your school. Research shows that individual and group emotions influence satisfaction, commitment, and performance outcomes (Men & Robinson, 2018; James, 2019; Salloum et al., 2018). Leithwood et al. (2017), in their Four-Path model of schools, suggest that the emotional path is an underutilized focus of school improvement for school leaders, as teachers' emotions influence every other path in schools and underscore the importance of teacher emotions in responding to their environment and engaging in effective classroom practices.

This strategy focuses on the individual and other distinct levels within the TRM. These levels include the following:

- **Personal level**: Focuses on individual differences in emotional awareness and self-management in response to affective events.
- **Interpersonal level**: Focuses on the differences between people in terms of emotions and builds strong communication and emotional regulation between individuals.
- **Team level**: Focuses on the emotions of teams and how leaders can influence a team's mood by encouraging positive emotional interactions among team members, such as sharing positive energy and reducing conflict.
- **Organizational level**: Aims to create a healthy, positive emotional climate across the school through developing common emotions like trust. Researchers suggest this level is the aggregate sum of the previous levels (Ashkanasay & Dorris, 2017).

This strategy focuses on helping school leaders and educators develop a deeper and more integrated set of social-emotional skills, serving as a supportive resource for one another. This strategy uses short recipes based on the CASEL competencies (self-awareness, self-management, social awareness, relationship skills, and responsible decision-making) that can be practiced in action until they become a habit. For instance, a school leader may focus on developing their self-management, with a key emphasis on emotional regulation. Simultaneously, these short processes or recipes can also be used by teachers individually and on teams as a focus for the continual development of the adult social-emotional climate in a school. For example, a whole school could use breathing exercises before every meeting to reduce stress and take note of emotions to develop greater emotional awareness.

Relative to the common elements of the TRM, the developing adult social-emotional skills strategy in this example focused on increasing emotional regulation by the school leader and reducing stress through breathing by the staff, and developing a better emotional climate, which can act as an ongoing resource to balance demands across all areas of the school. The exact skills and process for increasing adult social-emotional climate will be explored more in Chapter 3.

Reducing Demands

This strategy assesses whether the demands placed on teachers are realistic. Teachers need most of their energy focused on what matters most: teaching, preparing lessons, and analyzing student progress. However, many additional tasks, such as meetings, administrative duties, or dealing with negative colleagues, drain their energy and add stress. Educators' energy levels can be considered a constraint in work design and potential change. As a constraint, school leaders should be aware that adding an initiative will require teachers to expend additional energy and should attempt to reduce other demands to better balance their workload.

To help reduce unnecessary demands, the TRM suggests using a simple process called **Plan-Do-Study-Act (PDSA)**. Here is how it works:

- **Plan**: Identify a demand, like frequent meetings, and create a plan to reduce it.

- **Do**: Implement the change (e.g., reduce meetings and give teachers more planning time).
- **Study**: After a month, review the data to determine if reducing the number of meetings lowered teacher stress.
- **Act**: Decide if the change was effective and plan the next steps.

Relative to the common elements of the TRM, the reducing demands strategy in this example focused on (1) reducing the demands of meetings to (2) increasing time as a resource, (3) focused on minimizing the stress of teachers, and (4) building the adult social-emotional climate by using a simple, focused process and sharing data which helps to build more collective efficacy and trust among the adults. Reducing demands should always focus on giving teachers more time and energy to devote to their primary task: teaching. The exact protocol and process for removing demands will be explored more in Chapter 3.

Increasing Resources

Increasing resources does not always mean asking for more money. This strategy aims to determine what can help people do their job better and more effectively to balance the demands. These might include personal resources (such as social-emotional skills like resilience or relationship skills), classroom resources (such as classroom supports like technology or behavioral support), or workplace resources (such as supportive leadership or cohesive teams).

The TRM also recommends utilizing the PDSA process (Bennett et al., 2022) to increase resources. For example, if a team's PLC is experiencing conflict, you could

- **Plan**: Identify the necessary changes to enhance team collaboration.
- **Do**: Implement those changes and track how the team is improving.
- **Study**: After gathering data, analyze whether team collaboration improved.
- **Act**: Determine the next steps based on the findings of the data.

Relative to the common elements in the TRM, the increasing resources strategy in this example focused on enhancing team coherence and collaboration to reduce conflict, thereby acting as a demand on teams and individuals. This new resource can help reduce the stress of teachers and building the adult social-emotional climate, by using a simple, focused process and sharing data, which in turn helps build collective efficacy and trust among adults. By increasing resources, you're helping teachers feel more supported, which reduces stress and improves job satisfaction. The exact protocol and process for removing demands will be explored more in Chapter 4.

Conclusion

As school leaders, we have two choices: either let the current unintentional turnover system continue or start building an intentional retention system. You can build an intentional retention system by using the TRM to understand how to retain teachers and use the three key strategies to put the model in action: (1) decreasing demands, (2) increasing resources, and (3) developing the adult social-emotional climate to minimize teacher turnover. When we pay attention to these elements, school leaders can significantly enhance the well-being of our teachers and reduce the likelihood of their leaving.

In the following chapters, we will dive deeper into each strategy and provide actionable steps to help you create the intentional retention system your school needs.

Leadership Considerations

- Do you have an unintentional turnover system in your school or an intentional retention system? How do you know?
- Which key ideas in the Teacher Retention Model resonate most with you?
- Which key ideas are you struggling with?
- What are the greatest demands on your teachers right now? Do you know the impact of those demands?
- Which demands are critical and which are not?
- What can people in your school depend on for support?
- What else might they need to feel more support?

- How would you describe the emotional climate among adults in your school? Are emotions discussed and dealt with or pushed aside?
- What do you, as a school leader, see as your role in leading the adult social-emotional climate?

References

Ainsworth, S., & Oldfield, J. (2019). Quantifying teacher resilience: Context matters. *Teaching and Teacher Education*, 82, 117–128. DOI: 10.1016/j.tate.2019.03.012

Allen, C. D., Cunningham, G.K., & Klinger, J.M. (2009). Systems thinking for strategic leaders. https://apps.dtic.mil/sti/tr/pdf/ADA592793.pdf

Ashkanasay, N. M., & Dorris, A. D. (2017). Emotions in the workplace. *Annual Review of Organizational Psychology and Organizational Behavior*, 4, 67–90. DOI: 10.1146/annurev-orgpsych-032516-113231

Baker, W. E. (2019). Emotional energy, relational energy, and organizational energy: Toward a multilevel model. *Annual Review of Organizational Psychology and Organizational Behavior*, 6, 373–396. DOI: 10.1146/annurev-orgpsych-012218-015047

Bakker, A. & Albrecht, S. (2018). Work engagement: Current trends. *Career Development International*, 23(2), 4–11. doi: 10.1108/CDI-11-2017-0207

Bakker, A. B. & Demerouti, E. (2007). The jobs demands-resources model: State of the art. *Journal of Managerial Psychology*, 22(3), 309–328. DOI: 10.1108/02683940710733115

Bakker, A.B., Demerouti, E., & Sanz-Vergel, A. (2023). Job demands-resources theory: ten years later. *Annual Review of Organizational Psychology and Organizational Behavior*, 10(1), 25–53. https://doi.org/10.1146/annurev-orgpsych-120920-053933

Bennett, B., Grunow, A. & Park, S. (2022). *Improvement science at your fingertips: A compilation of resources for coaches of improvement science*. Improvement Collective.

Collie, R. (2021). A multilevel examination of teachers' occupational commitment: The roles of job resources and disruptive student behavior. *Social Psychology of Education*, 24(2), 387–411. DOI: 10.1007/s11218-021-09617-y

Collie, R. J., Malmberg, L. E., Martin, A. J., Sammons, P. & Morin, A. J. S. (2020). A multilevel person-centered examination of teachers' workplace demands and resources: Links with work-related well-being. *Frontiers in Psychology*, 11, 1–19. doi: 10.3389/fpsyg.2020.00626

Demerouti, E., & Bakker, A. B. (2023). Job demands-resources theory in times of crises: New propositions. *Organizational Psychology Review*, 13(3), 209–236. DOI: 10.1177/20413866221135022

Ford, T. G., Olsen, J., Khojasteh, J, Ware, J., & Urick, A. (2019). The effect of leader support for teacher psychological needs on teacher burnout, commitment, and intent to leave. *Journal of Educational Administration*, 57(6), 615–634. DOI: 10.1108/jea-09-2018-0185

Gomez-Leal, R., Holzer, A., Bradley, C., Fernandez-Berrocal, P, & Patti, J. (2022). The relationship between emotional intelligence and leadership in school leaders: A systematic review. *Cambridge Journal of Education*, 52(1), 1–21. DOI: 10.1080/0305764X.2021.1927987

Granziera, H., Collie, R. & Martin, A. (2021). Understanding teacher well-being through job demands-resources theory. In Mansfield, C.F. (ed) *Cultivating teacher resilience*. Springer.

Gui, G. E. (2019). Teacher attrition and school leaders' capacity for leading, practices and behaviors: A comparative study. *European Journal of Social Science Education and Research*, 6(1). DOI: 10.26417/ejser.v6i1.p111-122

Hase, A., aan het Rot, M., de Miranda Azevedo, R. & Freeman, P. (2020). Threat-related motivational disengagement: Integrating blunted cardiovascular reactivity to stress into the biopsychosocial model of challenge and threat. *Anxiety, Stress and Coping*, 33(4), 355–369. DOI: 10.1080/10615806.2020.1755819

Ingersoll, R. M., Merrill, E., Stuckey, D., & Collins, G. (2018). Seven Trends: The transformation of the teaching force. *CPRE Research Reports*. https://repository.upenn.edu/cpre_researchreports/108

James, C. (2019). Organising in schools: It's all about emotion. In Oplatka, I. & Arar, K. (eds), *Emotion Management and Feelings in Teaching and Educational Leadership: A Cultural Perspective*. Emerald Publishing. doi: 10.1108/978-1-78756-010-920191002

Leithwood, K., Anderson, S. F. Mascall, B., & Strauss, T. (n.d.) School leaders' influences on student learning: The four paths. https://www.leadershippartnerstx.com/files/1_school_leaders_influence_4_paths_to_learning.pdf

Leithwood, K., Sun, J., & Pollock, K. (2017). *How school leaders contribute to student success: The four paths framework*. Springer.

Mahfouz, J., Greenberg, M. T., & Rodriguez, A. (2019). *Principals' social and emotional competence: A key factor for creating caring schools*. University Park, PA: Edna Bennett Pierce Prevention Research Center,

Pennsylvania State University. https://prevention.psu.edu/sel/issue-briefs/principals-social-and-emotional-competence-a-key-factor-for-creating-caring-schools/

McCarthy, C. J., Lambert, R. G., Lineback, S., Fitchett, P. & Baddouh, P. G. (2016). Assessing teacher appraisals and stress in the classroom: Review of the classroom appraisal of resources and demands. *Educational Psychology Review*, 28, 577–603. DOI: 10.1007/s10648-015-9322-6

Men, L. R. & Robinson, K. L. (2018). It's about how employees feel! Examining the impact of emotional culture on employee-organization relationships. *Corporate Communications*, 23(4), 470–491. DOI: 10.1108/CCIJ-05-2018-0065

Mercer (2024). *How much turnover is too much?* https://www.imercer.com/articleinsights/workforce-turnover-trends

Merrimack College (2024). The teachers are not all right: Improving the mental well-being of teachers and their students. https://www-edweek-org.proxy2.library.illinois.edu/research-center/reports/the-teachers-are-not-all-right-improving-the-mental-well-being-of-teachers-and-their-students/2024/08

Pew Research Center (2024, April 4). *What's it like to be a teacher today?* https://www.pewresearch.org/social-trends/2024/04/04/whats-it-like-to-be-a-teacher-in-america-today/

Price, H. (2021). Weathering fluctuations in teacher commitment: leaders relational failures, with improvement prospects. *Journal of Educational Administration*, 59(4), 493–513. DOI: 10.1108/JEA-07-2020-0157

Quinn, R. W., Spreiter, G. M. & Lam, C. F. (2012). Building a sustainable model of human energy in organizations: Exploring the critical role of resources. *The Academy of Management Annals*, 6, 337–396. DOI: 10.5465/19416520.2012.676762

Salloum, S. J., Goddard, R. D. & Berebitsky, D. (2018). Resources, learning, and policy: The relative effects of social and financial capital on student learning in schools. *Journal of Education for Students Placed at Risk*, 23(4), 281–303, DOI: 10.1080/10824669.2018.1496023

Seppala, E. & Cameron, K. (2022, April 18). The best leaders have a contagious positive energy. *Harvard Business Review*. https://hbr.org/2022/04/the-best-leaders-have-a-contagious-positive-energy

Tran, H. (2022). Revolutionizing school HR strategies and practices to reflect talent-centered education leadership. *Leadership and Policy in Schools*, 21(2), 238–252. DOI: 10.1080/15700763.2020.1757725

Zhou, S., Slemp, G., & Vella-Brodrick, D. (2024). Factors associated with teacher wellbeing: A meta-analysis. *Educational Psychology Review*, 36(2), 1–48. DOI: 10.1007/s10648-024-09886-x

The Role of Adult Social-Emotional Skills in Retention

Principal Paul Bridges began to feel a growing knot in his stomach as he looked at his school's annual climate survey results on his computer screen. For the second consecutive year, the percentage of staff members reported that overall trust had decreased, and teachers' sense of efficacy in meeting students' needs had also declined. In written comments, some teachers expressed their concerns about their colleagues' resistance during meetings and the overall lack of caring and kindness. Others shared that teacher morale was at a low point and that, regardless of the type of improvements they were trying, not everyone was willing or on board. When it came to his leadership communication and openness to new ideas from staff, he was again shocked by the percentage of staff who had marked him in the lower categories. The knot in the pit of his stomach grew larger as he thought about a meeting with one of his school teams where he had snapped at them this morning. He also thought back to a professional learning community meeting he had recently observed, where two teachers began to argue about the best way to introduce a task. Even though the instructional coach tried to mediate, both teachers shut down while the others tried their best to finish the task without starting another conflict. He felt he needed to intervene, so he openly criticized the group's actions in a firm tone. As the bell rang, one of the teachers leaving mumbled, "What a waste of time." Although he felt a lot of pressure to improve his school performance, he thought

> they were on the right track with all their new initiatives. But with the continual turnover of teachers over the past few years, it seemed like the climate at his school was getting worse instead of better.

Anyone who has worked in schools or as a school leader will recognize the issues presented in the opening scenario. Teaching and leading schools are people-intensive endeavors, and without the development and use of adult social-emotional skills, the multitude of interactions that teachers and leaders have with students, colleagues, and others during the day can create more demands on energy than act as a resource. These ongoing interactions and decreases in energy can affect teachers' well-being and, ultimately, their decision to stay in a school or leave.

Researchers have increasingly recognized the impact of a school's social and emotional climate on teacher turnover. For example, Nguyen et al. (2020) found that teachers were more likely to stay when they felt supported by administrators and worked in a collaborative environment. Gundlach et al. (2024) noted that teachers' feelings of job satisfaction and motivation, along with school-wide factors such as leadership, culture, and collegiality, play a major role in whether they choose to stay or leave.

School leaders' social and emotional skills are especially important in reducing teacher stress and turnover. Gui (2019) demonstrated that principals' experiences, attitudes, and practices significantly influence teachers' decisions to remain at a school. Similarly, Shell et al. (2023) found that principal support, encouragement, clear communication, recognition, and fairness are key factors in retaining teachers. Ford et al. (2019) demonstrated that when principals address teachers' psychological needs by minimizing burnout and fostering commitment, teachers are less likely to consider leaving their school. Providing personal support, such as promoting teacher autonomy, and building organizational support, like fostering a sense of collective efficacy, can influence a teacher's decision to stay or leave.

Why is the adult social and emotional climate so critical for reducing teacher turnover, and why is leading this climate a key strategy for retaining teachers? Barsade and Gibson (2007) explained that

Affect permeates organizations. It is present in the interdependent relationships we hold with bosses, team members and subordinates. Affective processes (emotions) create and sustain work motivation. Strong affective feelings are present at any time we confront work issues that matter to us and our organization.

This chapter employs a systems perspective on school social-emotional factors as a primary strategy to enhance your teacher retention blueprint (see Appendix A) by expanding Key Ideas #1, #2, and #3 of the Teacher Retention Model (TRM). As a reminder,

- **Key Idea #1** centers on how teaching is an energy-intensive profession.
- **Key Idea #2** centers on the interaction of the social environment with the individual's psychology and biology to make stress a biopsychosocial process.
- **Key Idea #3** focuses on how emotions affect the energy and well-being of teachers.

Understanding the Social-Emotional Climate of Your School Exercise

To get a clear picture of the emotional climate in your school, use the following exercise. Your responses may not be exact but will give you a place to begin your analysis of your climate. Below is a list of core emotions and associated secondary emotions. Think of a typical school day with all the interactions between students and teachers, teachers and other teachers, school leaders and teachers, and parents or guardians. Imagine that 100% represents all the emotions expressed by adults in a day from these various interactions. List what percentage you believe is associated with each core emotion, either felt or expressed daily. List examples that come to mind for why you listed the percentage you did (Table 3.1).

Debrief this exercise with yourself or others. Which emotion did you mark as highest and lowest? What might that indicate about your school?

Table 3.1 Emotional Climate Exercise

Core Emotion	Secondary Emotion Examples	Estimated Daily Percentage Felt or Expressed by Adults in the School	Examples
Happy	Content Peaceful Optimistic		
Sad	Lonely Vulnerable Hurt		
Disgusted	Disappointed Revolted Judgmental		
Angry	Humiliated Aggressive Frustrated		
Fearful	Anxious Insecure Threatened		
Surprise	Excited Confused Amazed		

The Social-Emotional Influences on Teacher Well-being

The TRM (see Figure 3.1 below) proposes that teacher well-being is the primary outcome of a healthy and robust emotional climate; however, affective dimensions, such as teacher personalities, teacher emotions, colleague and student relationships, and the social-emotional skills of school leaders, can also directly influence this well-being. Note in Figure 3.1 that the emotional path sits directly between the demands and resources processes in the TRM and can directly influence the well-being of individuals and the school itself. In this section, we explore these relationships.

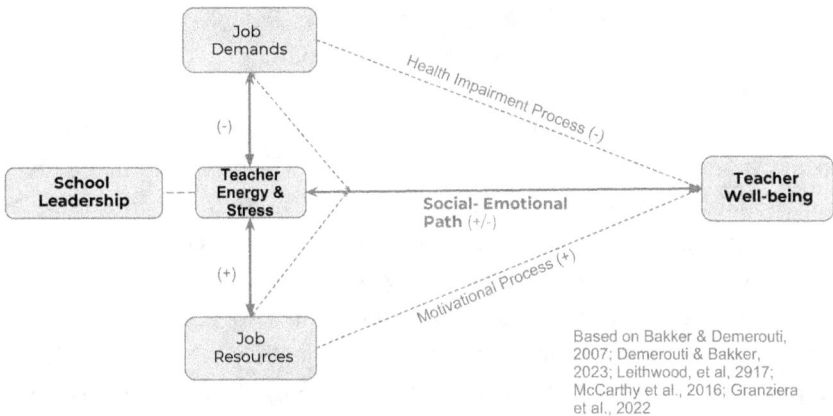

Figure 3.1 The Teacher Retention Model.

Teacher Well-being

Why is well-being such an important element of teachers' practice to consider? Let's change the analogy from teaching to physical performance. Imagine teachers as "learning athletes." Athletes need rest, steady focus, and enough energy to perform at their best. Similarly, teachers must manage various types of energy—physical, cognitive, psychological, and emotional—to effectively plan lessons, engage students, and maintain positive interactions with colleagues. If teachers are concerned about their performance or other stressors, their energy is depleted toward addressing those concerns, and their work suffers. In contrast, Cameron (2021) talks about the heliotropic effect, which means that all people are more inclined toward positive energy or "that which is life-giving".

The amount of energy required for teaching is a common complaint among teachers. Teaching can be exhausting: standing on your feet all day, making rapid decisions, managing student behavior, collaborating with colleagues, and keeping students engaged and motivated. These daily energy drains are rarely discussed in the press or policy circles as a problem to be solved, but they are a common complaint among teachers. Research often uses terms such as "stress," "burnout," and "exhaustion" to describe what happens when a teacher's energy is depleted. Conversely, feeling "vital" or "alive" at work is associated with stronger motivation and lower attrition. In this sense, the continuous maintenance of energy, Key Idea #1 in the TRM, is directly connected to a teacher's sense of well-being.

Researchers define well-being in various ways, but most agree it involves having the emotional, physical, and social resources needed to meet life's demands, inside and outside the classroom. McCallum et al. (2017) emphasize that teacher well-being refers to a person's ability to manage both positive and negative work factors over time, which in turn affects their emotional and cognitive states. Collie (2023) captures this in a broader sense: feeling good and functioning well in one's professional life.

Many scholars also discuss the positive side of well-being, what it means to flourish, not just avoid stress or burnout. Cann et al. (2022) mention the importance of positive emotions and life satisfaction, while Dreer (2023) applies the PERMA model (Positive Emotions, Engagement, Relationships, Meaning, and Accomplishment) to educators. Hascher and Waber (2021) note that although focusing on strengths is vital, schools also have their share of negative emotions that must be acknowledged.

Given that Key Idea #1 in the TRM relates to energy, many concepts explored through research connect energy to well-being. Numerous studies have linked well-being to a sense of "vigor," characterized by high energy combined with resistance to distractions (Bermejo-Toro et al. 2016). Kern et al. (2014) describe work engagement, characterized by vigor for tasks, as the opposite of burnout. In addition, Zhou et al. (2024) and Collie (2023) refer to "subjective vitality", feelings of aliveness and energy that boost resilience in challenging classrooms.

For clarity, Viac and Fraser (2020) offer a straightforward definition of teacher well-being as "the capacity for teachers to respond to the cognitive, emotional, health, and social conditions pertaining to their work and their profession" (p. 18). Any response in a classroom or school environment requires various types of energy – physical, cognitive, social, and psychological-emotional – that shape teachers' overall health and growth. When teachers have enough energy in these domains, they can sustain their performance and manage stress more effectively, resulting in a sustained commitment to the school and profession.

This energy-oriented view highlights four major dimensions of well-being – psychological and emotional, social, cognitive, and physical – emphasizing that well-being extends beyond simply avoiding burnout; it involves nurturing the sources of energy that teachers need to thrive in today's complex educational environment. Without well-being in all its forms, teachers are more prone to stress, burnout, and eventual decisions to leave the school or profession.

This energy-focused definition of well-being centers on four major dimensions of well-being. Individuals can assess their well-being using the tool in Appendix B, and this tool can also be used to aggregate individual well-being levels into a school-wide estimate.

- **Psychological and emotional well-being** involves cultivating a healthy balance of positive and negative emotions, developing a clear sense of purpose and meaning in both professional and personal life, and maintaining a sense of optimism. It also encompasses resilience in the face of challenges, self-awareness of emotional states, and the ability to manage stress adaptively. This dimension requires integrating cognitive, psychological, and emotional resources to sustain a sense of fulfillment and prevent burnout.
- **Social well-being** is characterized by meaningful and supportive relationships within and beyond the school context, a sense of belonging to a community, and effective collaboration with peers, families, and students. It includes feeling valued, accessing social and professional support networks, and making positive contributions to the social environment. Achieving social well-being requires cognitive, psychological, and emotional energy to foster and maintain constructive interactions and a supportive teaching ecosystem.
- **Cognitive well-being** involves sustaining intellectual engagement and curiosity, maintaining mental agility and focus, and continuously developing professional competencies. It includes managing cognitive load effectively, leveraging reflective practices for growth, and feeling competent in handling the demands of teaching. This dimension draws on physical, psychological, and emotional energy to adapt to evolving curricular, technological, and classroom challenges.
- **Physical well-being** encompasses maintaining overall physical health, vitality, and energy through sufficient rest, healthy nutrition, and active stress management. It promotes an awareness of how the work environment and teaching-related stressors can impact the body, emphasizing proactive self-care and organizational support (e.g., ergonomic classroom design and reasonable workloads). Physical well-being requires coordinating physical, cognitive, psychological, and emotional resources to maintain and enhance teachers' daily functioning.

Emotional Energy

Emotional energy is a vital resource that teachers rely on to perform their jobs effectively and maintain their well-being. In recent years, the importance of emotional energy has received increasing attention across different fields, including education, where the role of emotions in teaching has a long history of study (Frenzel et al., 2021; Hargreaves, 1998; Nguyen, 2021; Tsang, 2011; Yin, 2015). As Barsade and Gibson (2007) point out, emotional energy "permeates organizations" and is always present in the relationships that connect teachers to their students, colleagues, and school leaders.

Bakker (2019) describes emotional energy as the capacity to work when the driving force behind that work is affect or caring for those in your charge. In teaching, this means that if teachers must use and manage a variety of emotions to both engage students and regulate their feelings (Frenzel et al., 2021; Ye & Chen, 2015), then the "fuel" behind their labor is inherently emotional energy. Such energy can be boosted or depleted at multiple levels:

1. Micro (Personal): A teacher's choices, thoughts, or personal activities (e.g., anticipating a positive interaction with a student or feeling grateful after a good week)
2. Meso (Interpersonal): Encounters with colleagues or others (e.g., a supportive discussion in the teachers' lounge that offers fresh ideas)
3. Macro (Collective): Broader group connections (e.g., when coworkers rally around a teacher dealing with family illness or when an unpopular policy decision frustrates the entire staff)

Emotions and emotional energy have a significant influence on a teacher's psychological and emotional well-being, largely through interactions with students, colleagues, and school leaders (Hascher & Waber, 2021). Positive relationships can serve as resources that heighten emotional energy. For instance, feeling supported, trusted, and respected, along with a strong sense of belonging, can increase happiness and reduce stress

(Cann et al., 2022; Hartcher et al., 2023; Viac & Fraser, 2020). Cameron (2021) also suggests that human beings are naturally inclined toward the positive energy of relationships, and social or relational energy can be elevated and intensified through positive interactions. This type of energy and well-being has been shown to better predict long-term health than many other factors (Premman et al., 2019).

In contrast, negative relationships can act as stressors that decrease a teacher's emotional energy. For example, student misbehavior may lead to discouraging emotions that undermine psychological well-being (McCallum et al., 2017; Zhou et al., 2024). Likewise, a perceived lack of support, ongoing challenges, or social isolation (McCallum et al., 2017; Viac & Fraser, 2020) can erode a teacher's emotional and social well-being. Ultimately, nurturing collegial relationships that foster collaboration, encouragement, and positive emotions is essential for teachers to stay energized and thrive in their roles (Cann et al., 2022).

The Impacts of Emotions on Teacher Well-being

Key Idea #3 in the TRM suggests that reduced teacher well-being often arises from stress when educators perceive they lack the resources to meet the social or emotional demands of teaching. This stress can intensify and negatively affect their well-being if they do not have the social or emotional support they need, whether dealing with challenging relationships with students, colleagues, or administrators. Such a dip in psychological-emotional and social well-being has internal and external consequences. Internally, it can manifest as heightened stress and burnout, leading to emotional fatigue, disengagement, and apathy (McCallum et al., 2017). As burnout grows, teachers may experience lower job satisfaction, weaker occupational commitment, increased turnover intentions, negative emotions, and a reduced sense of self-efficacy (Hartcher et al., 2023; Viac & Fraser, 2020; Zhang et al., 2024; Zhou et al., 2024).

Externally, chronic exposure to negative social situations and emotions can diminish teachers' performance, decision-making, creativity, and even attendance. It may also weaken their prosocial behavior, teamwork, and leadership abilities (Asaloei et al., 2020; Barsade & Gibson, 2007;

Salvador & Nebria, 2023). Other studies have shown that decreases in well-being can lower teacher self-efficacy and instructional quality, which, in turn, can undermine student well-being and academic achievement (McCallum et al., 2017; Viac & Fraser, 2020).

In short, teacher energy and well-being, encompassing psychological-emotional, social, cognitive, and physical domains, are foundational to effective teaching and reducing turnover. A meta-analysis by Zhou et al. (2024) reports that high levels of teacher well-being strongly correlate with job satisfaction, occupational commitment, and work engagement while negatively correlating with turnover. The study also reveals that improved teacher well-being is associated with lower stress and burnout and that physical health is the most significant predictor of overall well-being.

The Adult Social-Emotional Path in Schools

Key Idea #3 of the TRM also suggests that if all forms of well-being, but especially psychological-emotional and social forms, are vital for teachers to teach effectively and avoid burnout, then improving a school's **adult social-emotional path** (Leithwood et al., n.d.) becomes a key strategy in your blueprint for increasing teacher retention. Previous research on the "emotional path" and emotional leadership (Berkovich & Eyal, 2021; Leithwood et al., n.d.; Leithwood et al., 2020) suggests that educational leaders can influence teacher emotions and thereby affect critical cognitive processes, such as perception, attention, memory, and judgment, ultimately affecting teachers' well-being.

Over the past three decades, numerous studies have investigated the impact of large-scale educational changes on teacher turnover and attrition. However, the affective revolution (Ashkanasy & Dorris, 2017; Parke & Seo, 2017), which focuses on the role of emotions in organizational settings, has received comparatively less attention in the context of schools than in other fields. One notable exception is Leithwood's work (Leithwood et al., 2010; Leithwood et al., n.d.; Leithwood & Sun, 2018), which explores how educational leaders might leverage the "emotional path" to influence teacher emotions related to schools and change. However, this research does not fully explain how the emotional path functions, what the adult social-emotional path means, or why its development is essential for teachers and school leaders today.

The Emotional Path

The emotional path is one part of the widely studied Four Paths Framework (Leithwood et al., n.d.), which explains how school leadership indirectly influences student learning through four interconnected areas that leaders can shape. These "paths" are groupings of mediating variables identified by research that link leadership actions to teacher, organizational, and student outcomes.

1. **Rational path**: This is considered the technical core of education, encompassing teachers' knowledge and skills related to curriculum, instruction, and assessment. Because of its direct link to student achievement, the rational path often has the strongest effect on student outcomes (Leithwood & Azah, 2017; Leithwood et al., 2010; Leithwood & Sun, 2018; Leithwood et al., 2020).
2. **Organizational path**: By focusing on structures, policies, and standard operating procedures, this path shapes teachers' working conditions. When these elements function effectively, they can have a positive influence on teacher emotions (Leithwood et al., 2019, 2020).
3. **Family path**: This path examines how the home environment, specifically parents' expectations, parent–child communication, and parents' social and intellectual resources, can be influenced by schools to enhance student success (Leithwood et al., 2019, 2020).
4. **Emotional path**: Central to this path are teachers' perceptions, dispositions, and everyday emotional states, which guide their thinking and behavior. Emotions significantly impact attention, memory, and judgment, making them crucial to how teachers adapt to their environments and deliver effective instruction (Leithwood et al., 2010; Leithwood & Sun, 2018; Leithwood et al., 2020; Salvador & Nebria, 2023).

Although research consistently indicates that the rational path has the most immediate effect on student achievement, the emotional path exerts a substantial, indirect influence by shaping what happens along the rational path. The logic is that when teachers feel positive about their workplace and their relationships with students, they engage more deeply in teaching practices that boost learning. For instance, Leithwood and Sun (2018) found high correlations between collective teacher efficacy and trust with student achievement ($r = 0.52$ and 0.50, respectively). From a leadership standpoint, their findings revealed indirect but significant effects on student learning through both rational ($b = 0.38$) and emotional ($b = 0.40$) paths, primarily driven by collective teacher efficacy and trust.

In essence, although the rational path directly informs classroom practice, leaders also must attend to the emotional path if they wish to maximize the benefits to student learning. Since teacher emotions and perceptions shape cognitive processes, any changes introduced through the rational path may be greatly influenced by teachers' emotional reactions, either positively or negatively. Furthermore, when excessive stress and burnout undermine teacher well-being, performance and student outcomes can suffer (Alave & Bearneza, 2024; Opper, 2019; Zhou et al., 2024). Thus, without a deliberate focus on creating and maintaining a supportive emotional climate for teachers, efforts on the rational path risk being blocked or weakened.

How the Emotional Path Works

If we accept that a school's adult social-emotional path significantly influences how teachers think and manage their energy in the classroom, then we need to ask: How does the emotional path work in practice, and why is it so important? This question is central for school leaders because, as Ashkanasy and Humphrey (2011) point out, emotions play a crucial role in human life across various areas, including family, health, and work.

The emotional path begins with emotions, essentially psychological and biological responses to events or stimuli in our environment (Ashkanasy & Dorris, 2017). These responses involve physiological changes that help us adapt, similar to Key Idea # 2 in the TRM. Emotions are usually short-lived, whereas mood is more enduring. Constructs like job satisfaction, often labeled as emotions, reflect a more sustained state or belief that is formed over time. In the teaching profession, emotions are especially relevant because teachers engage in frequent, intense, and meaningful interactions with students and other adults (Ye & Chen, 2015). Teaching is characterized by the frequency and intensity of social interactions that manifest student learning as well as the interactions and emotions involved in dealing with other adults. These social interactions and emotions are at the heart of teacher well-being and are crucial in fostering it (Hascher & Waber, 2021).

Affective Events Theory (AET) helps explain how workplace interactions become "affective events" that spark emotional reactions (Weiss & Cropanzan, 1996), which is again linked to Key Idea #2 in the TRM. According to AET:

1. **Work events trigger emotions**: Any situation or event, from a student's remark to feedback from a principal, can prompt an emotional response that can influence biological reactions. Teachers are not simply reacting randomly; there is almost always a specific event or thought that initiates the emotional reaction.

2. **Behavioral implications**: Emotions can influence how a person responds to these events, guided by implicit rules about what is acceptable in an organization. For example, in most schools, teachers are expected not to display overt anger toward students, even when they are frustrated.

3. **Long-term effects on attitudes and well-being**: When challenging events accumulate, teachers may experience increased stress, decreased enthusiasm, or even burnout. Conversely, frequent positive encounters can strengthen engagement and well-being. For instance, if a teacher has to deal with disruptive students and continually becomes upset, they may exhibit less enthusiasm and engagement with their teaching work as well as a decreased sense of well-being.

AET also emphasizes that employees are active interpreters of events, rather than passive recipients, in the psychological aspect of the biopsychosocial process. AET moves beyond stable job features, such as salary and schedules, to the more dynamic influence of affective events, which are those events that produce emotional reactions in employees. Beyond stating that a teacher has a stable schedule and small class sizes, AET acknowledges that any event or situation a teacher faces during the day may trigger an emotional response. These events can be big or small, positive or negative, but because the role of an educator is to interact with other humans during the day, every situation is primed for an affective response. These examples are just snapshots of teachers' daily interactions with students, parents, and school leaders, but each event may provoke an affective reaction. Consider the following:

- One teacher starts the day with hugs from her students, while another begins with a meeting with a parent who is upset about her child's grade.
- One teacher starting a third-period class gets the students' immediate attention, while another has to raise his voice numerous times to begin his class.
- One teacher meets with the principal and receives glowing feedback, while another gets a list of issues that need correction.

Like many other emotion-focused theories and models, AET suggests that employees are not passive recipients of these environmental events but actively interpret and appraise them, giving rise to emotions. This notion further suggests that school leaders must understand the events on the social-emotional path and how they can trigger emotions. They should also help educators develop and use adult skills and practices on the social-emotional path to better understand and manage emotions in response to affective events.

Levels on the Emotional Path

We often think of emotions primarily as personal, internal states. However, a more systemic way to understand the emotional path in schools and the forces that shape teacher emotions comes from the five-level model of emotions in organizations (Ashkanasy & Humphrey, 2011). Grounded in the neurobiology of emotions, this model enables leaders and teams to understand how emotions function at multiple levels, ultimately guiding them in creating a supportive emotional climate.

The five-level model of emotions in organizations (Ashkanasy & Humphrey, 2011) theorizes that the role of emotions can be considered and examined at five distinct but interrelated levels:

1. **Level 1 (Within-person)**: This level examines how individuals experience and respond to emotional events at a neurobiological level. People vary in their susceptibility to stress, for example, and

may also differ in how moods and longer-lasting emotional states, such as depression, affect their work behaviors.

2. **Level 2 (Between-persons)**: Individual differences in emotional traits, social-emotional skills, attitudes, or leadership styles fall under this level. For instance, one teacher might openly share emotions with coworkers, while another tends to remain private. Researchers here focus on variations in how often and intensely people experience positive or negative emotions.

3. **Level 3 (Interpersonal)**: This level examines how emotions are expressed and communicated between individuals. One leader might feel comfortable showing anger in a meeting, while another avoids openly expressing frustration. Differences in interpersonal style have significant implications for school leadership and culture.

4. **Level 4 (Group or team)**: At this level, we examine how collective emotions and moods emerge within groups or teams, often through processes such as emotional contagion. One group may radiate enthusiasm and humor, while another shows consistent dissatisfaction. The group leaders' emotional skills and behaviors can influence a team's overall mood and performance.

5. **Level 5 (Organizational)**: The final level addresses how a flourishing emotional climate is formed and sustained across the organization. Scholars suggest that this climate reflects the combined effects of the previous four levels (Ashkanasy & Humphrey, 2011). In other words, organizational-wide attitudes and behaviors evolve from repeated affective events at Levels 1, 2, 3, and 4. When teachers perceive a high level of collective trust and efficacy, for example, it signals a supportive emotional climate extending throughout the school (Leithwood & Beatty, 2009).

Ashforth and Humphrey (2022) note that workplace life is saturated with emotion, which affects every aspect of organizational behavior. Over time, these emotions can become institutionalized, entrenched "habits" or collective emotional norms that can be hard to change. Like all organizations, schools can develop a dominant affective tone; some are persistently upbeat and collaborative, while others remain tense or negative. Such an entrenched emotional climate can undermine teacher well-being, erode trust, and lead to increased turnover.

This five-level model shows that an individual teacher's emotional state (Level 1) is not isolated; it interacts with personal differences (Level 2), interpersonal interactions (Level 3), team dynamics (Level 4), and the overall school climate (Level 5). Leaders often focus interventions on Levels 1 through 3, trying to improve individual skills or foster better one-on-one relationships, without recognizing how these changes may affect group and organizational emotions.

By paying attention to all five levels, school leaders can gain a clearer understanding of how emotions influence their schools. The emotional path is not just about personal or even interpersonal relations; it is about how emotions reverberate throughout teams and, ultimately, the entire school. If school leaders overlook the broader perspective on the emotional path, they risk underestimating the significant influence of emotions on shaping teacher well-being, team performance, and overall school culture.

Conclusion

This chapter explored the emotional path in schools and its role in teacher well-being and turnover, guided by concepts such as AET and multi-level organizational perspectives on emotions, to expand on Key Ideas #1, #2, and #3 of the TRM: how emotions impact energy and well-being through a biopsychosocial process. With that background in mind, we turn next to how school leaders can strategically develop these skills in themselves and others to enhance the Emotional Path and improve teacher retention.

Leadership Considerations

- What types of emotions are typically displayed in your school? Why?
- Are there other emotions that people show but that are not typically expressed?
- Why do you believe that affect or emotion is an important factor in understanding successful schools and teacher turnover?
- How do you see teacher emotions impacting their performance and well-being?

- What type of well-being is typically addressed in your school? Why?
- What form of your teachers' well-being is highest and lowest? How do you know?
- Do teachers express different emotions in teams or whole groups versus what they display with you or another teacher?
- What displays of emotion typically show up in team meetings?
- How high are your teachers' current energy levels? What is that impacting?

References

Alave, A. D., & Bearneza, F. J. (2024). Stress as a predictor of mathematics teachers' teaching performance. *International Journal of Advanced Multidisciplinary Research and Studies*, 4(5), 1122–1125. https://www.multiresearchjournal.com/arclist/list-2024.4.5/id-3376

Asaloei, S. I., Wolomasi, A. K., & Werang, B. R. (2020). Work-related stress and performance among primary school teachers. *International Journal of Evaluation and Research in Education*, 9(2), 352–358. DOI: 10.11591/ijere.v9i2.20335

Ashforth, B. E., & Humphrey, R. H. (2022). Institutionalized affect in organizations: Not an oxymoron. *Human Relations*, 75(8), 1483–1517. DOI: 10.1177/00187267221083093

Ashkanasy, N. M., & Dorris, A. D. (2017). Emotions in the workplace. *Annual Review of Organizational Psychology and Organizational Behavior*, 4, 67–90. DOI: 10.1146/annurev-orgpsych-032516-113231

Ashkanasy, N. M., & Humphrey, R. H. (2011). Current emotion research in organizational behavior. *Emotion Research*, 3(2), 214–224. DOI: 10.1177/1754073910391684

Bakker, W. E. (2019). Emotional energy, relational energy, and organizational energy: Toward a multilevel model. *Annual Review of Organizational Psychology and Organizational Behavior.*, 6, 373–395. DOI: 10.1146/annurev-orgpsych-012218-015047

Barsade, S. G., & Gibson, D. E. (2007). Why does affect matter in organizations? *Academy of Management Perspectives*, 21, 36–59. DOI: 10.5465/AMP.2007.24286163

Berkovich, I. & Eyal, O. (2021). *A model of emotional leadership in schools: effective leadership to support teachers' emotions*. Routledge.

Bermejo-Toro, L., Prieto-Ursúa, M. & Hernández, V. (2016). Towards a model of teacher well-being: personal and job resources involved in teacher burnout and engagement. *Educational Psychology*, 36(3), 481–501. DOI: 10.1080/01443410.2015.1005006

Cameron, K. (2021). *Positively energizing leadership: Virtuous actions and relationships that create high performance*. Berrett-Koehler Publishers.

Cann, R. F., Sinnema, C., Daly, A.J., Rodway, J. & Liou, Y.H. (2022). The power of school conditions: Individual, relations and organizational influences on educator wellbeing. *Frontiers in Psychology*, 13. https://www.frontiersin.org/journals/psychology/articles/10.3389/fpsyg.2022.775614/full

Collie, R. (2023). Job demands and resources, teachers' subjective vitality, and turnover intentions: an examination during COVID-19. *Educational Psychology*. DOI: 10.1080/01443410.2022.2036323

Dreer, B. (2023). On the outcomes of teacher wellbeing: A systematic review of research. *Frontiers in Psychology*, 14. https://www.frontiersin.org/journals/psychology/articles/10.3389/fpsyg.2023.1205179/full

Ford, T. G., Olsen, J., Khojasteh, J., Ware, J., & Urick, A. (2019). The effects of leader support for teacher psychological needs on teacher burnout, commitment, and intent to leave. *Journal of Educational Administration*, 57(6), 615–634. https://doi.org/10.1108/JEA-09-2018-0185

Frenzel, A. C., Daniels, L., & Buric, I. (2021). Teacher emotions in the classroom and their implications for students. *Educational Psychologist*, 56(4), 250–264. DOI: 10.1080/00461520.2021.1985501

Gui, G. E. (2019). Teacher attrition and school leaders' capacity of leading, practices, and behaviors: A comparative study. *European Journal of Social Science Education and Research*, 6(1), 111–122. DOI: 10.26417/ejser.v6i1.p111-122

Gundlach, H. A. D., Slemp, G. R., & Hattie, J. (2024, May). A meta-analysis of the antecedents of teacher turnover and retention. *Educational Research Review*, 44. DOI: 10.1016/j.edurev.2024.100606

Hargreaves, A. (1998). The emotional practice of teaching. *Teaching and Teacher Education*, 14(8), 835–844.

Hartcher, K., Chapman, S., & Morrison, C. (2023). Applying a band-aid or building a bridge: Ecological factors and divergent approaches to enhancing teacher wellbeing. *Cambridge Journal of Education*, 53(3), 329–356. DOI: 10.1080/0305764X.2022.2155612

Hascher, T., & Waber, J. (2021). Teacher well-being: A systematic review of the research literature from the year 2000–2019. *Educational Research Review*, 34. DOI: 10.1016/j.edurev.2021.100411

Kern, M. L., Waters, L., Adler, A., & White, M. (2014). Assessing employee wellbeing in schools using a multifaceted approach: Associations with physical health, life satisfaction, and professional thriving. *Psychology*, 5, 500–513. DOI: 10.4236/psych.2014.56060

Leithwood, K., Anderson, S.F. Mascall, B., & Strauss, T. (n.d.). School leaders' influences on student learning: The four paths. https://www.leadershippartnerstx.com/files/1_school_leaders_influence_4_paths_to_learning.pdf

Leithwood, K., & Azah, V. N. (2017). Characteristics of high-performing school districts. *Leadership and Policy in Schools*, 16(1), 27–53. DOI: 10.1080/15700763.2016.1197282

Leithwood, K., & Beatty, B. (2009). *Leading with teacher emotions in mind*. Corwin Press.

Leithwood, K., Patten, S., & Jantzi, D. (2010). Testing a conception of how school leadership influences student learning. *Educational Administration Quarterly*, 46(5), 671–706. DOI: 10.1177/0013161X10377347

Leithwood, K., & Sun, J. (2018). Academic culture: A promising mediator of school leaders' influence on student learning. *Journal of Educational Administration*, 56(3), 350–363. DOI: 10.1177/10526846241258199

Leithwood, K., Sun, J., & McCullough, C. (2019). How school districts influence student achievement. *Journal of Educational Administration*, 57(5), 519–539. DOI: 10.1108/JEA-09-2018-0175

Leithwood, K., Sun, J., & Schumacker, R. (2020). How school leadership influences student learning: A test of "the four paths model". *Educational Administration Quarterly*, 56(4) 570–599. DOI: 10.1177/0013161X19878772

McCallum, F., Price, D., Graham, A., & Morrison, A. (2017). Teacher wellbeing: A review of the literature. *Association of Independent Schools of New South Wales*. www.aisnsw.edu.au/Resources/WAL%204%20[Open%20Access]/Teacher%20Wellbeing%20A%20Review%20of%20The%20Literature%20Faye%20McCallum%202017.pdf

Nguyen, T. D. (2021). Linking school organizational characteristics and teacher retention: evidence from repeated cross-sectional national data. *Teaching and Teacher Education*, 97, 103220. https://doi.org/10.1016/j.tate.2020.103220

Nguyen, T. D., Pham, L. D., Crouch, M., & Springer, M. G. (2020). The correlates of teacher turnover: An updated and expanded meta-analysis of the literature. *Educational Research Review*, 31, 100355. DOI: 10.1016/j.edurev.2020.100355

Opper, I. (2019). Teachers matter: Understanding teachers' impact on student achievement. *RAND*. https://www.rand.org/pubs/research_reports/RR4312.html

Parke, M. R., & Seo, M. G. (2017). The role of affect climate in organizational effectiveness. *Academy of Management Review*, 42(2), 334–360. DOI: 10.5465/amr.2014.0424

Premman, S. D., Jenkins, B., & Moskowitz, J. (2019). Positive affect and health: What do we know and where should we go next? *Annual Review of Psychology*, 70, 627–650. DOI: 10.1146/annurev-psych-010418-102955

Salvador, J. P., & Nebria, E. L. (2023). Teacher stress and school culture as predictors of teaching performance of public school teachers. *International Journal of Advanced Research*, 11(11), 671–688. DOI: 10.21474/IJAR01/17868

Shell, D. L., Hurt, C. S., & White, H. (2023). Principal characteristics' effect on teacher retention: A systematic review. *Educational Research and Reviews*, 18(6), 104–113. DOI: 10.5897/ERR2023.4318

Tsang, K. K. (2011). Emotional labor of teaching. *Educational Research*, 2(8), 1312–1316.

Viac, C., & Fraser, P. (2020). Teachers' well-being: A framework for data collection and analysis for PISA and TALIS. OECD Working Papers No. 213. www.oecd.org/content/dam/oecd/en.publications/reports/2020/01/teachers-well-being_bdafdeaf/c36fc9d3-en.pdf

Weiss, H. M. & Cropanzan, R. (1996). Affective events theory: A theoretical discussion of the structure, causes and consequences of affective experiences at work. *American Psychologist*, 44, 1–74.

Ye, M., & Chen, Y. (2015). A literature review on teachers' emotional labor. *Creative Education*, 6, 2232–2240. DOI: 10.4236/ce.2015.620230

Yin, H. (2015). The effect of teachers' emotional labour on teaching satisfaction: Moderation of emotional intelligence. *Teachers and Teaching*, 21(7), 789–810. DOI: 10.1080/13540602.2014.995482

Zhang, L., Chen, J., Li, X., & Zhan, Y. (2024). A scope review of the teacher well-being research between 1968 and 2021. *Asia-Pacific Educational Research*, 33, 171–186. DOI: 10.1007/s40299-023-00717-1

Zhou, S., Slemp, G., & Vella-Brodrick, D. (2024). Factors associated with teacher wellbeing: A meta-analysis. *Educational Psychology Review*, 36(2), 1–48. DOI: 10.1007/s10648-024-09886-x

Developing the Adult Social-Emotional Path as a Retention Strategy

> Reviewing his climate survey results later that night, Principal Paul Bridges wondered what he could do to improve his school's social-emotional climate. Was the way the adults were treating each other and not supporting each other a major reason teachers kept leaving the school? Or was the way he was treating others the reason teachers kept leaving? He had tried different things like dress-down Fridays and staff lunches once a month, but he realized that these efforts were not enough. Teachers appreciated these gestures, and morale seemed to improve temporarily, but he had come to the realization that it may be people's differing personalities, beliefs, needs, and social-emotional skills, including his own, that were influencing the school's climate and well-being. He had thought about doing a training on their next professional development day but knew one training would do little to develop these skills in the long term. The question of how he might develop better adult social-emotional skills as habits and where to begin remained on his mind all night as he continued to stare at his computer screen.

As we examined in the previous chapter, schools are filled with countless human interactions that can spark positive and negative emotions, creating ripples that affect teachers' well-being and, ultimately, their likelihood of staying or leaving. If leaders want to improve teachers' psychological-emotional and social well-being to reduce turnover, they must ensure that adult social-emotional skills are deliberately developed and strengthened.

Many adults assume that their social and emotional skills have been fully developed just by being an adult by their age. However, continual attention and practice of these skills can enhance overall adult development by increasing emotional understanding and regulation, shifting emotional priorities, and increasing emotional complexity.

This chapter continues using a systems perspective for developing and utilizing social-emotional skills in schools as a primary strategy to develop your teacher retention blueprint (see Appendix A). This chapter expands Key Idea #4 of the Teacher Retention Model (TRM), which centers on how **social-emotional leadership skills** and the collective role of social-emotional skills of all educators can help increase teacher retention. This chapter also details the specific skills and practices that schools can develop and use to improve the adult social-emotional path (Leithwood et al., n.d.) at distinct levels to improve the overall climate and influence teacher retention.

The TRM defines adult social-emotional skills and practices as *the research-based skills and practices that adults intentionally develop and use in school to enhance well-being*. To structure the social-emotional skills and practices, the TRM uses Ashkanasy and Humphrey's (2011) multi-level model of emotions in organizations and the five social-emotional competencies (self-awareness and management, social awareness, relationship skills, and responsible decision-making) of the Collaborative for Academic, Social, and Emotional Learning (CASEL, n.d.). Using this strategy as part of your blueprint requires knowledge of these skills and practices and insight into how to communicate their importance, develop them in practice, and determine their growth to make continuous improvement.

To simplify the multiple levels of emotions from Ashkanasy and Humphrey's (2011) multi-level model, the adult social-emotional skills and practices in the TRM are broken down into three levels: personal, interpersonal, and organizational (see Figure 4.1 below).

1. **Level 1 (Personal)** focuses on how individuals perceive themselves, experience, and respond to day-to-day emotional events and cope with stress to foster well-being. This level highlights the self-awareness and self-management components of the CASEL framework and acts as the base of the emotional path.
2. **Level 2 (Interpersonal)** concentrates on the skills and practices needed for effective communication and interaction between

Developing the Adult Social-Emotional Path

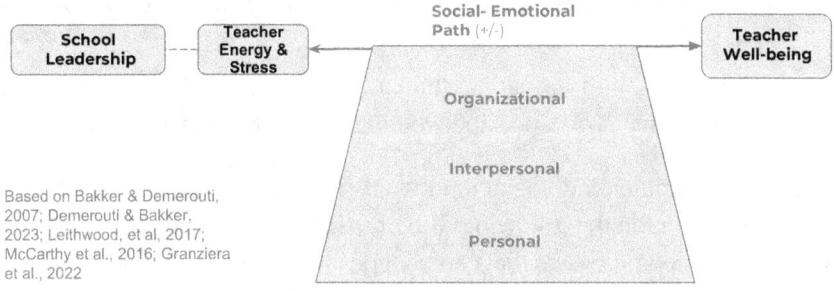

Figure 4.1 Three skill levels on the emotional path

educators to build well-being. This level emphasizes social awareness, relationship skills, and responsible decision-making from the CASEL model and acts in tandem with Level 1.

3. **Level 3 (Organizational)** examines how to create and sustain a positive school-wide social-emotional climate, relying on the skills from Levels 1 and 2. This level also underscores the importance of team or school leadership in managing group emotions and implementing more advanced social-emotional competencies across the entire organization. This level emerges from the previous two levels but also requires more advanced skills.

Each level is explored in more detail below, along with the corresponding skills and practices, potential strategies for developing them in a school, and ways to gauge their impact on individuals, relationships, and school culture.

Personal Level

In organizations like schools, people often have a mindset (a collection of beliefs and assumptions) that the social-emotional climate is about what the leader or employer does and not their role in creating that climate. However, schools are a collection of individuals whose collective actions and interactions work over time to create this climate. At the personal level, a mindset shift begins to happen when all educators, including leaders, realize that as individuals

- They can influence their understanding of emotions, their emotional thinking, and their emotional being.
- Influencing one's emotions, thinking, and being "shapes the world around them" and can shape well-being (Holdsworth & Wong, 2023)

The five recommended social-emotional skills and practices at the personal level include the following. The practices are all described below as four- or five-step processes that can be repeated to develop these behaviors into habits. The TRM uses research on habit development (Clear, 2018; Fogg, 2019), which targets using cues, actions, and rewards to internalize the habit. (See Appendices F and G for further explanation on habit development and how to create habit development plans.)

Skill: Understanding

One way to better understand yourself is through personality assessments and tests, which can help educators gain self-knowledge and insight into how they and others on their team operate. Given its solid research base, the Big Five personality model (Openness, Conscientiousness, Extraversion, Agreeableness, and Neuroticism) is a strong starting point. Other popular tools, such as the Enneagram, Gallup StrengthsFinder, or the Values in Action (VIA) Character Strengths Test, can also shed light on personal and interpersonal dynamics. Many of these tests are freely available online (e.g., at www.personality-quizzes.com). As individuals learn more about their personality traits, they can better appreciate the diversity of mindsets and emotional styles present in a school setting.

Practice	Steps
Using my strengths	1. Identify: Invite each person to name one of their personality strengths they want to lean on and how they will use it. 2. Connect: Ask participants to share how that identified strength can help the team's objectives. 3. Align: Briefly restate the shared purpose of the meeting. 4. Invite: Invite everyone to actively bring their strength forward during the discussion. 5. Reflect: Conclude with a 1- to 2-minute reflection on who felt they used their identified strength and any insights on how it impacted the discussion.

Skill: Breathing

Breathing exercises provide another effective strategy for reducing stress and enhancing focus during the workday. Fincham et al. (2023) meta-analysis suggests that breathwork can help mitigate stress and improve mental health. Similarly, studies by Shaw-Metz (2022) and Peterson et al. (2017) indicate that various simple breathing techniques can boost well-being by lowering perceptions of stress. Whether it's a brief pause between classes or a mindful moment before a meeting, deliberate breathwork can help educators remain centered and calm.

Practice	Steps
Box breathing	1. Inhale for a count of 4. 2. Hold for a count of 4. 3. Exhale for a count of 4. 4. Hold for a count of 4. 5. Repeat.
Belly breathing	1. Place one hand on your chest and abdomen. 2. Inhale through your nose for 4 seconds. 3. Hold for 2 seconds. 4. Exhale through your mouth for 6 seconds. 5. Repeat feeling your chest and abdomen move.

Skill: Labeling

A broader emotional vocabulary likewise supports well-being. Labeling emotions more precisely by consulting a "feelings wheel" or similar tool helps individuals better identify and manage their emotional reactions. Research demonstrates that having a robust vocabulary for describing emotional states, particularly positive ones, is linked to improved physical and mental health (Vine et al., 2020). Programs like RULER have similarly shown promise in guiding individuals to understand their emotional experiences more fully (Hoffmann et al., 2020), strengthening their capacity for emotional intelligence.

Practice	Steps
Feelings wheel	1. Pause and notice: Take a moment of stillness to recognize you are experiencing a feeling. This might be triggered by a physical sensation or an internal reaction.
2. Pinpoint the core emotion: Look at the center of the Feelings Wheel to find a core emotion that best matches your feelings.
3. Move outward: Move outward on the Feelings Wheel to find a more specific and nuanced emotion related to the core emotion you identified.
4. Validate: Acknowledge and accept the feeling for what it is: neither good nor bad. Share it.
5. Decide: Determine how you want to respond to the feeling now that it is clearly identified and validated. You can talk it out, take a break, adjust your environment, or simply note it and move on.
RAIN strategy	1. **R**ecognize and name the emotion.
2. **A**llow it to be; don't push it down or aside.
3. **I**nvestigate why and the thoughts creating the emotion.
4. **N**on-identify with the emotion; remember you are not the emotion.
5. Determine how you want to respond to the emotion now.

Skill: Reflecting

Reflection enhances social-emotional skills by fostering self-awareness and a deeper understanding of personal and professional experiences. Reflective practice can involve focusing on a specific social-emotional competency, such as Self-Awareness, or a challenging event during the school day (Bailey & Weiner, 2021). Research by White et al. (2015) indicates that taking a self-distanced perspective while reflecting on upsetting events can decrease emotional reactivity and promote more adaptive outcomes. Similarly, Ardelt and Grunwald (2018) highlight how reflection aids in recovering from trauma and building greater self-awareness, and Gerace et al. (2017) suggest that, overall, reflection represents a valuable tool for adult emotional development.

Practice	Steps
Prompting reflection [Note: Bailey and Weiner (2021) offer a selection of prompts to use.]	1. Read and pause: Take a moment to read the prompt or quote carefully. Pause briefly before responding. 2. Identify: Note keywords or themes related to the skill or emotion being discussed. 3. Connect: Ask yourself how the keywords or ideas relate to me and my role. Consider a recent situation or challenge you are facing. 4. Explore: Reflect on how the prompt or quote makes you feel. Consider what new insights emerge about yourself or others. 5. Apply: Decide how to apply any insights to your life or work. This might involve setting an intention, writing a small goal, or writing a reminder to yourself.
After action review	1. Recount the situation: Describe the event or incident in clear factual terms. Stick to who, what, where, and when, avoiding judgments or interpretations. 2. Identify and validate emotions: Name the emotion you experienced. 3. Analyze reactions: Explore what might have triggered these emotions, such as certain words, actions, behaviors, and think about how you responded in the moment (physically, verbally, behaviorally). 4. Extract insights: Consider the positive and negative outcomes. Ask "What did I do well?" and "What could have been done differently?" Focus on lessons learned and potential improvements. 5. Plan: Decide on specific next steps or changes and ensure that you understand your role in implementing these changes.

Skill: Expressing

Finally, expressing gratitude daily, whether spoken aloud or written, can yield multiple benefits. Adair et al. (2020) found that gratitude interventions alleviate emotional exhaustion and depression while promoting subjective happiness and emotional well-being. Likewise, Davis et al. (2015) identified improvements in psychological health stemming from various gratitude interventions. When teachers regularly acknowledge their work's positive aspects or recognize colleagues' support, they are more likely to experience sustained well-being.

Practice	Steps
Three good things	1. Find five minutes at the end of your day. 2. Review your day, noting the good things that happened. 3. List three good things that happened that day. These can be events, people, or things. 4. Consider why those things made you grateful. 5. Search for patterns over time in the things that make you grateful.
Gratitude letter	1. Reflect on the recipient: Think about why a chosen person matters to you. Recall situations, qualities, or actions that make you feel grateful toward them. 2. Choose a theme: Pick one central reason or theme for your gratitude. 3. Craft a first draft: Take 5–10 minutes and write down your appreciation, describing how this person has positively impacted you and why it matters. 4. Revise for clarity and warmth: Read through your draft, ensuring that the message is clear, personal, and warm, and add specific anecdotes or examples that illustrate your gratitude. 5. Deliver the letter.

Developing the Personal Level in Practice

To begin shifting mindsets at the personal level and boosting teacher well-being, school and team leaders can employ what we might call "emotional leadership moves." Rather than developing these skills and practices through isolated activities typically seen in short professional development sessions, leaders can weave them into daily routines so they become part of the school's social-emotional climate. The key is to keep these moves concise so they do not consume substantial time yet allow for regular practice and consistent reinforcement of the habit.

- As a school leader, explain why these skills and the adult social-emotional climate are important for increasing teacher well-being and retaining teachers. Use ideas from this book and others you may have thought about as you have read. Speak from the heart and find spaces to share your personal vision for this work.
- Begin with your leadership team, discuss what the skills and practices are at the personal level, and determine how and where they could be embedded. Give team leaders the agency to decide which skills they will use in their meetings, but set the expectations for the skills and practices to be used.
- Before the start of school, have your teachers take the personality assessment. Use the time during your before-school in-service days to explore and make meaning of the personality assessment results. Create a whole school or team chart listing each individual's results. Use these and the *Using My Strengths* practice in team meetings or individual discussions with situations or scenarios to understand how people might react to them or process them through social and emotional situations. Look at common patterns of strengths to build on and areas of difference to determine how you might work through various situations.
- Set a common norm that, before any meeting, you will review the personality profile of participants and use the *Using My Strengths* practice, noting which traits each individual wants to focus on.
- Use signature practices for every gathering of two or more people, like starting every meeting with breathing exercises to help people center and calm themselves before discussions begin. Or use an emotion labeling check-in to start and a labeling check-out to end a meeting.
- Use reflection prompts like: Which emotion was most expressed today in our meeting, or which emotion was I feeling but not expressing today? How did my personality strengths or weaknesses show up today? Or, as you debrief situations that happen, use the After Action Review practice to reflect on which emotions were used the most.
- Use gratitude frequently. Start your day with a gratitude list or start an email chain in which somebody starts expressing gratitude to somebody, which is then forwarded to another person, who expresses gratitude to another person, and so on. Another tactic for showing gratitude is to start a meeting by asking people to express gratitude or create a weekly gratitude board that people can add to.

Assessing Growth at the Personal Level

These methods can be used to gather information to know if personal-level skills and practices are becoming embedded and integrated into your school's climate.

- Have your staff take the Personal Level Diagnostic (Appendix B) to determine areas of strength and need.
- Use the social-emotional walk-through tool (Appendix H) and take some time to observe meetings and interactions to assess if and how teams and individuals are using these skills. Note which skills and practices are being used, and note which ones are not being used. Use this data to report to your leadership team and brainstorm how to reinforce the skills being used and how to begin including others.
- Use a tool like the Concerns-Based Adoption Model (CBAM) Levels of Use (Hall & Hord, 2011) to survey where individuals and teams are in their level of use of the practices at various times throughout the year. Use this data with your leadership team to determine the next steps.
- Last, you want to see if the practices are helping improve the well-being of your teachers. Use the Teacher Well-being measures in Appendix B up to three times per year to gauge the impact of these skills and practices on teacher well-being.

Interpersonal Level

Given the intensity of human interactions in schools, the interpersonal skills of educators can either bolster or diminish their well-being. Although there are many such skills to develop, the highlighted skills focus on what teachers and school leaders need most to support teachers' well-being. This list of skills is not exhaustive, reflecting choices from research and our experience based on developing educators' social and emotional well-being and minimizing the number of skills needed to learn and practice over time. These skills act like a user's manual for individuals, as they help give insight into how their emotions work in their brains.

At the interpersonal level, the mindset shift centers on how interactions with others add to or detract from their energy and well-being, even when addressing problems. At the interpersonal level, the mindset shift happens when all educators, including leaders, begin to realize that

- What they say and how they interact with others can influence their emotions, their emotional thinking, and their emotional being.
- This understanding of influencing others and their emotions can shape each other's well-being and sense of belonging.

At the interpersonal level, the recommended social-emotional skills and practices are explored below. Interpersonal skills can be developed through practices described below as four- or five-step processes that can be repeated to develop these behaviors into habits. (See Appendices F and G for further explanation on habit development and how to create habit development plans.)

Self-awareness: Mindfulness

Even though self-awareness is noted as a "self" skill, becoming more aware of and mindful in the moment with another person helps support good interpersonal skills. For example, people who know their triggers in conversations with others can avoid them and produce better interpersonal responses. The benefits of becoming more mindful of your tendencies and emotions are supported by Dahl et al. (2020). Their meta-analysis suggests that self-awareness, as attention to internal cues, can be strengthened through intentional training and "enhances self-regulation and corresponding networks in the brain."

Practice	Steps
Unpacking the emotion	1. Consider a big challenge or issue you are facing. 2. Recognize the feeling and name the emotion. 3. Ask what information that feeling or emotion has for you? What is it trying to tell you? 4. Ask what is happening in my body as I think about the issue. What might that be telling you? 5. Ask what feels like a next move or best step and why?
Change your inner dialogue	1. Notice your inner voice and what it is saying or telling you. 2. Ask yourself: Is that true or not? 3. Remind yourself it is just a thought and not you. 4. Change the thought and attend to it.

Self-management: Emotional Regulation

Managing one's emotions is an essential skill as an educator, given the multiple affective events that can occur during a normal school day. For instance, school leaders who listen to parent issues or teachers who deal with technology not working need to regulate their emotions to overcome natural responses that can decrease their energy levels. Farhi and Rubinstein's (2024) study showed that emotional regulation mediates the link between stress and well-being, and Socastro et al. (2022) found that using flexible emotional regulation strategies can lower stress intensity.

Practice	Steps
Tell a different story	1. Pause and breathe. 2. Notice the feeling and sensation. 3. Name the emotion and get curious. 4. Consider the story you are telling yourself. For example, I am feeling _____ because _____. 5. Choose a different response.
Recalibrate your anger	1. Notice the feeling of anger and slow down or disconnect for a while. 2. Ask: What am I valuing here? 3. Consider what the other(s) may be valuing. 4. Mentally zoom out to see what is at stake. 5. Choose deliberate words to discuss the value difference.

Social-Awareness: Positive Communication

Almost all affective events and interactions between people contain some form of communication that can highly influence interpersonal relations in a school. Very few educators are trained in the using positive communication skills, but this skill is especially critical for school leaders who must continually communicate effectively and positively to influence what happens in their school. Research done on Mirvel and Lyon's (2023) framework for positive communication shows that using the six positive communication behaviors serves as a "foundational mechanism to create connection" and can help establish better employee relationships.

Practice	Steps
Greeting	1. Approach with openness: Make eye contact, maintain relaxed body language, and smile. 2. Use their name: Personalize the greeting by using their name. 3. Offer a short positive statement: Set a welcome tone and express enthusiasm. 4. Check for readiness to engage: Observe verbal or nonverbal cues to see if the other person is open to engaging. 5. Invite next steps.
Asking questions	1. Establish genuine interest: Signal your curiosity about their perspective or experience. 2. Use open-ended starters: To prompt more detailed responses, use "What", "How", "Can you tell me about...?" 3. Listen actively: To demonstrate respect, maintain eye contact, nod, and remain attentive as they respond. 4. Seek clarification: Ask follow-up questions and restate key points: "So you're saying...?" 5. Show appreciation: Thank them for sharing or comment on their insight, "That's really helpful to know..."
Complimenting	1. Spot something genuine: To foster authenticity, identify a trait, behavior, or accomplishment you genuinely admire. 2. Be specific: To make the compliment more meaningful and believable, clearly state what you noticed. 3. Explain the impact: To show the broader significance and deepen the appreciation, briefly mention how their action or quality affected you or others. 4. Match the moment: Deliver the compliment privately or publicly in a way that suits the situation and person's comfort level to ensure the recipient feels respected. 5. Invite a response: Pause to let them react and follow up if it fits the context.

(Continued)

Practice	Steps
Disclosing	1. Assess the context and level of trust: Reflect on the appropriateness and comfort level of sharing personal information in this setting to ensure that the disclosure does not jeopardize the relationships. 2. Set a purpose: To help show relevance and intention behind your disclosure, briefly explain why you are sharing. 3. Share authentically: To build trust and foster a deeper connection through honesty, use clear, genuine language to describe your experience or perspective. 4. Express emotions: To validate the experience and encourage others, note how you felt. 5. Invite dialogue: Encourage the other person to share their thoughts or experiences.
Encouraging	1. Recognize effort: To validate their existing efforts, start by noting what the person has already accomplished or tried. 2. Emphasize potential: Highlight their strengths or possibilities to help them see their own capabilities and feel more confident. 3. Offer support: Ask how you can help or provide resources to show genuine investment in their success. 4. Share belief in them: To help reinforce their self-efficacy and motivation, convey genuine confidence in their abilities. 5. Follow up: To demonstrate long-term support, check back to see their progress.
Listening	1. Prepare to listen: To set the stage for attentive listening, remove distractions. 2. Show attentiveness: Maintain eye contact, nod, and use encouraging facial expressions or brief verbal affirmations to signal genuine interest and encourage them to keep speaking. 3. Reflect or paraphrase: Summarize what you heard to confirm understanding and clarify any confusion. 4. Validate feelings: Acknowledge their emotions to build empathy and trust. 5. Invite further sharing: Ask open-ended follow-ups to show you value their input and create more room for deeper conversation.

Relationship Skills: Relational Energy

Social well-being depends on emotional energy, the uplifting boost that people get from positive interactions (Cameron, 2021). The simple idea behind relational energy is that all humans can flourish in the presence of positive energy, which can be labeled as relational energy (Cameron, 2021). This relational energy is fostered between people through virtuous actions like generosity, compassion, kindness, or gratitude (Cameron, 2021). Relational energy is also the "extent to which a relationship is elevating, uplifting, and enriching" (Cameron, 2021). While many teachers and leaders discuss the need for strong relationships in schools, the question is are the relationships full of relational energy or more transactional in nature? And do the relationships increase well-being or detract from it?

Practice	Steps
Energy Focused Conversations	1. Set a positive intention: before engaging with someone, take a moment to visualize a supportive, uplifting exchange and remind yourself of your respect for the other person to help you approach the interaction with openness and genuine positivity. 2. Authentically acknowledge: Early in the conversation, provide a sincere acknowledgment or greeting. 3. Focus on strengths and potential: Spotlight the person's existing strengths, past successes, or future possibilities and ask them what they are excited about. 4. Create a two-way flow: invite active participation: ask questions, listen deeply, and respond with empathy and encouragement. 5. Build momentum and gratitude: Conclude by recognizing what was accomplished or clarified and express gratitude or positive expectations going forward.
Think compassion and kindness	1. Observe and notice: Pay attention to body language and verbal cues. 2. Acknowledge and validate: Use statements to show you understand or notice, "I can see something is bothering you." 3. Offer support or assistance: Ask "How can I help?" 4. Encourage care: Remind the person it's okay to step away or take a break. 5. Follow up: Check back in with the individual, "How are things going now?"

Responsible Decision-Making: Psychological Flexibility

Educators make countless decisions daily, from responding to student needs to designing lessons and shaping school policies. These decisions require not only solid information but also psychological flexibility. Similarly, the ability of teachers and leaders to overcome stressful situations sometimes requires psychological flexibility (McCracken et al., 2021). Work done by Pyszkowska (2020) also finds that psychological flexibility is a fundamental personal resource to adapt to and interact with changes in the environment.

Practice	*Steps*
Take it to the village	1. Think about two or three different ways to frame a decision.
	2. Consider whom you should talk to about the decision.
	3. As you talk to people, don't ask what they think about the two or three options. Instead, ask how they would feel if each decision were made.
	4. Using the emotional feedback, choose the option that gives the best emotional response.
Cultivating flexibility	1. Pause and notice when you feel distress or mental resistance around a decision. Check in with your thoughts, emotions, and bodily sensations.
	2. Allow the uncomfortable thoughts or feelings to be there to reduce the emotional intensity.
	3. Defuse from your thoughts and treat your thoughts as passing events, not absolute truths to create distance from unhelpful thoughts.
	4. Reconnect with values: Reflect on goals, values, and what matters most to better align your decisions with meaningful versus only emotional choices.
	5. Take committed action: Choose a small action consistent with your values to pair awareness with intentional behavior.

Developing the Interpersonal Level in Practice

Affective events and the emotions they generate significantly affect teacher well-being, but they also help sustain it (Hascher & Waber, 2021). Recognizing this central premise of the emotional path, school leaders, as well as all teachers, must prioritize the development of interpersonal skills. To encourage the mindset shift needed at the interpersonal level and improve teacher well-being, school and team leaders can introduce a series of "emotional leadership moves." These strategies focus on embedding new skills into everyday routines and emphasize habit formation to create lasting change.

- As you did with the personal skills, add to your reasons why interpersonal skills and the adult social-emotional climate are important for increasing teacher well-being and retaining teachers. Use other ideas in this book and explain why interpersonal skills are critical to the adult social-emotional path. Find new spaces to share your personal vision for this work.
- Have everybody at your school take the diagnostic in Appendix C to find collective areas of strength and development needs and set a commitment for growth. If diverse needs are evident, starting with a common skill to develop together is always easiest. Emotional regulation and positive communication are usually the best place to begin.
- Use the Habit Formation Guide in Appendices F and G to discuss with your teachers how skills like the interpersonal ones discussed previously become habits through habit cycles.
- Have teachers review the specific practices for the chosen skill area and create products to help them remember the practice and habit formation steps. Give them situations or scenarios to practice the skill.
- Put teachers into pairs or triads for a natural period, like a semester, as accountability partners.
- To help with cues or triggering the habit development cycle:
  - Have teachers determine two or three spaces where they most want to use the practice.

- - Set a norm that team leaders will give reminders to engage in the chosen practice at the start of all meetings.
  - Have teachers brainstorm other ways they will cue themselves to practice.
- To help with the actions being taken:
  - Create accountability partnerships.
  - Do monthly check-ins with accountability teams on progress and have teachers add to their habit development plans.
  - As leaders work on observations and feedback, use that time for check-ins on the chosen skills.
  - Troubleshoot the practice steps to see where people may be getting stuck and brainstorm solutions.
  - As the school leader, model your successes and failures as you also work to create new interpersonal habits. Share your goals and how you feel the climate is growing.
- To help reward the development of the skills:
  - Remind people of the growth you are seeing and its impact.
  - Individually or collectively, point out examples you have seen.
  - Create a small incentive system to reward those you see who are demonstrating the skill.
- After the period ends, have teachers use the diagnostic again (Appendix C) to see if they have grown. Teachers can choose a new skill or practice or stay on the one they originally chose.

Assessing Growth

- For individual teachers, the self-diagnostic (see Appendix C) offers a simple way to determine their growth. Journals can also be used to document specific times the skills were used and reflect on successes or opportunities for growth.

- Create an intentional meeting closing that asks participants to share examples of how these skills were used during meetings or other interactions.
- School or team leaders can create Innovation Configurations (Hall & Hord, 2011) for each skill and collect observational data to look at the use of skills in real scenarios (e.g., team meetings, staff meetings, professional learning communities, parent conferences, or hallway interactions).
- Use open-ended surveys to gather feedback from staff.
- Use the social-emotional walk-through tool (Appendix H) and take some time to observe meetings and interactions to assess if and how teams and individuals are using the interpersonal skills. Note which skills and practices are being used most and note which ones are not being used.

Collective Level

Schools can foster a more positive overall climate by developing the personal and interpersonal skills of all educators. Research suggests that improving self-awareness, self-management, social awareness, and relationship skills among educators will, over time, influence collective behaviors, whether at the team or whole-school level. There are, however, other common affective states that go beyond individual skills. These more advanced affective states can emerge from the personal and interpersonal work done at a school, but their importance and impact on well-being suggest that more advanced skills need to be employed.

At the organizational or team level, the advanced skills tied to these affective states align closely with what teachers have identified as critical emotional supports (Leithwood & Beatty, 2009; Leithwood et al., n.d.). These skills are especially important for school leaders and leadership teams. Because leadership is a primary factor in teacher turnover (Price, 2021; Shell et al., 2023), focusing on these higher-level emotional dynamics is another key to your blueprint for retaining teachers and sustaining a positive school culture.

At this level, the mindset shift centers on how the overall perceptions of important affective states like trust, efficacy, satisfaction, and recovery from stress add to teachers' energy and well-being. At the collective level, the mindset shift happens when all educators, including leaders, begin to realize that

- The collective climate can influence and support collective emotions, collective emotional thinking, and collective emotional being.
- This understanding of the collective influencing of emotions can shape teachers' well-being, sense of belonging, and ultimate decision to stay or leave.

At the collective level, the recommended social-emotional skills and practices include the following, which are explored below. More specific practices for each are listed below.

Skill: Create Trust through Empowerment

Teacher trust in school leaders is a key emotional factor that strongly influences teacher well-being and retention. In their meta-analysis, Sun et al. (2023) showed that school leadership has a powerful effect on teacher trust and that supportive, collegial leadership produces the highest levels of trust—an important finding since trust also moderately boosts student learning. Meanwhile, research by Da'as (2021) indicates that when principals use clear thinking when adding change initiatives and encourage participatory decision-making, they build affective trust and raise teacher job satisfaction. Tschannen-Moran (2014) similarly argues that those with greater power in hierarchical environments like schools must lead in creating and maintaining trust. A crucial skill in fostering that trust is empowering teachers. Bureaucratic approaches rely on hierarchy and authority, whereas professional models depend on trusting educators' expertise (Tschannen-Moran, 2014). Lack of trust and autonomy ranks among the top reasons that teachers leave the profession, so focusing on genuine empowerment is vital for both trust-building and teacher retention.

Practice	Steps
Team empowerment	1. Clarify purpose and shared vision, ensuring that everyone clarifies how their individual roles connect to the collective purpose. 2. Provide autonomy and resources: Give individuals the freedom to make decisions with clear boundaries. 3. Foster transparent communication: Encourage open dialogue about challenges, successes, and concerns to reduce suspicion and secrecy. 4. Encourage growth and risk-taking: Invite team members to try new ideas and frame mistakes as learning opportunities for learning and openly discuss how to improve for the future. 5. Recognize and celebrate contributions: Publicly acknowledge individual and group achievement, including efforts made and lessons learned to build morale.
Distributing leadership	1. Identify delegation opportunities: Review priorities to see which tasks, roles, or projects can be delegated to help expand leadership capacity. 2. Match roles to strengths and interests: Consider team members' skills, goals, and interests to align tasks to cultivate distributed leadership. 3. Define clear responsibilities and boundaries: Set explicit objectives, deadlines, and success metrics. Clearly outline what decisions can be made independently versus when they should consult or ask for help to prevent confusion and build trust. 4. Offer resources, training, and support: Provide initial training, documents, and contacts and set an agreed-upon communication routine like weekly check-ins. To reinforce a distributed leadership and empowerment culture, remain accessible but avoid micromanaging. 5. Monitor progress and reflect together: Schedule regular touchpoints to discuss progress, obstacles, and any adjustments needed. Celebrate achievements and share constructive feedback.

Skill: Create Collective Efficacy through Mastery Experiences

Collective teacher efficacy has long been linked to improved student outcomes (Hattie, 2023), showing the highest effect size (1.34) in some meta-analyses. When teachers believe they can positively influence student learning, they are more persistent in overcoming obstacles and more likely to succeed. For example, Goddard et al. (2017) found that high levels of collective efficacy improved math performance and cut academic disadvantages for Black students by half. Principals play a major role in creating this sense of collective efficacy. Some debate remains about whether collective efficacy is an end goal or develops from effective improvement processes that produce repeated successes (Hoogstein, 2020). In the TRM, we believe that effective leaders build team processes, like clear goal-setting, collaborative work around student data, and reflective instructional analysis, that can lead to these mastery experiences, ultimately strengthening collective efficacy. Rather than leaving success to chance, strong leaders carefully guide teams to recognize and celebrate their progress.

Practice	Steps
Cycles of inquiry	1. Set purposeful and attainable goals with teams for a defined period of time: Identify a specific challenge and break it down into small, clear objectives that feel meaningful and doable. 2. Design scaffolded, collaborative tasks: Provide structure through timelines, checklists, or protocols to help team members know how to begin and proceed. 3. Offer ongoing support: Be available for quick consultations or feedback and celebrate mistakes as part of growth. Invite other experts to consult as needed. 4. Reflect and celebrate progress: After each phase, hold a debriefing session asking what went well, what we learned, and what we can improve. Acknowledge the effort, collaboration, and interpersonal skills along the way. 5. Iterate: Incorporate lessons learned from each cycle into the next round of goals and encourage staff to share successes with the broader community.

Skill: Create Satisfaction through Reinforcing Meaning

A major benefit of a healthy adult social-emotional climate is increased job satisfaction. This sense of satisfaction can arise from intrinsic sources (e.g., helping students grow, feeling a sense of belonging, and enjoying one's daily work) and extrinsic factors (e.g., pay, professional status, and leadership support). According to Toropova et al. (2021), job satisfaction is closely tied to workload, teacher collaboration, and the school's approach to student discipline. Other studies highlight the link between meaningful work and job satisfaction. For instance, Turner and Thielking (2019) report that teachers who see their work as deeply meaningful, especially in shaping students' lives, experience higher satisfaction. Van Wingerden and Poell (2019) further show that finding meaning in one's work can boost teacher resilience and engagement. As growing accountability measures have limited teacher autonomy (Zhou et al., 2024), school leaders need to underscore a larger purpose beyond test scores, helping educators find renewed meaning in their profession.

Practice	Steps
Meaning for individuals	1. Open with appreciation: To link effort to impact, express gratitude for something specific the teacher has done recently. 2. Highlight a tangible win: Share a concrete positive outcome from the teacher's work and the impact it had on students. 3. Invite personal reflection: To help reconnect with their internal motivators and passion for teaching, ask the teacher to share one moment of success this week that reminded them why they became an educator. 4. Link to the larger mission: Briefly connect the teacher's work to the broader mission of the school or district. 5. Encourage next steps and growth: Close by asking the teacher about a personal goal or a small next step they would like to take. Offer your support.

(Continued)

Practice	Steps
Meaning for teams and whole schools	1. Open with collective appreciation: To set a positive tone and reminder that everyone's combined efforts matter, start by acknowledging a recent team-wide or school-wide accomplishment. 2. Highlight school-wide wins: Present data, stories, or visible outcomes that show the impact of the groups' work, emphasizing collective efforts to let everyone see how their daily contributions add up to meaningful progress. 3. Invite group reflection: Pose a simple prompt like "What's one moment from this past month that reminded you why you're here?" Encourage small-group discussions and then invite volunteers to share. 4. Link to the larger school mission: Connect recent achievements and reflections back to the broader mission or core values of the school and share a brief reminder of how everyone's role supports that overarching mission. 5. Encourage collaborative next steps: To help everyone feel they have a role in continuing forward momentum, ask the group to identify one or two actions that will build on current successes.

Skill: Create Recovery from Stress through Reframing and Reappraisal

As discussed previously, stress significantly affects teachers' energy and well-being. Like elite athletes, teachers as "learning-athletes" often need structured recovery from stress. Berkovich and Eyal (2021) argue that leaders must guide how teachers interpret events, helping them rethink challenges more constructively. While school leaders cannot easily give teachers extra days off to recover, they can help them reframe and reappraise stressful circumstances, reducing harmful rumination and preventing further energy loss. Studies by Denny and Ochsner (2013) show that reappraisal is a trainable skill that lowers negative emotions, and Crum et al. (2017) find that seeing stress as a positive force can improve coping. Similarly, other researchers (Wang & Hall, 2021; Liu et al., 2019) confirm that providing stress-reappraisal support for teachers can effectively reduce burnout and lower intentions to leave the profession.

Practice	Steps
Individual reframing	1. Invite the teacher to share: Begin by asking the teacher to describe the stressful situation in detail. Encourage them to speak freely to reduce the immediate tension. 2. Validate their experience: To keep the teacher open to reframing, acknowledge the teacher's feelings of frustration and normalize their reaction by noting that stress is common in challenging situations. 3. Identify underlying thoughts or assumptions: Gently ask any assumptions the teacher might be making, like "Are you assuming that the student's behavior is your fault?" or "Do you think your colleagues might view you negatively?" Uncovering these underlying narratives and beliefs reveals where a reframing opportunity exists. 4. Guide a shift in perspective: Offer alternative viewpoints or encourage the teacher to own the reframes. For instance, use "How else might we see this?" or "What if this challenge is an opportunity to try something different?" These reframes allow the teacher to see possibilities and different interpretations.
Know your ABCs (based on Reivich & Shatte, 2002)	1. Help the person calm down through breathing deeply. 2. Adversity: Ask what the event was that pushed your buttons. 3. Beliefs: Ask what thoughts and beliefs ran through your head? How aware were you of these thoughts and beliefs? Ask why you think those beliefs came up. 4. Consequences: Ask what feeling or emotion emerged from your thoughts and beliefs. 5. Discuss how beliefs led to consequences and potential next steps.

Developing the Collective Level In Practice

- As you did with the other two skill levels, explain why organizational skills and the adult social-emotional climate are important for increasing teacher well-being and retaining teachers. Use other ideas in this book and explain why this level of skills is essential for the adult social-emotional path. Find new spaces to share your vision for this work.
- Have your leadership team at your school take the diagnostic in Appendix D to find collective areas of strength and development needs. Set a commitment for growth in one area together.
- Create an accountability system with the other leaders at your meetings to check in and troubleshoot your growth as a team in the chosen area.
- Using the practices above, have leadership team members create habit development plans based on habit development steps of cues, behavior, and rewards. Emphasize the nature of routines so the practices become an embedded habit.
- To help with cues or triggering the habit development cycle:
    - Have team leaders determine two or three spaces where they most want to use the practice. Discuss natural routines during the day where these practices can become embedded.
    - Determine a set of cues to engage in the chosen practice at the start of all meetings or individual discussions by team leaders.
- To help with the actual practice or action taken:
    - Do monthly check-ins with your leadership team on progress and have leaders add to their practice charts.
    - Do individual check-ins with the other leaders to gauge their progress.
    - Troubleshoot the practice steps together to see where team leaders and others are struggling. Brainstorm solutions.
    - As a school leader, model transparency and vulnerability, admit mistakes, and share your growth journey so the other leaders see you growing.

- To help with the rewarding aspect of developing these skills:
  - Remind people of the growth you are seeing and its impact.
  - Individually or collectively, point out examples you have seen.
  - Create a small incentive system to reward those you see who are demonstrating the skill.

Assessing Growth

- For individual leaders, using the self-diagnostic (see Appendix D) offers a simple way to self-report their growth. Journals can also be used to document specific times the skills were used and to reflect on successes or opportunities for growth.
- Create an intentional leadership team meeting closing that asks participants to share examples of how these skills were used during the meeting or other interactions.
- Observe team meetings and how the team leader uses the practices during the meeting.
- Use open-ended surveys to gather feedback from team leaders and other school leaders.
- Multiple times during the year, use the Collective Affective State diagnostic in Appendix D to determine how staff perceive these common affective states.

Conclusion

Since the 1980s, educational leadership has focused on developing "instructional leaders" who raise student achievement through various methods. However, with rising teacher turnover, emotional leadership skills may be just as crucial, if not more so. According to Leithwood et al. (2020), the rational path of improving teaching and learning is heavily influenced by actions on the emotional path. In practical terms, when leaders successfully build personal and interpersonal skills, trust, and collective efficacy on the emotional path, they strengthen the rational path and drive school improvement.

This chapter examined personal, interpersonal, and organizational levels of emotions and the related skills and practices that can nurture a healthier social-emotional climate for adults, thereby reducing teacher turnover. The chapter also examined how leaders' social-emotional leadership skills and the role of social-emotional skills of all educators matter for teacher retention.

Berkovich and Eyal (2021) argue that people who do not receive care and support are unlikely to offer it to others, concluding that "positive emotional influence is a main influence on successful schools." True emotional leadership goes beyond small gestures like casual Fridays or monthly pizza lunches. When formal and informal leaders consistently practice emotional leadership, they foster meaningful work, belonging, and well-being, key factors in helping teachers stay and flourish.

Leadership Considerations

- How do the diagnostics help you better understand the strengths and needs of your social-emotional climate?
- How easy or difficult will it be to introduce the need for increased social-emotional skills in your school? Where might you begin?
- Why does how you communicate the role and need of the social-emotional path matter?
- How would you rate your current emotional leadership skills and your ability to develop these in others?
- How is developing habits in individuals and teams different from most professional learning?
- What do you want to add to your blueprint for retaining your teachers?

References

Adair, K. C., Kennedy, L.A. & Sexton, J.B. (2020) Three good tools: Positively reflecting backwards and forwards is associated with robust improvements in wellbeing across three distinct interventions. *The Journal of Positive Psychology*, 15(5), 613–622, DOI: 10.1080/17439760.2020.1789707

Ardelt, M., & Grunwald, S. (2018). The importance of self-reflection and awareness for human development in hard times. *Research in Human Development*, 15, 187–199. DOI: 10.1080/15427609.2018.1489098

Ashkanasy, N.M., & Humphrey, R.H. (2011). Current emotion research in organizational behavior. *Emotion Research*, 3(2), 214–224. DOI: 10.1177/1754073910391684

Bailey, J. A. & Weiner, R. (2021). *The daily SEL leader: A guided journal.* Corwin Press.

Berkovich, I., & Eyal, O. (2021) *A model of emotional leadership in schools: Effective leadership to support teachers' emotions.* Routledge.

Cameron, K. (2021). *Positively energizing leadership: Virtuous actions and relationships that create high performance.* Berrett-Koehler Publishers.

CASEL (n.d.). *What is the CASEL framework?* https://casel.org/fundamentals-of-sel/what-is-the-casel-framework/

Clear, J. (2018). *Atomic habits: Uneasy & proven way to build good habits & break bad ones.* Avery.

Crum, A. J., Akinola, A., Martin, A. & Faith, S. (2017). The role of actress mindset in shaping cognitive, emotional, and physiological responses to challenging and threatening stress. *Anxiety, Stress & Coping*, 30(4), 379–395. DOI: 10.1080/10615806.2016.1275585

Da'as, R. (2021). School principals' skills and teacher absenteeism during Israeli educational reform: Exploring the mediating role of participation in decision-making, trust and job satisfaction. *Journal of Educational Change*, 22, 53–84. DOI: 10.1007/s10833-020-09385-0

Dahl, C., Wilson-Mendenhall, C. D. & Davidson, R.J. (2020). The plasticity of well-being: A training-based framework for the cultivation of human flourishing. *Proceedings of the National Academy of Sciences*, 117(51), 32197–32206. DOI:10.1073/pnas.2014859117

Davis, D. E., Choe, E., Meyers, J., Wade, N., Vrajas, K., Gifford, A., Quinn, A., Hook, J. N., Van Tongeren, D. R., Griffin, B. J. & Worthington, E. L. (2015). Thankful for the little things: A meta-analysis of gratitude interventions. *Journal of Counseling Psychology*, 63(1), 20–31. DOI: 10.1037/cou0000107

Denny, B.T. & Ochsner, K.N. (2013). Behavioral effects of longitudinal training in cognitive reappraisal. *Emotion*, 14(2), 425–433. DOI:10.1037/a0035276

Farhi, M. & Rubinstein, O. (2024). Emotion regulation skills as a mediator of STEM teachers' stress, well-being, and burnout. *Scientific Reports*, 14, 15615. DOI: 10.1038/s41598-024-63228-z

Fincham, G. W., Strauss, C., Montero-Marin, J., & Cavanagh, K. (2023). Effect of breathwork on stress and mental health: A meta-analysis of randomised-controlled trials. *Scientific Reports*, 13(1), 1–14. DOI: 10.1038/s41598-022-27247-y

Fogg, B. J. (2019). *Tiny habits: The small changes that change everything*. Harvest Publishers.

Gerace, A., Day, A., Casey, S., & Mohr, P. (2017). 'I think, you think': understanding the importance of self-reflection to the taking of another person's perspective. *Journal of Relationships Research*, 8. DOI: 10.1017/jrr.2017.8

Goddard, R. D., Skrla, L., & Salloum, S. J. (2017). The role of collective efficacy in closing student achievement gaps: A mixed methods study of school leadership for excellence and equity. *Journal of Education for Students Placed at Risk (JESPAR)*, 22(4), 220–236. DOI: 10.1080/10824669.2017.1348900

Hall, G. E., & Hord, S.M. (2011). *Implementing change: Patterns, principles and potholes*. Pearson

Hascher, T., & Waber, J. (2021). Teacher well-being: A systematic review of the research literature from the year 2000–2019. *Educational Research Review*, 34. DOI: 10.1016/j.edurev.2021.100411

Hattie, J. (2023). *Visible learning the sequel: A synthesis of over 2,100 meta-analyses relating to achievement*. Routledge

Hoffmann, J. D., Brackett, M. A., Bailey, C. S. & Willner, C. J. (2020). Teaching emotion regulation in schools: Translating research into practice with the RULER approach to social and emotional learning. *Emotion*, 20(1), 105–109. DOI: 10.1037/emo0000649

Holdsworth, L., & Wong, N. (2023). *Human work: Five leadership mindsets for humanising the workplace*. Human work Publishing.

Hoogstein, T. J. (2020). *Collective efficacy: Toward a new narrative of its development and role in achievement*. Palgrave Communications. DOI: 10.1057/s41599-019-0381-z

Leithwood, K., Anderson, S. F., Mascall, B. & Strauss, T. (n.d.) School leaders' influences on student learning: The four paths. https://www.leadershippartnerstx.com/files/1_school_leaders_influence_4_paths_to_learning.pdf

Leithwood, K., & Beatty, B. (2009). *Leading with teacher emotions in mind*. Corwin Press.

Leithwood, K., Sun, J., & Schumacker, R, (2020). How school leadership influences student learning: A test of "the four paths model". *Educational Administration Quarterly*, 56(4), 570–599. DOI: 10.1177/0013161X19878772

Liu, J. J. W., Ein, N., & Gervasio, J., Vickers, K. (2019). The efficacy of stress reappraisal interventions on stress responsivity: A meta-analysis and systematic review of existing evidence. *PLoS ONE*, 14(2). https://journals.plos.org/plosone/article?id=10.1371/journal.pone.0212854

McCracken, L. M., Badinlou, F. Buhrman, M., & Brocki, K. C. (2021). The role of psychological flexibility in the context of COVID-19: Associations with depression, anxiety, and insomnia. *Journal of Contextual Behavioral Science*, 19, 28–35. DOI: 10.1016/j.jcbs.2020.11.003

Mirvel, J. C., & Lyon, A. (2023). *Positive communication for leaders*. Rowman & Littlefield.

Peterson, C. T., Bauer, S. M., Chopra, D., Mills, P. J., & Maturi, R. K. (2017). Effects of shambhavi mahamudra kriya, a multicomponent breath-based yogic practice (pranayama), on perceived stress and general well-being. *Journal of Evidence-based Complementary & Alternative Medicine*, 22, 788–797. DOI: 10.1177/2156587217730934

Price, H. (2021). Weathering fluctuations in teacher commitment: leaders relational failures, with improvement prospects. *Journal of Educational Administration*, 59(4), 493–513. DOI 10.1108/JEA-07-2020-0157

Pyszkowska, A. (2020). Personality predictors of self-compassion, ego-resiliency and psychological flexibility in the context of quality of life. *Personality and Individual Differences*, 161. DOI: 10.1016/j.paid.2020.109932

Reivich, K., & Shatte, A. (2002). *The resilience factor: 7 keys to finding your inner strength and overcoming life's hurdles*. Harmony

Shaw-Metz, J. L. (2022). Coming up for air: Breathwork practice for stress management in the healthcare setting. *Journal of Interprofessional Education & Practice*, 30(4). DOI: 10.1016/j.xjep.2022.100594

Shell, D. L., Hurt, C. S., & White, H. (2023). Principal characteristics' effect on teacher retention: A systematic review. *Educational Research and Reviews*, 18(6), 104–113. DOI: 10.5897/ERR2023.4318

Socastro, A., Everaert, J., Boemo, T., Blanco, I., Rodriguez-Carajal, R., & Sanchez-Lopez, A. (2022). Moment to moment interplay among stress appraisals and emotion regulation flexibility in daily life. *Affective Science*, 3, 628–640. DOI: 10.1007/s42761-022-00122-9

Sun, J., Zhang, R., & Forsyth, P. B. (2023). The effects of teacher trust on student learning and the malleability of teacher trust to school leadership: A 35-year meta-analysis. *Education Administration Quarterly*, 1–67. DOI: 10.1177/0013161X231183662

Toropova, A., Myrberg, E., & Johansson, S. (2021). Teacher job satisfaction: The importance of school working conditions and teacher characteristics. *Educational Review*, 73(1), 71–97. DOI: 10.1080/00131911.2019.1705247

Tschannen-Moran, M. (2014). *Trust matters: Leadership for successful schools*. Jossey Bass.

Turner, K., & Thielking, M. (2019). How teachers find meaning in their work and effects on their pedagogical practice. *Australian Journal of Teacher Education*, 44(9). DOI: 10.14221/ajte.2019v44n9.5

Van Wingerden, J., & Poell, R. F. (2019). Meaningful work and resilience among teachers: The mediating role of work engagement and job crafting. *PLoS ONE*, 14(9). DOI: 10.1371/journal.pone.0222518

Vine, V., Boyd, R.L., & Pennebaker, J.W. (2020). Natural emotion vocabularies as windows on distress and well-being. *Nature Communications*, 11. DOI: 10.1038/s41467-020-18349-0

Wang, H. & Hall, N. C. (2021). Exploring relations between teacher emotions, coping strategies, and intentions to quit: A longitudinal analysis. *Journal of School Psychology*, 86, 64–77. DOI: 10.1016/j.jsp.2021.03.005

White, R. E., Kross, E., & Duckworth, A. L. (2015). Spontaneous self-distancing and adaptive self-reflection across adolescence. *Child Development*, 86(4), 1272–1281. https://doi.org/10.1111/cdev.12370

Zhou, S., Slemp, G. & Vella-Brodrick, D. (2024). Factors associated with teacher wellbeing: A meta-analysis. *Educational Psychology Review*, 36(2), 1–48. DOI: 10.1007/s10648-024-09886-x

Reducing Demands as a Retention Strategy

Principal Bridges turned the corner after school one day and heard a group of teachers talking about an email they had all received from their department of instructional services asking for volunteers to begin a new technology initiative. He could hear snippets of their conversation as he slowly made his way down the hall. "My plate is full. I don't know how I could do one more thing." "What about all of the other things going on? How does this fit with everything else?" "Don't we have enough to do already? I can't imagine trying to fit this into my classes. They are short enough already." "Just reading that email gave me stress. I thought about it all day." "I just don't have the energy to do one more thing with all we're asked to do. Maybe if they would hire more people to help with some of the other duties, I could see working on using technology more effectively, but I just don't have the mental energy anymore." "Yeah, I try and give all of my energy to my students who are really struggling. This seems like a lot. Maybe if we quit doing something, it might not be that bad, but to pile on one more thing?" "With my kids in sports after school, and my husband on night shifts now, there is no way I have any extra time for something like this until summer." Principal Bridges took a deep breath to calm himself before he engaged with this group. He asked himself why the central office leaders hadn't talked to all of the principals before they rolled this out, so he could have smoothed the way. He took another deep breath, reminded himself to stay calm, then entered the conversation.

DOI: 10.4324/9781003628767-5

The opening scenario for anyone who has led schools for any time will be a familiar refrain. Leaders attempt to create new change initiatives to help move schools forward, while teachers try to determine how new ideas or programs fit into their current way of thinking, daily schedules, and energy levels. Teachers manage the daily interaction between their work and personal lives, attempting to balance these in some way that does not shortchange the other.

In Chapters 3 and 4, we looked at a primary factor causing teachers to leave their role: the relationship between emotional and social energy and well-being and the school's social-emotional path. However, the demands of teaching coupled with people's innate personalities and how they respond to those demands are other primary causes leading to excess stress, burnout, and eventual turnover of teachers.

The job demands-resources (JDR) model (Bakker & Demerouti, 2007, 2017), which underlies our Teacher Retention Model (TRM, Figure 5.1), has demonstrated that every job has specific risk factors or job demands associated with energy depletion and stress. *Job demands* are defined as the "physical, psychological, social, or organizational aspects of a job that require sustained physical and psychological (cognitive and emotional) effort or skill, and are therefore associated with certain physiological or psychological costs" (Bakker & Demerouti, 2007).

Teaching and leading schools present specific risk factors associated with stress and energy depletion that differ from other occupations. According to the JDR model, if demands become too extreme, they can impede performance (Collie et al., 2020). The more demands placed on the educator, the more energy is required to meet those demands, leading to increased stress as teachers question if they have the personal and organizational resources to meet them.

You can easily see how this plays out in the opening scenario. Teachers trying to balance their current demands (personal, classroom, and school) have just been asked to add another demand to their already-full day, causing an appraisal of time and energy toward the initiative. In many teachers' minds, this new demand will outpace their current resources, leading to stress, which can eventually lead to burnout. It is a simple formula: teachers will have less stress and more energy when resources exceed demands. When demands are greater than perceived resources, more stress emerges, and less energy is available for teaching.

Reducing Demands as a Retention Strategy

School leaders who are busy and stressed themselves may not connect the overall stress and energy of the school climate to the health, well-being, and flourishing of their staff. This juncture is where the TRM can help school leaders begin to have a more systemic view of teacher retention. To build an intentional retention system, school leaders need to understand the concept of demands, their influence on teacher stress and energy, and how reducing demands is a second key strategy for retaining teachers.

This chapter builds on the TRM by further examining stress and energy and then explores the types of demands evident in schools from a review of research. This chapter also examines how these demands, stress, and energy work systemically to create the health impairment process, often creating burnout and teacher turnover. This system is shown in Figure 5.1, where the demand level of the TRM is highlighted. The Key Ideas discussed in this chapter include the following:

Key Idea #1: Teaching is **energy-intensive**.
Key Idea #2: Stress is a **biopsychosocial process** that can drain energy.
Key Idea #5: **Job demands** drain energy by creating excess stress.
Key Idea #6: Excess demands can lead to **health impairment** through stress and burnout.

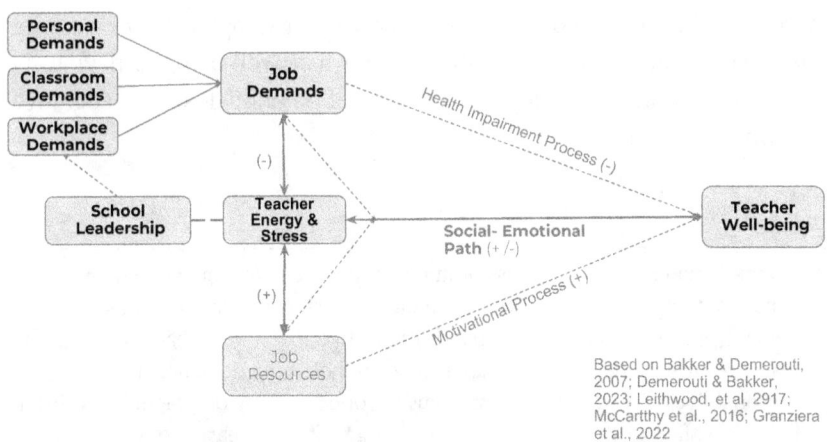

Figure 5.1 The Teacher Retention Model and Job Demands.

This chapter also describes a simple process that school leaders can use to reduce demands. This process describes removing demands intentionally using simple plan-do-study-act (PDSA) cycles. This process includes two data tools that schools can use to determine areas of the largest demand and the stress and energy of teachers.

Analyzing Demands in Your School Exercise

To begin, use the following exercise yourself or with a team to determine the current demands in your school or district. Remember, a demand is any factor that costs excess time or energy (Table 5.1).

1. Now, rank order each type of demand based on how much extra time and energy it takes teachers. Use a rating system of 1 (low), 3 (medium), and 5 (high) for each demand you listed.
2. Discuss any patterns you see and how much time and energy these demands are taking from your teachers.

Other Forms of Educator Energy

In Chapter 2, we discussed the Key Ideas supporting the TRM, emphasizing that teaching requires multiple forms of energy: physical, cognitive, social, psychological, and emotional (Key Idea #1). In Chapter 3, we explored the energy–well-being relationship, noting that well-being is having the energy to respond to the job's psychological-emotional, social, cognitive, and physical demands.

Table 5.1 Analyzing Demands Exercise

Personal demands:	**Classroom demands:**	**Workplace demands:**
What are the greatest demands most of your teachers have in their personal lives? Try to list at least five.	What are the greatest demands most of your teachers have in their classrooms beyond normal teaching? Try to list at least five.	What are most of your teachers' greatest demands in their workplace? Try to list at least five.

Beyond the social, psychological, and emotional forms of energy, other forms also play a major role in teacher well-being. These types of energy are essential for interacting with students and other adults and sustaining engagement and motivation in the complex world of education today. Quinn et al. (2012), for instance, identified physical energy as a primary energy source. He defined physical energy as the "capacity to do work" derived through complex physiological processes that convert chemical energy from food into mechanical energy (Jéquier & Flatt, 1986). The expenditure of physical energy is a complex process influenced by genetics, physiology, lifestyle, daily exercise, and occupational activity (Donahoo et al., 2004). According to Donahoo et al. (2004), a person's total daily energy expenditure varies due to differences in non-exercise activity, including occupation and environment. While many believe teaching is a fairly sedentary activity, teaching can be a physically demanding profession with lots of standing and walking. One teacher in a non-scientific study expressed:

> I have to walk my kids to and from lunch, to and from the bathroom (three times a day) and to and from specials and to the buses at the end of the day. The steps add up pretty quickly. There will be some days when I will have over 7,000/8,000 steps before 11 AM. I usually get 10,000 steps easily at work. Though I average around 14,000 at work a day. The most I got in one day was 17,000. While I have gotten over 20,000 steps on a workday, I usually get that because I get home having around 14,000–15,000 steps and get over 20,000 by walking around my apartment and working out.
>
> (Myfitnesspal, 2015)

Teachers also need substantial cognitive energy. The ability to remember and recall information, analyze and respond to questions, and make hundreds of decisions each hour requires ongoing cognitive energy. Given the mental energy needed to teach, a concept that helps us understand teachers' cognitive energy is cognitive load (Feldon, 2007; McCarty et al., 2021). Cognitive load centers on the idea that working memory, responsible for conscious information processing, has limited capacity and is the number of mental activities imposed on a teacher's working memory. For example, keeping the flow of a lesson in mind while listening for student misconceptions and answers to further prompt students while tracking student engagement are all cognitive processes happening in a teacher's working memory. When a teacher's cognitive load is flooded, cognitive overload happens with the demands on working memory surpassing its capacity, causing stress.

Cognitive load and energy in teaching consist of three categories. First, intrinsic load refers to the content knowledge and pedagogical strategies needed for a lesson. Second, extraneous load refers to distractions or irrelevant information that occupy a teacher's working memory, like a classroom disruption or being preoccupied with an upcoming meeting. Last, germane load is the ideal state, meaning the intrinsic load plus any necessary extraneous load does not overload the working memory (Feldon, 2007). Over time, with experience, many skills and processes of teaching become automatic and do not require conscious processing. However, under a high cognitive load, teachers may default to previous behavior, which can interfere with decision-making, causing unintended biases. For example, imagine a teacher who argued with their child, making them late for work, having a meeting during their planning period, and dealing with a parental complaint. All of these events combined may overload the extraneous load, limiting the working memory of a teacher who may revert to default behaviors in dealing with the students in their class.

As previously discussed, schools are ripe with social interactions. These interactions are primary and fundamental to schools and educating children, but these interactions and relationships require energy. Hall et al. (2023) discuss what makes social interaction or events like meetings or daily classes energy-intensive interactions. First, they suggest that energy is a fundamental commodity of human interaction and that the principle of energy investment suggests that individuals will invest their energy to attain the goals they seek, like a teacher wanting to get their students to a level of performance. Social energy involves perceiving and understanding others, the arousal from these interactions, and energy for managing self-presentation and motor displays such as gesturing (Hall et al., 2023). The intensity of social energy usage comes from personal investment, interaction length, the topic of the conversation, specific people, and feelings of connection (Baker, 2019; Hall et al., 2023). Last, as previously discussed, emotional energy is another primary form of energy that teachers rely on to fuel their work.

In sum, physical, cognitive, social, and emotional energy are highly intertwined and form the basis of the TRM's Key Idea #1. Simply stated, these forms of energy are the key resource needed for teaching and working with students. As educators, energy systems are taxed daily with movement, cognition, and relational-emotional demands that drain their human batteries. When these demands overwhelm their energy resources, teachers feel stress and decreased energy. Unfortunately, unlike our phone batteries, teachers can recharge but cannot replace their batteries by purchasing a new one. They burn out.

The Impact of Stress on Educator Energy and Well-Being

Teaching can be demanding, often draining a teacher's energy and well-being. Technically, stress and burnout arise from the interplay of biological, psychological, and social factors, often labeled as a "biopsychosocial process" (Hase et al., 2020), Key Idea #2 in the TRM. In simpler terms, this means that the social world that teachers live and work in is filtered through their thoughts and emotions, which then can affect their physical health.

A key part of the stress response is how teachers perceive challenges and evaluate whether they have the resources to manage them (McCarthy et al., 2016). Too much work or too many demands can overwhelm a teacher's resources and sense of control, triggering the body's stress response. This stress response includes the release of hormones like adrenaline and cortisol, which can lead to long-term health problems if stress becomes chronic (Wettstein et al., 2021). Over time, ongoing stress can disrupt these hormonal systems, lowering teachers' energy levels and increasing their risk for health issues (Epela et al., 2018; Staufenbiel et al., 2013).

Many educators talk about feeling "drained" or "running on fumes," especially during busy times of the school year (von der Embse et al., 2017). Research shows that excessive stress negatively affects teachers' health and well-being, which is closely connected to their energy levels. When teachers are stressed, they may feel emotionally exhausted, making it harder to engage with their work or maintain positive interactions with students and colleagues (Chang, 2009; Montgomery & Rupp, 2005; Jennings & Greenberg, 2009; Muylaert et al., 2023; Skaalvik & Skaalvik, 2018; Yin, 2015). Under high stress, teachers might use maladaptive coping strategies, such as avoiding tasks or withdrawing from responsibilities, which can further drain their energy and harm their mental and physical health (Agyapong et al., 2022; Chang, 2009; Gooden et al., 2023).

Long-term stress can also lower teachers' job satisfaction and motivation, which, in turn, reduces their energy (Granziera et al., 2021). Feeling overwhelmed or lacking control at work can weaken their sense of purpose and accomplishment, potentially leading to decreased effort and a higher desire to leave the profession (Bottiania et al., 2019; Simon & Moore-Johnson, 2015; Skaalvik & Skaalvik, 2018). Diminished job satisfaction contributes to emotional exhaustion and further erodes energy levels and well-being. Over time, these factors can lead to burnout, which includes emotional exhaustion, cynicism or detachment, and reduced personal accomplishment (Agyapong et al., 2022). Burnout can intensify negative effects on teacher energy and well-being and increase the likelihood of health problems like high blood pressure, sleep issues, chronic fatigue, gastrointestinal problems, and headaches (Taylor et al., 2024; von der Embse & Mankin, 2021).

When teachers' energy and well-being decline due to stress or burnout, their job performance usually suffers. Even highly skilled teachers can struggle with decision-making and instructional practices if overwhelmed. For example, Bottiania et al. (2019) showed that stressed teachers who lack coping skills and self-confidence can have more conflicts with students and find it harder to handle challenging behaviors. Stress can also limit innovative teaching methods, leading to less effective student learning experiences (Bottiania et al., 2019; Mennes et al., 2023).

Relative to the TRM's Key Idea #6, teachers with high stress levels often report physical and mental health problems, leading to more absences and potentially disrupting student learning (Herman et al., 2020; Howard & Howard, 2020). In some cases, teachers may feel pressure to come to work despite being ill, known as "presenteeism", which also reduces the quality of their instruction and can negatively affect student engagement and learning (Howard & Howard, 2020; Taylor et al., 2024). Chronic stress can reduce teachers' motivation, leading them to make more mistakes, show negative behaviors at work, and take longer to complete tasks. All of this can lower student satisfaction, motivation, and the overall quality of instruction (Viloria, 2023).

High stress in teachers can also harm student learning, achievement, and motivation in several ways. For example, stressed teachers tend to have weaker relationships with students, which can result in lower academic and behavioral outcomes (Herman et al., 2018). When teachers lack the emotional energy to support students, it often decreases student motivation and engagement (Klusmann et al., 2016; Schmidt & Jones-Fosu, 2019). Burned-out teachers may become withdrawn and cynical, offering less encouragement, providing fewer positive behavior supports, and potentially increasing behavioral problems in the classroom (Herman et al., 2018; Madigan & Kim, 2020). Over time, these patterns can contribute to lower student achievement in math and reading (Herman et al., 2018; Madigan & Kim, 2020).

Key Idea #2 of the TRM describes stress as a biopsychosocial process. Research shows that high or prolonged stress levels can seriously harm teachers' well-being and job performance, affecting student success. These negative effects align with Key Idea #6, the health impairment process, which states that "the severity of job demands leads to increased effort, depleting teachers' physical, cognitive, and emotional resources and possibly leading to exhaustion and health problems" (Bakker et al., 2023). But rather than burdening teachers to decrease their stress, leaders who want to create a more intentional retention system in their schools can begin to question the demands that cause the stress. The next section explores the job demands that may contribute to these health impairments.

Types of Demands

If stress and burnout are a biopsychosocial process, then the social environment in which teachers exist creates a set of demands that teachers must respond to daily to educate their students. Key Idea #5 of the TRM centers on the demands of teaching and how excess demands can lead to stress and a long-term health-impairment process: Key Idea #6 (Bakker & Demerouti, 2007; Demerouti & Bakker, 2023).

As previously defined, demands are "physical, psychological, social, or organizational aspects of a job that require sustained physical and psychological (cognitive and emotional) effort or skill, and are therefore associated with certain physiological or psychological costs" (Bakker & Demerouti, 2007). As shown in Figure 5.1, teachers' daily demands can be placed into three distinct categories: personal, classroom, and workplace. The most common demands found in research in each of these areas are explored below. These are not exhaustive, and each school or district may have unique demands in these categories.

Personal Demands

While we would love it if educators would direct all their energy toward teaching, they also have a life outside school that demands time and energy. The surveyed research shows that younger teachers struggle to balance the demands of raising a young family and their careers. More experienced teachers may struggle with balancing health issues and trying to give the same energy to their teaching as when they were younger. Many other teachers struggle to balance the emotional demands between home and work and create a separation between the two. All of these demands can and do detract from a teacher's energy.

Managing Time

Over the past few decades, research has shown that teachers' personal lives and abilities to manage time can impact their stress, energy, and well-being levels. For example, responsibility for childrearing and childcare duties often falls to the female partner who, if teaching full-time, can exacerbate their stress (Thomas et al., 2003). The number and age of a family's children can also increase family stress on teachers (Thomas et al., 2003).

Labor Division

Societal expectations for labor divisions between male and female married partners can be another personal demand placed especially on female teachers. On average, female teachers spend more time on household chores as unpaid work. This greater workload can add to teachers' stress levels and reduce their energy, leaving less energy for teaching (Stengard et al., 2021). Female teachers also have less time for leisure activities, which limits time for relaxation, recovery, and stress reduction (Stengard et al., 2021).

Work & Family Conflict

Family and work conflicts are often present because of the amount of work associated with a teacher's job (DeCarlo et al., 2019). Teachers may struggle to meet work demands, often having to bring work home, which conflicts with family attention and commitments, leading to stress and decreased energy (Kinman & Jones, 2008). Older, middle-aged teachers may also have multiple roles besides their teaching role. This group of teachers may be acting as a parent for their children, a spouse, and a caretaker for older parents in addition to increasing health issues (Torenbeek & Peters, 2017). Similarly, with the increased communication technology, Park et al. (2018) found that teachers seemed to be on call to respond to parents, students, or administrators outside of regular school hours. This perceived expectation can lead to enhanced strain for teachers and blur the lines between being at work and home. Finally, research done by Rahimi and Arnold (2024) found that the work–family conflict of teachers in Australia who intend to leave and stay is significantly higher than the general workforce.

Personality Traits

Teachers' personalities can also contribute to their stress levels. Everyone has unique personality traits that influence how they perceive and respond to stress; teachers are no exception. The Big Five personality model – consisting of the traits of openness, conscientiousness, extraversion, agreeableness, and neuroticism – helps explain these differences. Research shows that neuroticism, which involves being more prone to negative emotions and anxiety, is strongly linked to stress. Teachers who find it challenging to manage emotions or set high expectations for themselves may be more likely to experience stress and burnout. In short, some teachers are naturally more susceptible to stress in their personal lives and at school (Bardach et al., 2022).

In brief, personal demands are one category of demands that can impact a teacher's stress and energy levels. Role strain between home and work can often create a work–life imbalance, creating more emotional labor and additional stress along with inherent personality traits.

Classroom Demands

Our review of research identified four main classroom demands, adding extra pressure to the work of teachers. First, many teachers feel a loss of control due to high-stakes testing and pressure to boost student achievement, reducing their sense of autonomy and raising stress. Second, the increased need for managing and supporting students since the pandemic has placed extra stress on teachers to develop new behavioral management skills.

Third, the daily emotional and mental demands of working with students can be highly stressful. Fourth, frequent changes and requirements to use technology have created "technostress," leading to more anxiety for teachers. These rising demands in the classroom contribute to a range of emotions that heighten stress and drain teachers' energy.

Minimized Autonomy

Teachers face significant stress from accountability policies that demand higher student performance, often limiting their autonomy and sense of agency (Gundlach et al., 2024), which can act as an antecedent for stress and turnover. These policies emphasize standardized testing, bringing standardized curricula, pacing guides, and prescribed instructional models that restrict teachers' instructional choices (Lambert et al., 2018). Parcerisa et al. (2022) found that teachers feel pressured to focus on test scores over other valuable outcomes, reducing their autonomy. This increased accountability, which scrutinizes classroom practices, has also contributed to teacher stress and burnout by curbing instructional freedom (Darling-Hammond & Rustique-Forrester, 2005; Nguyen et al., 2024). Lambert et al. (2018) observed that states with strict accountability measures limiting teachers' time and decision-making reported higher stress levels.

Additionally, linking teacher evaluations and quality to student performance often leads to burnout symptoms, and teachers in the U.S. reported limited influence over key decisions compared with the OECD (Organization for Economic Cooperation and Development) average (Parcerisa et al., 2022). This trend has fostered feelings of de-professionalization and reduced job satisfaction. Further, von der Embse and Mankin (2021) noted that when test scores impact job evaluations, teachers feel increased stress and face potential burnout as their job security and professional standing hinge on these outcomes. Kraft and Arnold-Lyon (2024) found that the percentage of teachers worrying about their job security based on student test performance increased from 27% to 42% between 1999 and 2015.

Student Behavior

Managing disruptive student behavior is a major source of stress for teachers, demanding emotional and psychological resources. Studies, such as Dicke et al. (2017), highlight that handling social-psychological aspects of teaching, like managing student behavior and building teacher–student relationships, creates significant strain, particularly for new teachers. High numbers of classroom disruptions often lead to emotional exhaustion and decreased commitment to teaching. Additionally, poor attendance and behavioral issues can overwhelm teachers, amplifying stress. Negative emotions in these interactions can harm the teacher–student relationship, as excessive negativity may diminish students' self-beliefs (Frenzel et al., 2021). Gundlach et al. (2024) also find that a lack of student engagement is associated with teachers' intentions to leave the profession. Lambert et al.'s (2018) research found that teachers with less classroom control were less likely to continue teaching, and O'Brennan et al. (2017) identified factors like personal safety concerns and a lack of organized discipline as contributors to burnout.

Post-pandemic, teachers have reported even greater concerns about student behavior (Doan et al., 2024). Oxley et al. (2024) observed that returning students exhibited more conduct issues, with increased disruptions, greater defiance, and a heightened need for academic and emotional support, particularly among younger students. These behavioral challenges since the pandemic have negatively impacted teachers' emotional well-being, contributing to stress and burnout. Some research also points out that a school's socioeconomic level can influence teacher stress levels and intent to leave (Nguyen, 2021).

Emotional and Cognitive Demands of Teaching

Teaching is widely regarded as a high-emotion profession across various cultures, marked by stress, burnout, and emotional exhaustion (Chang, 2009), largely due to teachers' significant emotional investments (Hargreaves, 1998; Tavers, 2017). As job demands intensify, teachers experience increased emotional labor, which involves managing their emotions to conform to social expectations (Ye & Chen, 2015). This emotional labor often results in a disconnect between the emotions that teachers feel and those they display in the classroom, and surface acting, hiding true feelings, leads to higher emotional exhaustion, reduced well-being, and lower engagement (Tsang, 2011; Wang et al., 2019; Wang & Hall, 2021). Emotional challenges are exacerbated by student misbehavior, which triggers negative emotions like anger and anxiety that can have lingering effects (Frenzel et al., 2021). These challenges, coupled with the demands of emotional labor, often initiate a stress loop with both psychological and physiological impacts (Wang & Hall, 2021).

Beyond emotional demands, teachers face extensive cognitive demands, requiring mental energy to plan lessons, adapt curriculum, assess work, track lesson flow, respond to students, evaluate understanding, and manage classroom dynamics, all while being asked to perform administrative tasks like taking attendance or testing students. Teachers' noticing of classroom events (Bastian et al., 2024) and their ability to perceive relevant information necessary for deep pedagogy and learning is a critical cognitive demand that can be diminished without the necessary energy.

Technostress

Another significant classroom demand is "technostress," or the rising pressure on teachers to use technology as a teaching tool. Technostress can stem from several factors: the expectation to use technology without adequate training or support, a lack of control over which tools are used and how, and the constant need to update skills as technology evolves (Fernandez-Batanero et al., 2021). This demand is amplified by email, which allows constant access to teachers, adding pressure to frequently check for updates. Technostress can also be caused by inadequate or outdated equipment, sometimes forcing teachers to rely on personal devices (Rosyidah & Purwati, 2023). Malfunctioning technology, especially during critical tasks like testing or reporting, can lead to frustration, and concerns over data loss or viruses only add to the stress. Additionally, the line between work and home becomes blurred as technology enables teachers to access school networks remotely, prompting them to monitor student progress, complete administrative tasks, and respond to emails outside school hours, increasing stress at home.

In brief, classroom demands are another category of demands that can impact a teacher's stress and energy levels. The loss of autonomy, student needs, emotional and cognitive demands, combined with technostress, can cause severe stress and burnout and increase teacher turnover intentions.

Workplace Demands

Outside of the classroom, teachers exist in a work environment that may sometimes not be as hospitable as necessary to support teachers.

Conditions like unsupportive leadership, peer conflict, and parental issues also become perceived as demands on a teacher's energy. Coupled with the disciplinary environment, pace of change, and extra duties, the workplace demands can further limit the energy teachers need for working with students.

Increased Workload

An increased workload, largely driven by accountability policies, has become a significant demand, negatively impacting teachers. Beyond working directly with students, teachers face an "intensification" of their job. Extra tasks like grading, planning differentiated lessons, attending meetings, and completing professional development often extend beyond the regular school day (Findlay & Thompson, 2017). This increased workload stems from a "culture of performativity" that demands evidence of progress through standardized testing and accountability measures, adding paperwork and reporting requirements that divert focus from teaching (Fitzgerald et al., 2019). Additionally, the teaching role has expanded to addressing student mental health and well-being, and teachers are frequently expected to act as counselors, a role for which they lack training and time. Consequently, teachers' working hours have surged; in the U.S., teachers report working an average of 46 hours per week, one of the highest workloads worldwide (NCES, 2018), and recent studies indicate that this number has risen to 53 hours, exceeding the national average for other professions (Doan et al., 2024). This workload forces teachers to triage their responsibilities, prioritizing some tasks while neglecting others (Stacey et al., 2022).

Change and Pace of Change

With the mandate to continually raise the achievement of all students, teachers report constant stress from frequent curriculum changes or adaptations, new assessment tools, and instructional models, which require constant learning and adaptations of teaching materials and methods. These expectations for greater academic success and student support have resulted in the need for extra time and energy (Carroll et al., 2020). Other initiatives to support student well-being or meet the demands of the external environment have also left teachers feeling overwhelmed.

Parental Issues

As societal expectations for more students going to college increase, teachers feel stress due to heightened parental expectations around student performance and grades. Increased teacher stress stems from excessive communication with parents and negotiating individual expectations, which can be difficult to manage for teachers. Teachers also lament when parents challenge their professional judgment or when school leaders compromise their position of authority. The pressures to meet potentially unrealistic demands add to teacher stress and burnout (Carroll et al., 2020; Li & Yao, 2022).

Unsupportive Leadership

Unsupportive school leadership is one of the leading causes of teacher stress, burnout, and turnover (Ford et al., 2019; Gundlach et al., 2024). From the teachers' perspective, poor communication, a lack of consultation and communication around changes and issues, and frequent change leave teachers feeling disenfranchised, unsupported, and devalued (Gui, 2019). Inadequate support during evaluations, student behavior issues, and the need for classroom resources for new initiatives can lead to teacher frustration and stress (Humphrey et al., 2016; Gui, 2019). Limited opportunities for teacher leadership and input into decision-making can also impact teachers' feelings of value (Bartanen et al., 2024; Nguyen et al., 2020).

Interpersonal Problems with Colleagues

Difficult relationships with colleagues can contribute to stress for teachers and lead to turnover. Conflicts over beliefs and values or feelings of rivalry can create tension in the school workplace and contribute to a stressful work environment (Carroll et al., 2020). Different degrees of emotional intelligence have also been considered probable reasons for interpersonal conflict in the workplace (Bardach et al., 2022). Also, teachers express frustration over a lack of time for collaboration and the limited ability to support one another and collectively address challenges with students (Nguyen, 2021). A lack of perceived organizational support and trust from colleagues has been shown to link to higher intent to leave (Li & Yao, 2022).

Safety Issues

Gundlach et al. (2024) find that teacher safety has strong associations with lower stress levels in teachers and can be a factor in teacher retention. In contrast, teachers suggest that challenging behaviors can make them feel less safe and can be a significant source of stress, and they are more likely to leave when there are continual student disciplinary problems (Gundlach et al., 2024). Data further shows increases in teachers being threatened or physically attacked over the previous decade, and the more than 100 shooting incidents per year in schools between 2017 and 2022 made teachers feel less safe (Kraft & Arnold-Lyon, 2024).

Extra Duties

Extra duties beyond classroom teaching, like sponsoring extracurricular activities or taking on quasi-administrative roles like supervision duties, can also add to the normal stress and strain of teaching. These responsibilities often require that teachers spend additional hours at school, reducing their time for personal or family obligations and adding to feelings of burnout. Moreover, these roles frequently come without additional compensation or formal training, increasing frustration and the sense of being overburdened. Balancing these extra duties with core teaching responsibilities can overwhelm teachers, reducing their ability to focus on instructional quality and student support. Over time, these demands can erode job satisfaction and contribute to teachers' overall challenges in managing work–life balance.

In sum, the three categories of demands – personal, classroom, and workplace – systemically support one another as an increasing and dangerous set of causes for teacher stress, burnout, and eventual turnover. The sheer quantity of classroom and workplace demands work reciprocally over time to reduce perceptions of time to get everything done and drain energy, which begins to blur the line between work and home. These high demands and increasingly low autonomy for decisions have also been labeled as job strain or the combination of high demands and low control over work, which can impact physical and mental health (Netterstrom, 2012). Only by recognizing the most common demands and examining more specific demands in schools and districts can educational leaders begin to decrease these demands.

Using the Decreasing Demands Process

Schools are notorious for adding new programs, initiatives, or curricula, but they are not as good about evaluating their effectiveness and removing them when they do not provide the anticipated benefits. Humans generally find that adding things often answers organizational problems, but Klotz (2021) suggests that we often neglect subtraction as an improvement strategy because it is harder. School leaders are trained to initiate and manage change in schools, but little time is given to teaching leaders the benefits of removing demands or de-implementing things that are not working (Hamilton et al., 2023).

Given the busy nature of schools, school leaders and staff do not have an excessive amount of time for elaborate training or complex processes to decrease demands. Instead, the PDSA process (Bennett et al., 2022) and data tools explained below provide a concrete structure that leaders can use to reduce demands within the school's control. PDSA cycles are a method derived from improvement science (Bennett et al., 2022; Bryk et al., 2015; Langley et al., 2009) that can help leaders and teachers determine which demands are greatest in their schools and learn from their collective actions to reduce them and the impact the reduction has on teacher stress, burnout, and turnover intentions.

Based on improvement science, PDSA cycles use three simple questions in the model of improvement (Bennett et al., 2022; Langley et al., 2009). Modified to focus on reducing demands, these three questions are the following:

- What are we trying to accomplish in reducing demands for teachers?
- What change can we make that will result in less stress, burnout, and turnover for our teachers?
- How will we know the change improves stress, burnout, and turnover?

PDSA cycles are ultimately a process to learn about and discover new data and information by taking some action. Bennett et al. (2022) state that

> In the last 500 years, our ability to discover has greatly been accelerated by scientific thinking, the forming of theories and hypotheses, observation or experimentation and subsequent revision of our theories when our hypotheses failed to be correct in practice.

(p. 18)

Using PDSA cycles is a simple and practical way to use more scientific thinking about school turnover issues and understand that reducing demands can reduce stress, burnout, and turnover. The specific actions and questions in each phase of the PDSA cycle are detailed below (see Appendix K for the PDSA template).

Plan

In the Plan phase, leaders and teams seek to identify possible demands that can be reduced and determine their approach for reducing the demand. Table 5.2 below details the steps and questions to consider in the Plan phase. As you think about your first reduction in demands cycle, consider how Hamilton et al. (2023) define the types of reduction or de-implementation:

- Remove: Stop doing something altogether, like completely removing a meeting.
- Reduce: Change the frequency of doing something, like changing a meeting to one time a month instead of two times a month.
- Re-engineer: Change the reason why or how something is done, like making faculty meetings more about an instructional goal.
- Replace: Use a completely new form, like a short video weekly from the principal for faculty announcements.

Tool #1: The Job-Demands Diagnostic. This diagnostic helps school teams determine the specific demands causing the stress and what resources may be missing (see Appendix I). Based on Key Ideas #5–#8 of the TRM (job demands, resources, health impairment, and motivation), the JDR Diagnostic helps school leaders and teams determine where to focus their change efforts to lower demands.

Based on a thorough review of those demands that cause the most stress to teachers and those resources that best support teachers, the diagnostic is a simple diagnostic survey focusing on personal, classroom, and workplace demands. A few of the questions are shown below in Table 5.3, and the whole survey can be seen in Appendix I. When staff results are

Table 5.2 The Plan Phase of Reducing Demands

Steps	Questions to consider
1. Prepare your school to reduce demands.	1. How might I explain what reducing demands may do for teachers?
2. Use the **JDR Diagnostic** explained below to determine which demands are greatest in your school.	2. Which demands stand out as the greatest? Why do you think that is?
3. Determine which demand may most impact on lowering teacher stress and why.	3. Which demand may have the most impact on lowering stress?
4. Predict the impact of reducing the demand.	4. What is our prediction about what will happen if we reduce that demand?
5. Decide on the type of reduction: remove, reduce, re-engineer, or replace (Hamilton et al., 2023).	5. What type of reduction is needed for this demand? Why?
6. Determine if there may be any impact on student outcomes when the reduction happens.	6. Do we predict any impact on student outcomes if we make this reduction? Why?
7. Determine how you will measure the impact on teacher stress and energy (see Flash survey idea below).	7. What data should we collect to determine if the reduction is impacting stress and energy?
8. Create an action plan for communication of reduction and what this will look like for staff.	8. What steps must we take to make this reduction happen? Consider • Communication to staff • Exact expectations for reduction • Timeline • Data collection • Identifying other impacts • Other?

combined, this diagnostic can give school leaders insight into areas to reduce to help teachers gain more energy. The open-ended questions can get at more specific demands that are causing excess stress. Since the diagnostic is short, it is usually given at the end of the school's first and third quarters, leaving time to adjust demands.

Table 5.3 The Job Demands Diagnostic Sample Questions

Personal demand questions	Classroom demand questions	Workplace demand questions
1–5 Very low to Very high: In general, how demanding on your time and energy is each of the following currently: • Childcare issues • Trying to balance my work and outside family and personal life	1–5 Very low to Very high: In general, how demanding on your time and energy is each of the following currently: • Student behavior in my classroom • The number of digital tools and platforms I am required to use	1–5 Very low to Very high: In general, how demanding on your time and energy is each of the following currently: • The number of changes we are trying to implement • Interpersonal conflicts with colleagues

Do

In the Do phase, leaders and teachers begin to execute the plan for reducing the diagnosed demand with the expectation that teachers' overall burden will be reduced once the reduction is complete. Table 5.4 below details the specific steps and questions to consider in the Do phase.

Tool #2: Flash Surveys. Collecting some practical measures to determine the impact of the change idea is key to learning from your efforts to

Table 5.4 The Do Phase of Reducing Demands

Steps	Questions to consider
1. Communicate the plan and expectations to staff on the reduction.	1. How will we communicate the plan and expectations to staff?
2. Carry out the plan.	2. How will we know the plan and expectations for reduction are being followed?
3. Collect the practical measurement data.	3. How will we collect and store the data we are collecting?
4. Observe and note anything unexpected.	4. How can we attune ourselves to any unexpected impacts?

A Blueprint for Teacher Retention

reduce demands. You are trying to determine if reducing the demand will lessen stress and increase teacher energy, and simple measures can act as leading indicators of success. Based on Key Ideas #1 and #2 of the TRM, a simple flash survey is a one- or two-question survey that takes less than 30 seconds to complete. Since stress and energy are two central ideas in the TRM, continually assessing their levels can give school leaders a leading indicator of the No. 1 cause of burnout and teacher health issues. Ongoing stress is also known as a precursor to burnout and can diminish the amount of emotional support to students.

A flash survey is a simple rating of a teacher's stress or energy levels during the week and uses a simple 1–5 rating scale. Using the two questions below, determine how you would answer them based on your week at work.

1. On a scale of 1 to 5, how stressed did you feel this week?

1	2	3	4	5
Little stress				A great deal of stress

2. On a scale of 1 to 5, how much energy did you feel this week?

1	2	3	4	5
Little energy				A great deal of energy

Note that the two questions are designed to contrast with one another. As a school leader, you would want to see a low score on the stress scale and a high score on the energy scale. If done every week or every other week at a minimum during the school year, these data can show school leaders and their staff the perceived increasing or decreasing amounts of stress that can help leaders intervene around the demands placed on their staff.

Study

In the Study phase, data from the flash survey or other data are reviewed to determine if reducing the demand worked, and teacher stress was lowered. This phase also checks whether or not the intended goal of reducing demands has been met. Table 5.5 below details the steps and questions to consider in the Study phase.

Table 5.5 The Study Phase of Reducing Demands

Steps	Questions to consider
1. Collate and analyze the data collected.	1. What is the best way to analyze and display these data? Average, by week?
2. Compare the results to your predictions.	2. Was our prediction correct or not? Why?
3. Determine what was learned from your change idea.	3. What did we learn from our change idea?
4. Determine if there were any unintended consequences because of the reduction.	4. Were there any unintended consequences because of the reduction? How do you know?

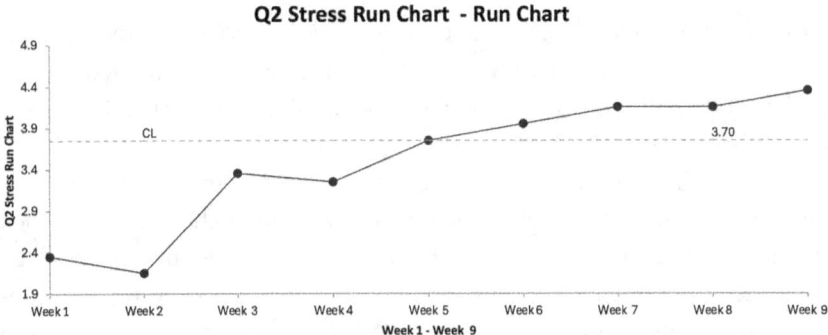

Figure 5.2 Run Chart of Stress Data Over a Quarter.

Figure 5.2 above shows a quarter's data on stress and energy using what is known as a run chart that shows a median of the ratings from teachers and how each week increased or decreased the aggregate stress level. Imagine you were the principal or part of the leadership team at this school and think about these two questions.

1. Which weeks show the highest amount of stress? In your experience, what might that be?
2. How would weekly data like this be helpful to you as a school leader?

Table 5.6 The Act Phase of Reducing Demands

Steps	Questions to consider
1. Discuss if you want to adopt the reduction in full and move to another reduction idea, adapt or modify the reduction idea, or abandon the reduction and focus somewhere else.	1. What should we decide?
2. Begin the plan phase again.	2. What is our next step?

Act

Last, in the Act phase, leaders and teachers decide to adopt (remove permanently), adapt (iterate on the demand), or abandon the reduction idea and try something else. Table 5.6 above details the specific steps and questions to consider in the Act phase.

By following the four-step PDSA cycle to reduce demands, school leaders and their teachers begin to generate knowledge about the demands causing stress and how teachers' stress can be impacted by the demands removed. The reducing demands strategy, however, should not be a one-time use of the PDSA cycles. Many demands on teachers and their time need to be reviewed and reduced. If you feel like you have gone through numerous cycles and reduced everything you can without secondary impacts, an ongoing review of demands still needs to be done to ensure the demand needle has not crept up again.

Conclusion

You would be hard-pressed to find teachers today who claim that teaching is easy and that the demands have not risen over the past few decades. Yet many of these demands have become normalized without realizing the unintended consequences of continually increasing them without the accompanying resources or structural changes to schools. The primary consequence is teachers leaving their schools or the profession entirely. Nguyen (2021) supports this claim as he found in national data that organizational characteristics and demands of schools positively influence retaining or losing teachers.

In short, the logical argument of how this occurs is supported by the four Key Ideas of the TRM.

> *Key Idea #1:* Teaching is **energy-intensive**.
> *Key Idea #2:* Stress is a **biopsychosocial process** that can drain energy.
> *Key Idea #5:* **Job demands** drain energy by creating excess stress.
> *Key Idea #6:* Excess demands can lead to **health impairment** through stress and burnout.

Understanding these four key ideas, the types of demands that can lead to greater stress in teachers, and a simple process for reducing demands may help to stem the tide of teacher turnover by creating a more intentional retention system.

Leadership Considerations

- What are the greatest demands that teachers face in your school or district? How do you know?
- Why is energy such an important idea for improving teacher performance?
- How is energy discussed or considered in your school or district?
- How does stress show up in your teachers? What are the obvious and not-so-obvious signs that stress is increasing over time?
- Which category of demands do you see as causing most of the stress in your teachers?
- What do you think teachers would suggest are their greatest demands?
- Has any obvious discussion of demands been done in your school or district? Why or why not?
- How might you involve your teachers in using the reducing demands strategies?
- How might you use the two data tools to inform the demand issues in your school or district?
- What is your role as the school and district leader in reducing demands on your teachers? How might you sponsor this idea for your teachers?

References

Agyapong, B., Obuobi-Donkor, G., Burback, L., & Wei, Y. (2022). Stress, burnout, anxiety and depression among teachers: A scoping review. *International Journal of Environmental Research and Public Health*, 19. DOI: 10.3390/ijerph191710706

Baker, W.E. (2019). Emotional energy, relational energy, and organizational energy: Toward a multilevel model. *Annual Review of Organizational Psychology and Organizational Behavior*, 6, 373–395. DOI: 10.1146/annurev-orgpsych-012218-015047

Bakker, A., Demerouti, E., & Sanz-Vergel, A. (2023). Job demands-resources theory: Ten years later. *Annual Review of Psychology and Organizational Behavior*, 10, 25–53. DOI: 10.1146/annurev-orgpsych-120920-053933

Bakker, A. B., & Demerouti, E. (2007). The jobs demands-resources model: State of the art. *Journal of Managerial Psychology*, 22(3), 309–328. DOI: 10.1108/02683940710733115

Bakker, A. B., & Demerouti, E. (2017). Job demands-resources theory: Taking stock and looking forward. *Journal of Occupational Health Psychology*, 22(3), 273–285. DOI: 10.1037/ocp0000056

Bardach, L., Klassen, R. M., & Perry, N. E. (2022). Teachers' psychological characteristics: Do they matter for teacher effectiveness, teachers' well-being, retention, and interpersonal relations? An integrative review. *Educational Psychology Review* 34, 259–300. DOI: 10.1007/s10648-021-09614-9

Bartanen, B., Husain, A. N., Liebowitz, D. D., & Rogers, L. K. (2024). The returns to experience for school principals. (EdWorkingPaper: 24-978). Annenberg Institute at Brown University: DOI: 10.26300/qq95-3q14

Bastian, A., Kaiser, G., Meyer, D., & Konig, J. (2024). The link between expertise, the cognitive demands of teacher noticing and experience in teaching mathematics in secondary schools. *International Journal of Science and Mathematics Education*, 22(2), 257–282. DOI: 10.1007/s10763-023-10374-x

Bennett, B., Grunow, A., & Park, S.(2022). *Improvement science at your fingertips*. Improvement Collective.

Bottiania, J. H., Duran, C. A. K., Pas, E. T., & Bradshaw, C. P. (2019). Teacher stress and burnout in urban middle schools: Associations with job demands, resources, and effective classroom practices. *Journal of School Psychology*, 77(1), 36–51. DOI: 10.1016/j.jsp.2019.10.002

Bryk, A. S., Gomez, L. M., Grunow, A., & LeMahieu, P. G. (2015). *Learning to improve: How America's schools can get better at getting better*. Harvard Education Press.

Carroll, A., Flynn, L., Sanders O'Connor, E., Forrest, K., Bower, J, Fynes-Clinton, S., York, A., & Ziaei, M. (2020). In their words: Listening to teachers' perceptions about stress in the workplace and how to address it. *Asia-Pacific Journal of Teacher Education*, 49(4), 1–15. DOI: 10.1080/1359866x.2020.1789914

Chang, M. L. (2009). An appraisal perspective of teacher burnout: Examining the emotional work of teachers. *Educational Psychology Review*, 21(3), 193–218. DOI: 10.1007/s10648-009-9106-y

Collie, R. J., Malmberg, L. E., Martin, A. J., Sammons, P., & Morin, A. J. S. (2020). A multilevel person-centered examination of teachers' workplace demands and resources: Links with work-related well-being. *Frontiers in Psychology*, 11, 1–19. DOI: 10.3389/fpsyg.2020.00626

Darling-Hammond, L., & Rustique-Forrester, E. (2005). The consequences of student testing for teaching and teacher quality. *Yearbook of the National Society for the Study of Education*, 104(2), 289–319. DOI: 10.1111/j.1744-7984.2005.00034.x

DeCarlo, A., Girardi, D., Falco, A., Dal Corso, L. & Di Sipio, A. (2019, May). When does teacher work interfere with teachers' private life? An application of the job demands-resources model. *Frontiers in Psychology*, 10, 1–13. DOI: 10.3389/fpsyg.2019.01121

Demerouti, E., & Bakker, A. B. (2023). Job demands-resources theory in times of crises: New propositions. *Organizational Psychology Review*, 13(3), 209–236. DOI: 10.1177/20413866221135022

Dicke, T., Stebner, F., Linninger, C., Kunter, M., & Leutner, D. (2017). A longitudinal study of teachers' occupational well-being: Applying the jobs-demand-resources model. *Journal of Occupational Health Psychology*, 23(2), 262–277. DOI: 10.1037/ocp0000070

Doan, S., Steiner, E. D., Woo, A., & Pandey, R. (2024). *State of the American teacher survey*. RAND. https://www.rand.org/pubs/research_reports/RRA1108-11.html

Donahoo, W., Levine, J., & Melanson, E. (2004). Variability in energy expenditure and its components. *Current Opinion in Clinical Nutrition and Metabolic Care*, 7, 599–605. DOI: 10.1097/00075197-200411000-00003

Epela, E., Crosswella, A. D., Mayera, A. A., Slavichb, E. P., & Mendesa, W. B. (2018). More than a feeling: A unified view of stress measurement for population science. *Frontiers in Neuroendocrinology*, 49, 146–169. DOI: 10.1016/j.yfrne.2018.03.001

Feldon, D. F. (2007). Cognitive load and classroom teaching: The double-edged sword of automaticity. *Educational Psychologist*, 42 (3), 123–137. DOI: 10.1080/00461520701416173

Fernandez-Batanero, J. M., Roman-Gravan, P., Reyes-Rebollo, M. M., & Montenegro-Rueda, M. (2021). Impact of educational technology of teacher stress and anxiety: A literature review. *International Journal of Environmental Research and Public Health*, 18 (2), 1–13. https://pmc.ncbi.nlm.nih.gov/articles/PMC7827099/

Findlay, P., & Thompson, P. (2017). Contemporary work: Its meaning and demands. *Journal of Industrial Relations*, 59(2). DOI: 10.1177/0022185616672251

Fitzgerald, S., McGrath-Champ, S., Stacey, M., Wilson, R., & Gavin, M.(2019). Intensification of teachers' work under devolution: A 'tsunami' of paperwork. *Journal of Industrial Relations*, 61(5). 613–636. DOI: 10.1177/0022185618801396

Ford, T. G., Olsen, J., Khojasteh, J., Ware, J., & Urick, A. (2019). The effects of leader support for teacher psychological needs on teacher burnout, commitment, and intent to leave. *Journal of Educational Administration*, 57(6), 615–634. DOI: 10.1108/jea-09-2018-0185

Frenzel, A. C., Daniels, L., & Burić, I. (2021). Teacher emotions in the classroom and their implications for students. *Educational Psychologist*, 56(4), 250–264. DOI: 10.1080/00461520.2021.1985501

Gooden, C., Zelkowski, J., & Smith, F. A. (2023). A systematic literature review on factors of stress, burnout and job satisfaction of secondary grades teachers at time of professional crisis. *The Clearing House: A Journal of Educational Strategies Issues and Ideas*. DOI: 10.1080/00098655.2023.2238880

Granziera, H., Collie, R., & Martin, A. (2021). Understanding teacher well-being through job demands-resources theory. In Mansfield, C.F. (Ed.) *Cultivating teacher resilience*. Singapore: Springer.

Gui, G. E. (2019). Teacher attrition and school leaders' capacity of leading, practices, and behaviors: A comparative study. *European Journal of Social Science Education and Research*, 6(1), 111–122. DOI: 10.26417/ejser.v6i1.p111-122

Gundlach, H. A. D., Slemp, G. R., & Hattie, J. (2024, May). A meta-analysis of the antecedents of teacher turnover and retention. *Educational Research Review*, 44. DOI: 10.1016/j.edurev.2024.100606

Hall, J. A., Dominquez, J., Merolla, A. J., & Otmar, C. D. (2023). Social bandwidth: When and why are social interactions energy intensive? *Journal of Social and Personal Relationships*, 40(8), 2614–2636. DOI: 10.1177/02654075231154937

Hamilton, A., Hattie, J., & William, D.(2023). *Making room for impact: A de-implemention guide for educators*. Corwin Press.

Hargreaves, A. (1998). The emotional practice of teaching. *Teaching and Teacher Education*, 14(8), 835–844. DOI: 10.1016/s0742-051x(98)00025-0

Hase, A., aan het Rot, M., de Miranda Azevedo, R., & Freeman, P. (2020). Threat-related motivational disengagement: Integrating blunted cardiovascular reactivity to stress into the biopsychosocial model of challenge and threat. *Anxiety, Stress and Coping*, 33(4), 355–369. DOI: 10.1080/10615806.2020.1755819

Herman, K. C., Hickmon-Rosa, J., & Reinke, W. M. (2018). Empirically derived profiles of teacher stress, burnout, self-efficacy, and coping and associated student outcomes. *Journal of Positive Behavior Interventions*, 20(2), 90–100. DOI: 10.1177/1098300717732066

Herman, K. C., Reinke, W. M., & Eddy, C. L. (2020). Advances in understanding and intervening in teacher stress and coping: The coping-competence-context theory. *Journal of School Psychology*, 78, 69–74. DOI: 10.1016/j.jsp.2020.01.001

Howard, J. T., & Howard, K. J. (2020). The effects of perceived stress on absenteeism and presenteeism in public school teachers. *Journal of Workplace Behavioral Health*, 35(2), 100–116. DOI: 10.1080/15555240.2020.1724794

Humphrey, R. H., Burch, G. F., & Adams, L. L. (2016). The benefits of merging leadership research and emotions research. *Frontiers in Psychology*, 7, 1022. DOI: 10.3389/fpsyg.2016.01022

Jennings, P. A., & Greenberg, M. T. (2009). The prosocial classroom: Teacher social and emotional competence in relation to student and classroom outcomes. *Review of Educational Research*, 79(1), 491–525. DOI: 10.3102/0034654308325693

Jéquier, E., & Flatt, J. (1986). Recent advances in human energetics. *Physiology*, 1, 112–114. DOI: 10.1152/physiologyonline.1986.1.3.112

Kinman, G., & Jones, F. (2008). A life beyond work? Job demands, work-life balance, and wellbeing in UK academics. *Journal of Human Behavior in the Social Environment*, 17, 41–60. DOI: 10.1080/10911350802165478

Klotz, L. (2021). *Subtract: The untapped science of less*. Flatiron Books.

Klusmann, U., Richter, D., & Ludtke, O. (2016). Teachers' emotional exhaustion is negatively related to students' achievement: Evidence from a large-scale assessment study. *Journal of Educational Psychology*, 108(8), 1193–1203. DOI: 10.1037/edu0000125

Kraft, M. A. & Arnold-Lyon, M. (2024). *The rise and fall of the teaching profession: Prestige, interest, preparation, and satisfaction over the last* half-century. (EdWorkingPaper: 22-679). Annenberg Institute at Brown University. DOI: 10.26300/7b1a-vk92

Lambert, R. G., McCarthy, C. J., Fitchett, P. G., & Eyal, M. (2018). Examining elementary teachers' risk for occupational stress: Associations with teacher, school, and state policy variables. *Teachers College Record*, 121(12), 1–42. DOI: 10.1177/016146811812001205

Langley, G. J., Moen, R. D., Nolan, K. M., Nolan, T. W., Norman, C. L., & Provost, L. P. (2009). *The improvement guide: A practical guide to enhancing organizational performance*. Jossey Bass.

Li, R., & Yao, M. (2022). What promotes teachers' turnover intention? evidence from a meta-analysis. *Educational Research Review*, 37(19). DOI: 10.1016/j.edurev.2022.100477

Madigan, D. J. & Kim, L. (2020). Does teacher burnout affect students? A systematic review of its associations with student achievement and student-reported outcomes. *International Journal of Educational Research*, 101174. DOI: 10.1016/j.ijer.2020.101714

McCarthy, C. J., Lambert, R. G., Lineback, S., Fitchett, P., & Baddouh, P. G. (2016). Assessing teacher appraisals and stress in the classroom: Review of the classroom appraisal of resources and demands. *Educational Psychology Review*, 28, 577–603. DOI: 10.1007/s10648-015-9322-6

McCarty, C., Redmond, P., & Peel, K. (2021). Teacher decision-making in the classroom: The influence of cognitive load and teacher affect. *Journal of Education for Teaching*, 47, 548–561. DOI: 10.1080/02607476.2021.1902748

Mennes, H., von der Embse, N., Kim, E., Sundar, P., Hines, D., & Welliver, M. (2023, November 13). Are "well" teachers "better" teachers? A look into the relationship between first-year teacher emotion and use of evidence-based instructional strategies. *School Psychology*. DOI: 10.1037/spq0000593

Montgomery, C., & Rupp, A. A. (2005). A meta-analysis for exploring the diverse causes and effects of stress in teachers. *Canadian Journal of Education*, 28, 458–486. DOI: 10.2307/4126479

Muylaert, J., Decramer, A., & Audenaert, M. (2023). How leaders' red tape interacts with employee's red tape from the lens of the job-demands-resources model. *Review of Public Personnel Administration*, 23(3), 430–455. DOI: 10.1177/0734371X221087420

Myfitnesspal. (2015, December). Teachers, do you take that many steps in the classroom? [Online forum post]. https://community.myfitnesspal.com/en/discussion/10304395/teachers-do-you-take-that-many-steps-in-the-classroom

NCES (2018). *TALIS 2018 U.S. highlights web report* (2018). U.S. Department of Education. Institute of Education Sciences, National Center for Education Statistics. https://nces.ed.gov/pubsearch/pubsinfo.asp?pubid=2019132

Netterstrom, B. (2012). Job strain as a measure of exposure to psychological strain. *The Lancet*, 380(9852), 1455–1456. DOI: 10.1016/s0140-6736(12)61512-8

Nguyen, D., See, B. H., Brown, C., & Kokotsaki, D. (2024, December). Leadership for teacher retention: Exploring the evidence base on why and how to support teacher autonomy, development, and voice. Oxford Review of Education. DOI: 10.1080/03054985.2024.2432635

Nguyen, T.D. (2021). Linking school organizational characteristics and teacher retention: Evidence from repeated cross-sectional national data. *Teaching and Teacher Education*, 97, 103220. DOI: 10.1016/j.tate.2020.103220

Nguyen, T. D., Pham, L. D., Crouch, M., & Springer, M. G. (2020). The correlates of teacher turnover: An updated and expanded meta-analysis of the literature. *Educational Research Review*, 31, 100355. DOI: 10.1016/j.edurev.2020.100355

O'Brennan, L., Pas, E., & Bradshaw, C. (2017). Multilevel examination of burnout among high school staff: Importance of staff and school factors. *School Psychology Review*, 46(2), 165–176. DOI: 10.17105/spr-2015-0019.v46-2

Oxley, L., Asbury, K., & Kim, L. E. (2024). The impact of student conduct problems on teacher wellbeing following the onset of the covid-19 pandemic: An interpretive phenomenological analysis. *British Educational Research Journal*, 50(1), 200–217. DOI: 10.1002/berj.3923

Parcerisa, L., Verger, A., Pages, M., & Browser, N. (2022). Teacher autonomy in the age of performance-based accountability: A review based on teaching profession. *Education Policy Analysis Archives*, 30(100). DOI: 10.14507/epaa.30.6204

Park, Y., Liu, Y., & Headrick, L. (2018). *Improving lives of teachers: Staying connected to work, work-family boundary control, and strain. 78th Annual Meeting of the Academy of Management*, AOM 2018. DOI: 10.5465/ambpp.2018.7

Quinn, R. W., Spreitzer, G. M., & Lam, C. F. (2012): Building a sustainable model of human energy in organizations: Exploring the critical role of resources. *The Academy of Management Annals*. DOI: 10.5465/19416520.2012.676762

Rahimi, M., & Arnold, B. (2024). Understanding Australia's teacher shortage: The importance of psychosocial working conditions to teacher turnover intentions. *The Australian Educational Researcher*. DOI: 10.1007/s13384-024-00720-5

Rosyidah, F. I., & Purwati, S. (2023). Technostress in secondary school teachers. *International Journal of Research Publications and Reviews*, 4(11), 1840–1846. DOI: 10.55248/gengpi.4.1123.113107

Schmidt, L. W., & Jones-Fosu, S. (2019). Teacher stress in urban classrooms: A growing epidemic. *Urban Education Policy and Research Annuals*, 6(2). DOI: 10.55370/uerpa.v6i2.907

Simon, N., & Moore-Johnson, S. (2015). Teacher turnover in high-poverty schools: What we know and can do. *Teachers College Record*, 117, 030308. DOI: 10.1177/016146811511700305

Skaalvik, E. M., & Skaalvik, S. (2018). Job demands and job resources as predictors of teacher motivation and well-being. *Social Psychology of Education*, 21(5), 1251–1275. DOI: 10.1007/s11218-018-9464-8

Stacey, M., Wilson, R., & McGrath-Champ, S. (2022) Triage in teaching: the nature and impact of workload in schools. *Asia Pacific Journal of Education*, 42(4), 772–785. DOI: 10.1080/02188791.2020.1777938

Staufenbiel, S. M., Penninx, B.W., Spijker, A.T., Elzinga, B.M., & van Rossum, E.F.C. (2013). Hair cortisol, stress exposure, and mental health in humans: A systematic review. *Psychoneuroendocrinology*, 38(8), 1220–1235. DOI: 10.1016/j.psyneuen.2012.11.015

Stengard, J., Mellner, C., Toivanen, S., & Nyberg, A. (2021). Gender difference in the work and home spheres for teachers and longitudinal associations with depressive symptoms in a Swedish cohort. *Sex Roles*, 86, 159–178. DOI: 10.1007/s11199-021-01261-2

Tavers, C. (2017). Current knowledge on the nature, prevalence, sources and potential impact of teacher stress. In T.M. McIntyre, S.E. McIntyre, & Francis, D.J. (Eds.), *Educator stress: An occupational health perspective* (pp. 23–54). Springer.

Taylor, L., Zhou, W., Boyle, L., Funk, S., & De Neve, J. E. (2024). *Wellbeing for Schoolteachers* (Report No. 2). International Baccalaureate Organization. https://www.ibo.org/research/wellbeing-research/wellbeing-for-schoolteachers-2024/

Thomas, N., Clarke, V., & Lavery, J. (2003). Self-reported work and family stress of female primary teachers. *Australian Journal of Education*, 47(1), 73–87. DOI: 10.1177/000494410304700106

Torenbeek, M., & Peters, V. (2017). Explaining attrition and decreased effectiveness of experienced teachers: A research synthesis. *Work*, 57(3), 397–407. DOI: 10.3233/WOR-172575

Tsang, K. K. (2011). Emotional labor of teaching. *Educational Research*, 2(8), 1312–1316.

Viloria, J. M. (2023). Extinguishing the fire: Occupational stress-coping mechanisms of high school teachers. *Journal of Interdisciplinary Perspectives*, 2(7), 24–33. DOI: 10.69569/jip.2023.0023

von der Embse, N., & Mankin, A. (2021). Changes in teacher stress and wellbeing throughout the academic year. *Journal of Applied School Psychology*, 37(2), 165–184, DOI: 10.1080/15377903.2020.1804031

von der Embse, N. P., Schoemann, A.M., Kilgus, S.P., Wicoff, M., & Bowler, M. (2017). The influence of test-based accountability policies on teacher stress and instructional practices: a moderated mediation model, *Educational Psychology*, 37(3), 312–331. DOI: 10.1080/01443410.2016.1183766

Wang, H., & Hall, N. C. (2021). Exploring relations between teacher emotions, coping strategies, and intentions to quit: A longitudinal analysis. *Journal of School Psychology*, 86, 64–77. DOI: 10.1016/j.jsp.2021.03.005

Wang, H., Hall, N. C., & Taxer, J. L. (2019). Antecedents and consequences of teachers' emotional labor: A systematic review and meta-analytic investigation. *Educational Psychology Review*, 31, 663–698. DOI: 10.1007/s10648-019-09475-3

Wettstein, A., Schneider, S., Grosse Holtforth, M., & La Marca, R. (2021, September). Teacher stress: A psychobiological approach to stressful interactions in the classroom. *Frontiers in Education*, 6, 1–6. DOI: 10.3389/feduc.2021.681258

Ye, M. L., & Chen, Y. (2015). A literature review on teachers' emotional labor. *Creative Education*, 6, 2232–2240. DOI: 10.4236/ce.2015.620230

Yin, H. (2015). The effect of teachers' emotional labour on teaching satisfaction: Moderation of emotional intelligence. *Teachers and Teaching*, 21 (7), 789–810. DOI: 10.1080/13540602.2014.995482

 Increasing Resources as a Retention Strategy

Principal Bridges felt a familiar tension building as he sat in the spring budgeting meeting with his leadership team. Each colleague had a suggestion for how to use the school's resources: "We need more teachers to reduce class sizes." "We need more administrators to handle the surge in behavior issues." "Let's use all new state funds for teacher salaries, so we can stop losing staff." "How about more paraprofessionals to maintain order in classrooms?" "Better professional development is essential." "Let's not forget technology that actually works."

While these ideas had merit, Principal Bridges noticed a pattern: to his team, additional funding seemed to be the sole solution. From their perspective, more money could buy more staff, more programs, and more equipment. But experience had taught him that pouring money into new hires and resources did not always create meaningful change. Last year, for example, they added an in-school suspension coordinator, yet behavior problems persisted.

Now, he wondered if the school needed a broader definition of "resources." Was there something beyond extra positions and new materials that could foster a healthier school climate—one where teachers felt supported, students felt engaged, and turnover rates declined? He realized that truly transforming the school might require more than a bigger budget; it might require rethinking how to build a place where people genuinely want to stay and thrive.

Many principal preparation programs include courses on resource management, like financial budgeting and staffing strategies. These are important skills; knowing how to allocate funds and position staff effectively can improve a school's operations. These "resources" are necessary but may not be sufficient to create the intentional retention system needed to retain more teachers year after year.

In the previous chapters, we explored the demands placed on teachers and how these demands can drain their energy and well-being, ultimately leading to burnout or attrition. The Teacher Retention Model (TRM), inspired by the Job Demands-Resources (JDR) theory (Demerouti & Bakker, 2023), shows that resources beyond funding and staff are critical for job satisfaction, motivation, reducing burnout, and ultimately retaining educators.

In the original JDR model, Bakker and Demerouti (2007) define job resources as physical, psychological, social, or organizational supports that can

- Help individuals reach work goals,
- Reduce job demands (and related physical or psychological strain), and
- Stimulate personal growth, learning, and development.

These resources can operate at several levels: organizational, interpersonal, within the work itself, or at the individual level. While money and staffing certainly matter, they are only part of a larger system. Other resources, such as social-emotional support, updated materials, and classroom assistance, can significantly reduce stress, promote motivation, and improve overall well-being (Kleine et al., 2019; Porath et al., 2022).

Building on our discussion of demands, this chapter focuses on the "positive side of energy," or thriving, as a form of high-level well-being, Key Idea #1. We then explore how job resources replenish teachers' energy, Key Idea #7, and how these resources boost motivation and engagement over time, leading to thriving, Key Idea #8. Figure 6.1 below highlights how the resource level fits within the TRM. The Key Ideas discussed in this chapter are

Key Idea #1: Teaching is **energy-intensive**.
Key Idea #7: **Job resources** replenish energy.
Key Idea #8: Resources promote a **motivational process** and thriving.

A Blueprint for Teacher Retention

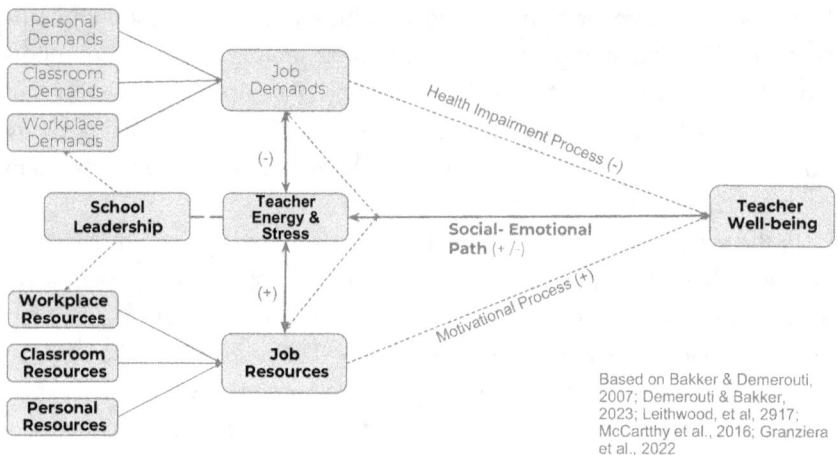

Figure 6.1 The Teacher Retention Model and Job Resources.

This chapter also outlines a simple, practical process to increase and refine resources in your school using plan-do-study-act (PDSA) cycles. Included are two data tools you can use to identify which resources are most needed and gauge your teachers' overall level of thriving. By following these steps, school leaders can act more intentionally to foster an environment where educators feel supported, motivated, and ready to stay for the long term.

Analyzing Resources in Your School Exercise

To begin, use the following exercise yourself or with a team to determine the current greatest resource needs in your school or district. Remember, a resource is any element that can help teachers achieve work goals, reduce demands and energy costs, and stimulate personal growth. Remember, these do not have to be financial or personnel resources (Table 6.1).

Thriving as an Educator

Energy is essential for effective teaching and for retaining teachers over time. Earlier chapters explained how persistent, excessive demands, such as heavy workloads, emotional stress, and insufficient support, can deplete a teacher's energy. When these demands continually surpass the teacher's

Table 6.1 Analyzing Resources Exercise

Personal resource: What personal resources might teachers need to help achieve work goals, reduce demands, or stimulate personal growth that may not be in place now? Try to list at least five.	**Classroom demands:** What classroom resources might teachers need to help achieve work goals, reduce demands, or stimulate personal growth that may not be in place now? Try to list at least five.	**Workplace demands:** What workplace resources might teachers need to help achieve work goals, reduce demands, or stimulate personal growth that may not be in place now? Try to list at least five.

capacity to recover, burnout becomes more likely, leading some to leave their school or the profession.

On the other side of the TRM, resources can provide a "charge" that helps teachers maintain or boost their energy. While the demand side treats energy as a limited store, the resource side highlights a more dynamic view: energy can be replenished or expanded through positive interactions, emotional support, and other forms of energetic activation (Quinn et al., 2012).

Quinn et al. (2012) describe this energetic activation as the subjective sense of vitality, vigor, or enthusiasm, those moments when teachers feel excited to collaborate with colleagues or experience a breakthrough with students. Baker (2019) refers to a similar concept, emotional energy, which can be heightened by cultivating positive emotions or reducing negative ones.

Klijn et al. (2021) extend this understanding of personal energy by identifying four key dimensions: physical, emotional, mental, and spiritual. Their research also links an array of factors, such as clear goals, strong relationships, autonomy, and a shared sense of purpose, to "thriving" at work, a state closely tied to feeling energized. These findings reinforce that school conditions can shape energy levels and are changeable over time.

In short, while demands drain a teacher's energy, well-designed and utilized resources can help replenish it and foster thriving. Understanding how to maximize these resources is central to creating schools where teachers remain motivated, engaged, and eager to stay.

Perspectives on Thriving

In stark contrast to the energy drain caused by excessive demands, using the right resources effectively can increase teacher thriving and well-being. But what exactly is "thriving"? Emerging from positive psychology (Porath et al., 2022), thriving goes beyond simply removing stressors. It involves actively fostering psychological states, behaviors, and resources that promote growth (Spreitzer et al., 2005). While different authors have offered various definitions, nearly all emphasize psychological growth, vitality, and a sense of positive momentum.

A frequently cited definition comes from Spreitzer et al. (2005), who describe thriving as "the psychological state in which individuals experience both a sense of vitality and a sense of learning at work." Vitality involves having sufficient energy and feeling positive emotions, whereas learning refers to acquiring new knowledge and skills (Okros & Virga, 2025). Together, these dimensions fuel self-development and provide a sense of forward momentum (Spreitzer et al., 2005).

Kleine et al. (2019) likewise define thriving as a positive state of vitality, learning, and forward momentum that helps individuals adapt to challenges and produce positive outcomes. Their meta-analysis shows that thriving at work is strongly linked to employee engagement, a supportive workplace climate, coworker support, supportive leadership, and organizational support all play important roles. Thriving is also associated with lower burnout and higher commitment and job performance (Kleine et al., 2019). Porath et al. (2022) further suggest that thriving buffers against stress and distractions, leading to stronger resilience, better physical health, and improved focus.

Thriving is especially critical for teachers, who face high demands daily. According to Goh et al. (2021), thriving fosters personal growth, physical and emotional well-being, and organizational effectiveness. When teachers thrive, they seek new ways to build their skills, experience higher satisfaction in their work, and show greater commitment: factors that reduce turnover intentions (Goh et al., 2021; Walumbwa et al., 2017).

Thriving is viewed as a dynamic rather than permanent trait (Goh et al., 2021; Istiningtyas et al., 2025; Spreitzer et al., 2005). People experience ebbs and flows in their energy and sense of momentum, often influenced by levels of support they receive and opportunities for growth. A study by Porath (2022) found that only 36% of workers felt they were thriving, underscoring how fragile thriving can be in the face of long work hours, isolation, loneliness, and deteriorating mental health. These findings highlight why creating conditions that sustain thriving is essential, especially in schools looking to support and retain their teachers.

Types of Resources

What conditions, structures, systems, or resources are needed if school leaders want to create an environment where teachers truly thrive? Many assume that money is the primary resource. Increasing teacher salaries can play a crucial role in attracting and retaining talent. However, even with significantly higher pay, the complex realities of teaching mean that other forms of support are also needed for thriving to become a natural and permanent state for all teachers across the country.

Spreitzer et al. (2005) emphasize that thriving is not determined solely by individual factors; the broader social context heavily influences it. Teachers become more aware of changes in their well-being as they "navigate and change their work contexts to promote their own development." In this model and related research, resources such as knowledge, positive meaning, strong relationships, and psychological capital (Okros & Virga, 2025; Spreitzer et al., 2005) are key to enabling thriving.

In the updated JDR theory, Demerouti and Bakker (2023) defined resources as aspects of the job that help achieve work goals, reduce demands and related stress, or encourage personal growth and development. Resources also work in an interdependent manner. Demerouti & Bakker (2023) explain that organizational, job, home, and personal resources interact with, support, and reinforce one another. In simpler terms, when one resource is low, a teacher can draw upon other sources for motivation. The more resources a teacher can draw upon, the less dependent they are on a particular resource, and the more likely they are to thrive, increasing their well-being.

Demerouti and Bakker (2023) further explain that educators with abundant personal resources, such as a sense of self-efficacy or strong coping skills, can better address job demands and make full use of available job resources. Leaders also play a significant role in buffering the impact of demands and amplifying resources, especially during challenging times (Demerouti & Bakker, 2023).

With this background on thriving and the importance of resources, we next explore the day-to-day resources teachers require to thrive in their work. We group these resources into three categories – personal, classroom, and workplace – similar to the demand categories. While common themes appear in the categories from the research, every school and district may have other unique resources to draw upon.

Personal Resources

Despite significant changes in curriculum, pedagogy, and technology over the past 50 years, teacher stress and burnout have consistently undermined well-being and contributed to turnover. While various supports benefit teachers, the JD-R theory highlights the pivotal role of personal resources or "personal capacities that reflect employees' potential to influence their working environment" (Bakker & Demerouti, 2017). These resources, which teachers can cultivate within themselves, are closely linked to thriving and overall well-being at work. Research identifies five main categories of personal resources that teachers can draw upon for thriving and well-being.

Social-Emotional Competencies

Similar to the previous discussions on the social-emotional path in Chapter 3, extensive research underscores the significance of social-emotional competencies in promoting teacher well-being (Bidi et al., 2024; Braun & Hooper, 2024; Collie, 2021; Wang et al., 2024). Many studies indicate that higher self-management and social awareness levels predict lower burnout rates. In particular, teachers who demonstrate stronger self-management skills exhibit reduced exhaustion and cognitive impairment, factors often associated with burnout (Jugović et al., 2025; Mornar, 2024). These competencies also function as psychological resources that help mitigate negative outcomes (Mornar, 2024).

Moreover, high levels of social-emotional competence correlate with a stronger professional identity, contributing to a deeper sense of purpose and commitment among teachers (Zhou et al., 2024). Zhang et al. (2023) find that teacher social-emotional competence negatively correlates with burnout, suggesting that enhancing these skills can bolster well-being. Finally, Furtună (2024) shows that emotional regulation fosters greater acceptance of others, positively influencing classroom climate, the effectiveness of teaching, and student outcomes.

Psychological Capital

Psychological capital has attracted growing interest for its role in enhancing teacher well-being. Defined as a state-like personal resource that can be developed through targeted interventions, it consists of four components: hope, optimism, resilience, and self-efficacy. Research indicates that psychological capital can significantly influence teachers' professional experiences. For instance, Granziera et al. (2019) highlight the importance of resilience in helping teachers cope with everyday challenges, while Elçiçek et al. (2022) associate higher levels of psychological capital with increased job satisfaction, even under less favorable economic conditions. Other studies show that psychological capital protects against burnout and psychological distress (Hazan-Liran & Karni-Vizer, 2023), improves stress management, and promotes healthier coping strategies (Soykan et al., 2019). Finally, Williams et al. (2015) find that psychological capital correlates with workplace well-being and happiness, underscoring its potential to foster greater thriving among teachers.

Self-Efficacy

Teachers' self-efficacy, a primary component of psychological capital, can significantly affect their personal and professional well-being. Research finds that teachers with higher self-efficacy exhibit stronger emotional regulation and adaptability, leading to better overall well-being (Lu et al., 2024). Lu et al. (2024) found that self-efficacy accounted for 61% of the variance in teacher well-being. Similarly, Bagdziuniene et al. (2023)

reported a direct link between self-efficacy and resilience, and resilience predicted well-being. Other studies demonstrate that self-efficacy positively influences job satisfaction, which in turn contributes to higher levels of well-being (Lazarides & Warner, 2020; Wang et al., 2024). Additionally, increases in self-efficacy bolster teaching satisfaction and the capacity to manage high-stakes testing, thereby reducing stress and enhancing emotional well-being (von der Embse et al., 2016; Wang et al., 2024).

Self-efficacy, however, can be undermined by excessive demands and inadequate support. Conversely, a supportive school climate, positive relationships, and effective resources can help sustain or increase it. In a comprehensive review spanning four decades, Zee and Koomen (2016) found that higher self-efficacy levels correlate with stronger instructional support, better classroom organization, and lower burnout rates, all of which benefit teacher well-being and student outcomes.

Multiple strategies have been identified for boosting teacher self-efficacy. Structured, sustained professional development targeting mastery of core instructional techniques has shown an effect size of 0.62 (Täschner et al., 2024). Well-designed mentorship and coaching programs can also markedly improve self-efficacy, particularly for beginning teachers (Gorghiu et al., 2024; Walsh et al., 2020), and ongoing, structured feedback from mentors proved to be crucial (Mok et al., 2023). Finally, targeted emotional competence and resilience training further strengthen self-efficacy (Pozo-Rico et al., 2022).

Coping Strategies

Coping strategies refer to the methods that teachers use to manage their work, emotions, and stress. When developed and applied effectively, these strategies can significantly mitigate school-based stressors. Research generally identifies three main categories of coping strategies.

First, problem-focused coping involves actively addressing the sources of stress. This category can include creating alternative lesson plans, experimenting with new engagement techniques (Krummenacher et al., 2024), or developing practical skills like time management and organization (Casungcad, 2024). Woods et al. (2023) found that problem-solving approaches accounted for 25% of the variance in teachers' stress levels, linking such strategies to higher job satisfaction and lower burnout.

Second, emotion-focused coping is particularly relevant when the source of stress cannot be easily resolved. Nwoko et al. (2024) identified various emotion-focused strategies among teachers, including setting boundaries, practicing mindfulness, balancing work and personal life, and integrating resilience-oriented pedagogies (Isidori et al., 2023). By contrast, Sáez-Delgado et al. (2023) showed that reliance on maladaptive strategies (e.g., denial and self-blame) can elevate anxiety and stress.

Third, maintaining a healthy work–life balance serves as a crucial coping mechanism. Common self-care practices include regular exercise or physical activity (Nwoko et al., 2024), hobbies (Conte et al., 2024), and leisure activities (O'Bryan, 2019). A study by Woods et al. (2023) of 2,347 teachers found that those prioritizing self-care reported greater job satisfaction and reduced burnout, highlighting the protective role these strategies can play in sustaining teacher well-being.

Classroom Resources

The classroom is the pivotal setting where teacher–student interactions unfold, often involving emotional, cognitive, physical, and social demands. Because these interactions form the basis of a school's climate, school leaders need to consider how best to support teachers in this space. Classroom resources, tangible (e.g., instructional materials) and intangible (e.g., supportive beliefs and expectations), are vital for helping teachers thrive and maintain their well-being. Research identifies numerous classroom resources, but seven key categories consistently emerged and will be explored in the following sections.

Autonomy and Value Fulfillment

One of the key demands highlighted in Chapter 4 is the loss of professional autonomy that many teachers experience due to high-stakes accountability policies. Standardizing curriculum and instructional practices can diminish a teacher's sense of agency and conflict with the personal values that originally drew them into the profession (DeYoung & Tiberious, 2023). Research consistently finds that reducing autonomy erodes teacher well-being but that granting teachers more professional discretion within reasonable boundaries can enhance their overall satisfaction (DeYoung & Tiberious, 2023).

DeYoung and Tiberious (2023) define well-being as "the effective pursuit of a set of nonconflicting values that are emotionally, motivationally, and cognitively suitable to the person." When teachers' values about teaching and learning align with their school's mission, thriving becomes more attainable. For example, a study by Sugrue (2019) discovered that K-12 educators can experience moral injury comparable to military veterans, leading to guilt, burnout, and ultimately an increased desire to leave the profession.

Johari et al. (2018) found that giving teachers control over methods and pacing improves motivation and job satisfaction and boosts job performance. Similarly, Gundlach et al. (2024) found that perceived autonomy was strongly associated with teachers intending to stay. Last, Collie et al. (2017) similarly report that teachers feel a stronger sense of well-being when leaders adopt an autonomy-supportive style.

Time

Time is a critical resource in K-12 education, where curriculum demands, school schedules, variability in student learning, and community constraints all shape how time can be used (Bergener & Santarius, 2021). The increasing workload for teachers and principals (Creagh et al., 2025) has contributed to a growing sense of "time poverty," defined as the gap between the volume of work and the complexity or stakes of teaching tasks (Creagh et al., 2025; Lagawid, 2024). This intensification often diverts teachers from their core instructional roles, leaving them feeling hurried and overwhelmed.

When teachers receive the implicit or explicit message that they must "teach more in less time" while handling additional responsibilities, this perception of time scarcity intensifies. A key resource, then, is not just the total amount of scheduled classroom time but also how much teachers can control and devote to teaching and learning. Schools that reduce extraneous workload demands and empower teachers to prioritize core instructional tasks can bolster teacher well-being and retention (Lagawid, 2024). Because time poverty is partly subjective, helping educators focus on high-impact instructional priorities and giving them more autonomy over their schedules can significantly shift how they experience time in the classroom.

Behavior Support

Classroom management significantly affects teachers' well-being (Collie, 2021). Although the emphasis on student achievement has sometimes overshadowed the importance of classroom management in educational research, recent findings suggest that effective management support is a vital classroom resource that can improve achievement. This support can take several forms. First, teachers perceive discipline support from their administrators as essential for managing classroom behavior, and teachers often cite consistent enforcement of discipline policies as a critical support. Gaston (2015) and Welsh (2023) found that inconsistencies in disciplinary actions across the school undermine teacher authority. Discipline support from school leaders is positively associated with occupational commitment, whereas disruptive behavior correlates with lower commitment (Collie, 2021).

Second, intentionally building rapport with students can help reduce behavioral problems and create a more positive learning environment. Wilkins et al. (2022) found that fostering a sense of connectedness among students reduced risky behaviors. Similarly, Gandzel (2022) reported that when students feel genuinely valued by their teachers, they are more likely to engage in learning, which contributes to better behavioral patterns. A study by Chan et al. (2023) found that teachers exhibiting lower-quality emotional support, classroom organization, and instructional support to students reported higher levels of stress, suggesting that the quality of teacher–student interactions is related to work-related stress. Last, teachers frequently express a need for ongoing training in classroom management methods and culturally responsive teaching (Welsh, 2023). Such professional development helps educators address diverse student needs, maintain a supportive classroom climate, and safeguard their well-being.

Differentiated Curriculum Materials

The increasing diversity of learners in U.S. classrooms has made it clear that a standardized curriculum rarely meets all students' needs. When materials are not differentiated, teachers often bear the additional responsibility of adapting or creating them for different needs. A study by Andrean (2023) in English language classrooms showed that teachers commonly modify existing resources or develop entirely new ones to accommodate varied learning levels and backgrounds. By contrast, when differentiated materials are readily available, they act as a valuable classroom resource, allowing teachers to tailor instruction more effectively while reducing their preparation time.

Support for Educational Technology Use

Educational technology has become integral to modern classrooms, but successfully integrating it requires multiple layers of support. Ongoing professional development helps teachers develop the skills to select and align digital tools with curriculum goals (Makgato, 2023; Mouza, 2022). Without adequate training, technology often goes underused or is misapplied. Additionally, reliable infrastructure and technical support, such as strong internet connections, functional devices, and responsive IT assistance, are essential classroom resources (Timotheou et al., 2022). When these supports are in place, technology can significantly enhance teaching and learning; when lacking, even the best tools may fail to improve outcomes.

Instructional Support

For many years, instruction was often treated as a "black box", viewed more as an art than a science. However, advances in our understanding of how students learn (Galea, 2024; Korisky et al., 2024) and the emergence of new pedagogical models such as blended learning, technology integration, project-based learning, and competency-based approaches show that instructional practices can be shaped and improved over time (Hill & Papay, 2022; Kraft et al., 2018; Peterson et al., 2018; Weddle, 2022). In light of this evidence, providing instructional support as a key resource for teachers has become paramount.

Research indicates that effective professional development, a central form of instructional support, should be ongoing, targeted, and aligned with specific teacher needs rather than relegated to one-off workshops (Hill, 2009). The Research Partnership for Professional Learning (RPPL) recently identified six design features of professional learning that consistently enhance instructional practice and student outcomes (Hill & Papay, 2022):

- Structured collaboration among teachers focused on improving instruction
- One-to-one coaching that provides observation and feedback
- Follow-up meetings to refine and adjust teaching approaches
- Subject-specific practice aimed at building deeper content expertise
- Concrete instructional materials that align with curricular goals
- Strong teacher–student relationships as a central component of classroom success

Each of these features is supported by extensive research. For example, Weddle's (2022) literature review confirms the benefits of teacher collaboration for both educators and students, while Kraft et al. (2018) report an average effect size of .49 for instructional coaching interventions. In addition, Hill et al. (2020) found that STEM (science, technology, engineering, and mathematics)-focused professional development is most effective when it targets specific knowledge that teachers can apply in the classroom, such as aligning curriculum materials, representing concepts for diverse learners, and understanding how students learn particular content.

Whether the focus of these forms of instructional support is for new teachers, literacy or math pedagogy, or technology integration, these design principles have shown effectiveness across numerous contexts (Hill & Papay, 2022). These six design elements suggest two guiding principles for their effectiveness across different studies and contexts. First, they support the day-to-day work of teachers in their classrooms with their specific students. Second, effective professional learning based on these design elements provides a form of social accountability for change and improvement.

In sum, emphasizing classroom resources represents a shift from many existing occupational models using the JDR framework, which often focus solely on personal and organizational supports. The classroom and interactions between teachers and students represent the core of the teaching and learning process. Although researchers have examined individual classroom supports, they have rarely been considered as a unified set of resources to support teachers' work. When thoughtfully integrated, these resources can reinforce one another, providing a comprehensive support system that fosters teacher vitality and growth. While the categories outlined may not be surprising in isolation, their collective, strategic use can significantly enhance teachers' capacity to thrive daily.

Workplace Resources

Workplace resources largely correspond to the working conditions that teachers experience and are closely tied to their job satisfaction and career decisions (Simon & Moore-Johnson, 2015). These resources include the social, psychological, and organizational factors that shape teachers' day-to-day work, ultimately influencing outcomes like well-being, overall satisfaction, and retention (Rahimi & Arnold, 2024). While these supports extend beyond individual or classroom-level considerations, they are pivotal in shaping how teachers perceive and cope with job demands. When available, workplace resources can assist teachers in coping with demands and increase thriving and well-being, but if not, teachers have little recourse but to rely on themselves.

Key workplace resources typically involve supportive school leadership, strong collegial relationships, effective professional learning communities (PLCs) or teams, a positive shared affective climate, and meaningful opportunities for teacher input. Although other elements may also be relevant, these have been consistently identified as central to fostering teacher well-being and encouraging long-term commitment to the profession.

School Leadership and Teacher Thriving

As Figure 6.1 illustrates, school leadership occupies a pivotal position at the intersection of teacher energy and stress, the social-emotional path, job demands, and job resources, giving them extensive influence on the thriving and well-being of their teachers. Numerous studies underscore that when principals cultivate supportive working conditions, teachers are more likely to thrive and remain at their schools (Gundlach et al., 2024; Nguyen, 2021; Nguyen et al., 2024; Simon & Moore-Johnson, 2015; Urick, 2016). In contrast, principals who fail to establish a strong, supportive environment often struggle with heightened turnover, forcing them to continually recruit and replace staff (Sartain & Estrera, 2023). Research also suggests that effective leaders who are supportive, empowering, and able to foster positive interpersonal relationships tend to create environments where teachers feel valued and engaged (See et al., 2024).

Supportive leadership stands out as a key factor in teacher retention. For instance, using the lens of positive psychology, Cameron et al. (2011) found that positive practices used by leaders in organizations, such as caring, compassionate support, forgiveness, inspiration, meaning, respect, integrity, and gratitude, showed a negative correlation with turnover and intent to leave. A study by Tran et al. (2023) suggests that different types of administrative supports matter across school levels, locales, and retention status. Their study examined the role of specific emotional, psychological, and organizational support in contrast to administrative support that has typically been used in general terms. This study found that teachers prioritize the following forms of support:

1. Respect
2. Discipline enforcement
3. Open-door policy
4. Communication
5. Resources
6. Collegial relationships
7. Professional appreciation
8. Trust in the professional
9. Agency over change
10. Coaching
11. Peer mentoring
12. Personal relationship
13. Community relationship

Another study, by Ford et al. (2019), showed that strong relational interactions between teachers and principals can foster organizational commitment, while creating a trusting work environment builds collective teacher efficacy. A structured review by See et al. (2024) revealed the importance of administrative support for beginning teachers, highlighting supportive communication as crucial. Earlier research by Simon and

Moore-Johnson (2015) also underscored that teachers' perceptions of their principal greatly influence career decisions.

Additional research highlights leadership practices that help retain teachers. First, consistently reaffirming a school's mission, particularly in high-poverty schools, can significantly motivate and inspire teachers, who often find deep meaning in serving these student populations (Lochmiller et al., 2024). Second, strong interpersonal relationships, emotional intelligence, and trust are essential to building commitment. Humphrey et al. (2016) emphasize that leadership is inherently emotional, and Price (2021) confirmed that when principals nurture authentic, trusting relationships, teachers are more likely to stay. Recognition of teachers' contributions is another powerful factor in retention (Lochmiller et al., 2024; Shell et al., 2023).

Third, leadership that empowers teachers by granting autonomy, involving them in decision-making, and promoting a sense of control can substantially boost teacher well-being and retention (See et al., 2024). Nguyen et al. (2024) found that providing professional freedom strengthens teachers' autonomy and increases job satisfaction, commitment, and the probability of remaining in the profession. Involving teachers in decisions that affect them can also help build a culture of shared responsibility (Ingersoll & Tran, 2023; Shell et al., 2023).

Collegial Relationships and Support

How teachers collaborate and support each other is a vital resource for retaining educators. Research shows that positive work relationships can mitigate the impact of job demands (Gilmour & Sandilos, 2023; Kaiser & Thompson, 2021). Collaboration also fosters a sense of belonging and advocacy, which helps reduce stress and provides both emotional and psychological support (Gilmour & Sandilos, 2023; Kaiser & Thompson, 2021). Strong collegial connections increase job satisfaction (See et al., 2024), create a sense of community, and help schools meet their goals (Bryant et al., 2023). When executed well, collaborative efforts promote professional growth through knowledge-sharing, feedback, and mutual observation of classroom practices, ultimately enhancing instructional quality and collective efficacy (Gilmour & Sandilos, 2023; Simon & Moore-Johnson, 2015).

Ample evidence links collegial support to teacher retention. For example, Nguyen (2021) found that teacher cohesion and collaboration strongly predict whether teachers remain in the profession. See et al. (2024)

similarly report that positive peer relationships boost job satisfaction and, in turn, the likelihood of staying at a school. Hu et al. (2024) discovered that teachers' collective innovation amplifies the beneficial effects of a supportive school climate on job satisfaction. In an international meta-analysis, Gundlach et al. (2024) concluded that collegiality reduces teachers' motivation to leave, while job satisfaction, reinforced by strong collegial bonds, is a key predictor of retention. These findings confirm that a positive social-emotional environment, marked by strong collegial relationships, is essential for fostering teacher job satisfaction, well-being, and long-term commitment.

Effective Teams and PLCs

Beyond the social and emotional benefits of collegial relationships, team-based collaboration, particularly through structures like PLCs, can be a powerful support system for teachers. When implemented effectively, PLCs create an environment for continuous professional learning, knowledge sharing, and emotional support, enhancing instructional practices and fostering a sense of belonging. For instance, in a review of empirical research, Nguyen et al. (2024) concluded that PLCs provide a strong platform for collaborative learning, professional development, and improved teaching efficacy while helping teachers build trusting relationships. Waters (2019) similarly found that participation in a PLC offered educators personal and emotional support, classroom problem-solving skills, and an increased intent to remain in the profession. In another study, the six core components of a PLC positively correlated with teachers' well-being (Liang et al., 2020). Owen (2016) likewise noted that analyzing PLCs through a positive psychology lens illustrates how they can foster a nurturing emotional climate. Finally, as educational change accelerates, organizing teaching and learning by teams has become increasingly important for promoting deep learning (Pinheiro & Alves, 2024) at the individual, team, and organizational level.

Research beyond education also underscores the impact of high-performing teams on retention: Yang et al. (2024) found that such teams significantly reduce turnover intention by enhancing employees' skills, motivation, and participation, particularly when overall job satisfaction is high. Moreover, high-performing teams can serve as a resource by providing collaboration, support, skill development, and greater psychological empowerment through shared decision-making. Further, recent findings suggest that team-level emotional dynamics, including emotional contagion, can influence the relationship between stress and well-being (Hernández Grande et al., 2024). These studies highlight the value of robust team structures in bolstering teacher resilience, professional growth, and retention.

One caution, however. Fullan et al. (2022) warn us that "collaboration directs attention too quickly to the processes of working together and not enough to the thinking disposition that must precede the process of collaboration itself." Instead, these authors believe that a better view of collaboration is found in connected autonomy, which captures the "dynamic equilibrium of being simultaneously autonomous from and connected to others" (Fullan et al., 2022). Connected autonomy requires that individuals and teams in a school keep some autonomy around the needs of their students but also have a sense of being connected to the larger direction and problems in a school. Connected autonomy also requires deeply understanding the role of individual, team, and organizational learning to influence joint action.

Common Affective States

In Chapter 4, we introduced three levels of the social-emotional path in schools, including the organizational level, which focuses on cultivating and maintaining a positive school-wide social-emotional climate. As discussed, this climate is shaped by four key affective states, identified by research and teachers as essential for emotional support (Leithwood & Beatty, 2009; Leithwood et al., n.d.). These affective states have been consistently linked to outcomes such as job satisfaction, well-being, and retention, making them critical resources for teachers. The four states are

1. Trust
2. Collective efficacy
3. Satisfaction
4. Recovery

Together, these dimensions help define a supportive environment that teachers can rely on to feel secure, motivated, and resilient in their work.

Teacher Input

A final workplace resource that can enhance teacher well-being and retention is teacher input in decision-making. Such input occurs when teachers have meaningful influence over policies and practices within their classrooms and the broader school environment. For example, Park et al. (2020) found that teacher involvement in instruction-related decisions correlated strongly with professional commitment, while influence over managerial decisions is more closely linked to job satisfaction. Similarly, Brezicha et al. (2020) reported that job satisfaction increases when teachers feel individually involved and empowered in school decisions. Somech and Bogler (2020) also found that teacher commitment varies depending on whether the decision-making domain is instructional or organizational.

Collie et al. (2020) suggest that teachers who have a say in key decisions feel more supported and see their professional needs being met, which is closely tied to well-being (Vangrieken et al., 2015). Additionally, Collie et al. (2020) found that schools classified as "Supportive" because of higher levels of resources also tended to provide greater opportunities for teacher input, leading to stronger job satisfaction and occupational commitment.

Using the Increasing Resources Process

As discussed, many resources that influence teacher well-being and retention cannot simply be bought or mandated. Whereas some resources, such as differentiated materials or additional staff, are tangible purchases, other intangible resources (self-efficacy, supportive leadership, time, and trust) are rooted in the psychological or social dynamics of schools. In line with the JD-R theory, resources comprise "physical, psychological, social, or organizational elements of the job that help achieve work goals, reduce the demands associated with physiological or psychological costs, or stimulate personal growth, learning, and development" (Granziera et al., 2021). Most resources fall under psychological or social aspects of a school's working conditions, requiring intentional development, mindset shifts, and cultural change, processes that take time to develop and sustain.

Because schools operate under tight schedules, expanding or strengthening these resources requires strategic thinking and a developmental mindset. Leaders and teachers must clarify what a resource looks like in practice, determine how it can improve teacher thriving, and explore how to develop and embed new habits and practices at both individual and organizational levels.

In Chapter 5, we introduced PDSA cycles as an action framework rooted in improvement science. To guide thinking for your blueprint, three guiding questions are key to using this strategy effectively:

1. What are we trying to accomplish by increasing resources for teachers?
2. What change can we make that will result in more thriving and well-being for our teachers?
3. How will we know the change is an improvement in thriving and well-being?

PDSA cycles encourage scientific thinking about turnover in schools by systematically examining whether initiatives to enhance resources effectively boost teacher thriving, well-being, and ultimately increase retention. Specific actions and guiding questions for each cycle phase are detailed below (see Appendix J for the PDSA template).

Plan

In the Plan phase, leaders and teams identify potential resources that can be developed or strengthened to better support teachers. Table 6.2 below outlines the specific steps and guiding questions for this stage. Although many of these resources may already exist in schools, they are often underutilized or insufficiently developed. When designing your first resource-expansion cycle, consider how resources might be

- **Refined**: The resource exists but needs enhancement or improvement to serve teachers more effectively.
- **Reconstructed**: The resource must be rebuilt or reestablished, such as boosting teachers' self-efficacy or revitalizing team structures after conflict.
- **Recultured**: The fundamental purpose or focus of the resource requires a shift, such as changing an instructional coaching program from a

Table 6.2 The Plan Phase of Increasing Resources

Steps	Questions to consider

1. Prepare your school to increase resources.
2. Use the **JDR Diagnostic** explained below to determine which resources are needed in your school.
3. Determine which resource may most impact increase teacher thriving and why.
4. Predict the impact of increasing the resource.
5. Decide on the type of increase: refining, reconstructing, reculturing, or reconnecting.
6. Study the resource concept, what it needs to look like in action, and how it is best developed.
6. Determine if there may be any impact on student outcomes when the increase happens.
7. Determine how you will measure the impact on teacher thriving and well-being (see Flash survey idea below).
8. Create an action plan for communication and development of the resource, and what this will look like for staff.
	1. How might I explain what increasing resources may do for teachers?
	2. Which resource need stands out as the greatest? Why do you think that is?
	3. Which resource may have the most impact on increasing thriving?
	4. What is our prediction about what will happen if we improve that resource?
	5. What type of increase is needed for this resource? Why?
	6. What would it look like or feel like if this resource were increased? How should it be developed?
	7. Do we predict any impact on student outcomes if we make this increase? Why?
	7. How will we know the impact on teacher thriving and well-being if we make the increase?
	8. What steps must we take to make this increase happen? Consider
	  • Communication to staff
	  • Development steps and processes
	  • Timeline
	  • Data collection
	  • Identifying other impacts
	  • Other?

narrow emphasis on test preparation to broader student engagement strategies.

- **Reconnected**: A previously effective idea, approach, or technique needs to be revived. Examples include a principal dedicating time to reestablish the core meaning of teaching or reconnecting staff with discipline-support strategies that have lapsed.

Tool #1: The Job-Resources Diagnostic

This diagnostic tool helps school teams identify the resources most urgently needed to boost teacher thriving and well-being (see Appendix I). Grounded in Key Ideas #7 and #8 of the TRM covering job resources and motivation, it guides school leaders and teams in determining where to direct their efforts to expand or enhance resources.

Drawing on a range of research-based supports for teachers, the diagnostic is a concise survey focused on personal, classroom, and workplace resources. When aggregated, the survey results offer valuable insights into which resources may best foster teacher thriving within the school context. Open-ended questions can further clarify the specific resources needed in a particular setting. Because the survey is brief, it can be administered at the end of the first and third quarters, allowing time to develop resource-improvement initiatives.

Do

In the Do phase, leaders and teachers carry out their plan to enhance the identified resource, aiming to bolster teachers' overall sense of support once the new or refined resource is in place. Table 6.3 outlines the specific steps and guiding questions for this phase.

Tool #2: Flash Surveys

Similar to the flash survey used to check stress and energy levels, brief measurement tools are essential for evaluating the impact of resource-related interventions. The goal is to see whether enhancing a specific resource boosts

Table 6.3 The Do Phase of Increasing Resources

Steps	Questions to consider
1. Communicate the plan and expectations to staff on the resource need and development. 2. Carry out the development plan. 3. Collect the practical measurement data. 4. Observe and note anything unexpected.	1. How will we communicate the plan and expectations to staff? 2. How will we know the plan and expectations for developing the resource are being done? 3. How will we collect and store the data we are collecting? 4. How can we attune ourselves to any unexpected impacts?

teacher thriving, and quick "flash surveys" can provide early indicators of success. Aligned with Key Ideas #1, #7, and #8 of the TRM, these surveys typically take under 30 seconds. Because thriving is treated as a positive energy state in the TRM, regularly measuring it can help school leaders detect rising vitality and learning, which in turn supports well-being.

A flash survey might ask teachers to rate their sense of thriving for the week on a 1–5 scale. Given that thriving combines vitality and learning, the two questions below can be used to gauge each dimension based on teachers' experiences over the past week.

1. During this past week, I felt energized and enthusiastic about my daily activities.

1	2	3	4	5
Strongly Disagree				Strongly Agree

2. During this past week, I felt I was learning new things or improving my skills.

1	2	3	4	5
Strongly Disagree				Strongly Agree

Study

In the Study phase, leaders and teams review data from flash surveys or other relevant sources to evaluate whether the increased or newly developed resource has boosted teacher thriving. This step also assesses whether the intended goals have been met by increasing the resource, recognizing that many of these resources require time to mature. Therefore, it is crucial to explore the effectiveness of the development process and identify any possible reasons for a lack of success. Table 6.4 below outlines the steps and guiding questions for the Study phase.

Act

In the Act phase, leaders and teachers determine whether to adopt the resource for continued development and impact monitoring, adapt it by refining the plan to increase the development of the resource, or abandon the idea altogether in favor of a different approach. Table 6.5 provides the specific steps and guiding questions for this phase.

A Blueprint for Teacher Retention

Table 6.4 The Study Phase of Increasing Resources

Steps	Questions to consider
1. Collate and analyze the data collected. 2. Compare the results to your predictions. 3. Determine what was learned from your change idea. 4. Determine if there were any unintended consequences of developing the resource. 5. Determine the success or next steps for the development plan of the resource.	1. What is the best way to analyze and display these data? Average, by week? 2. Was our prediction correct or not? Why? 3. What did we learn from our change idea? 4. Were there any unintended consequences because of trying to increase the resource? How do you know? 5. How successful has our development plan for the resource been?

Table 6.5 The Act Phase of Increasing Resources

Steps	Questions to consider
1. Review all data and compare to your initial thinking and plan. 2. Discuss if you want to fully adopt the resource (keep developing and monitoring), adapt the development plan, or abandon the resource development plan and focus elsewhere. 3. Begin the plan phase again.	1. What are the data telling us? 2. What should we decide? What is our rationale? 3. What is our next step?

By continuously applying the four-step PDSA cycle to increase resources, school leaders and teachers can concentrate on the "positive side" of the TRM and gather actionable insights from their efforts. This ongoing, data-informed learning method differs from typical approaches and demands a disciplined mindset. Often, development initiatives lose momentum when there is no clear data to guide decisions or when day-to-day school demands take precedence. Implementing a resource-building strategy requires extra time and effort, as it involves overcoming existing habits and shifting mindsets and behaviors. Moreover, it should not be viewed as a one-time intervention: success depends on sustained attention and periodic adjustments to ensure that teachers continue to thrive and experience improved well-being.

Conclusion

Even amid growing demands in K-12 education, some schools succeed in creating environments where teachers thrive and remain committed over the long term. In these settings, personal, classroom, and workplace resources converge into a supportive network, enabling teachers to rely on themselves, their colleagues, and their administrators to excel in their work. These schools have established intentional retention systems, consistently retaining a high proportion of their teaching staff from one year to the next. Numerous studies in this chapter show that although funding is important, a range of psychological, social, and organizational resources is equally vital for retaining quality educators.

The logical foundation for these findings aligns with three key ideas from the TRM:

- **Key Idea #1**: Teaching is energy-intensive.
- **Key Idea #7**: Job resources replenish energy.
- **Key Idea #8**: Resources promote a motivational process and thriving.

Understanding these three key ideas, the types of resources that can lead to greater teacher thriving, and a simple process for increasing resources may stem the tide of teacher turnover by creating a more intentional retention system over time.

Leadership Considerations

- Which resources discussed in this chapter are most or least apparent in your school or district? How do you know?
- How is thriving, as increased energy, different from stress as decreased energy?
- Does your school or district focus on thriving or stress more? What might that tell you?

- How does thriving show up in your teachers?
- Which category of resources do you see as causing the most thriving among your teachers?
- What would teachers suggest are their greatest resource needs?
- Has any obvious discussion of resources beyond money or personnel been done in your school or district? Why or why not?
- How might you involve your teachers in using the increasing resource strategies?
- How might you use the two data tools to inform the resource issues in your school or district?
- How would you plan to increase one of the resources mentioned in this chapter? What is the basis of the resource, and what specific steps and actions would you take to increase this resource?
- What is your role as the school and district leader in increasing resources for your teachers? How might you sponsor this idea for your teachers?

References

Andrean, C. (2023). Designing and adapting materials for differentiated instruction in English language classrooms: a literature review. *Tell-Us Journal: Teaching-English-Linguistics-Literature-Usage*. DOI: 10.22202/tus.2023.v9i3.6996

Bagdziuniene, D., Kazlauskienė, A., Nasvytienė, D., & Sakadolskis, E. A. (2023). Resources of emotional resilience and its mediating role in teachers' well-being and intention to leave. *Frontiers in Psychology*. DOI: 10.3389/fpsyg.2023.1305979

Baker, W. E. (2019). Emotional energy, relational energy, and organizational energy: Toward a multilevel model. *Annual Review of Organizational Psychology and Organizational Behavior*, 6, 373–396. DOI: 10.1146/annurev-orgpsych-012218-015047

Bakker, A. B., & Demerouti, E. (2007). The jobs demands-resources model: State of the art. *Journal of Managerial Psychology*, 22(3), 309–328. DOI: 10.1108/02683940710733115

Bakker, A. B., & Demerouti, E. (2017). Job demands-resources theory: Taking stock and looking forward. *Journal of Occupational Health Psychology*, 22(3), 273–285. DOI: 10.1037/ocp0000056

Bergener, J., & Santarius, T. (2021). A pace of life indicator. Development and validation of a general acceleration scale. *Time & Society*, 30(3), 273–301. DOI: 10.1177/0961463X20980645

Bidi, S. B., Bhat, V., Chandra, S. R., Dmello, V. J., Weesie, E., Gil, M. T., Kurian, S., & Rajendran, A. (2024) Decoding occupational well-being of teachers: Does psychological capital and coping mechanism impact perceived stress? *Cogent Psychology*, 11(1), 2409505. DOI: 10.1080/23311908.2024.2409505

Braun, S. S., & Hooper, A. L. (2024). Social and emotional competencies predict pre-service teachers' occupational health and personal well-being. *Teaching and Teacher Education*, 147, 104654. DOI: 10.1016/j.tate.2024.104654

Brezicha, K. F., Ikoma, S, Park, H, & LeTendre, G. K. (2020) The ownership perception gap: Exploring teacher job satisfaction and its relationship to teachers' principals' perception of decision-making opportunity. *International Journal of Leadership in Education*, 23(4), 428–456. DOI: 10.1080/13603124.2018.1562098

Bryant, J., Ram, S., Scott, D., & Williams, C. (2023, March 2). K-12 teachers are quitting. *What would make them stay?* McKinsey & Company. https://www.mckinsey.com/industries/education/our-insights/k-12-teachers-are-quitting-what-would-make-them-stay

Cameron, K., Mora, C., Leutscher, T., & Calarco, M. (2011). Effects of positive practices on organizational effectiveness. *The Journal of Applied Behavioral Science*, 47(3). DOI: 10.1177/0021886310395514

Casungcad, E. P. (2024). Inclusive teaching: stressors, impact of stress, and coping strategies of teachers in public schools. *Power System Technology*, 48(2), 383–404. DOI: 10.52783/pst.555

Chan, S., Poysa, S., Lerkkanen, L., & Pakarinen, E. (2023). Teachers occupational well-being in relation to teacher-student interactions at the lower secondary level. *Scandinavian Journal of Educational Research*, 68(6), 1137–1154. DOI: 10.1080/00313831.2023.2204114

Collie, R. J. (2021). A multilevel examination of teachers' occupational commitment: The roles of job resources and disruptive student behavior. *Social Psychology of Education*, 24(2), 387–411. DOI: 10.1007/s11218-021-09617-y

Collie, R. J., Malmberg, L.-E., Martin, A. J., Sammons, P. & Morin, A. J. S. (2020). A multilevel person-centered examination of teachers' workplace demands and resources. *Frontiers in Psychology*, 11, 626. DOI: 10.3389/fpsyg.2020.00626

Collie, R. J., Perry, N. E., & Martin, A. J. (2017). School context and educational system factors impacting educator stress. In T.M. McIntyre,

S.E. McIntyre & D.J. Francis (Eds.), *Educator stress: An occupational health perspective*, 3, 22. Springer.

Conte, E., Cavioni, V., & Ornaghi, V. (2024). Exploring stress factors and coping strategies in Italian teachers after COVID-19: Evidence from qualitative data. *Neveléstudomány*. DOI: 10.3390/educsci14020152

Creagh, S., Thompson, G., Mockler, N., Stacey, M., & Hogan, A. (2025) Workload, work intensification and time poverty for teachers and school leaders: A systematic research synthesis. *Educational Review*, 77(2), 661–680, DOI:10.1080/00131911.2023.2196607

Demerouti, E., & Bakker, A. B. (2023). Job demands-resources theory in times of crises: New propositions. *Organizational Psychology Review*, 13 (3), 209–236. DOI: 10.1177/20413866221135022

DeYoung, C. G., & Tiberious, V. (2023). Value fulfillment from a cybernetic perspective: A new psychological theory of well-being. *Personality and Social Psychology Review*, 27(1), 3–27. DOI: 10.1177/10888683221083777

Elçiçek, Z., Han, B., & Yildiz, S. (2022). Can teachers' job satisfaction be ensured despite economic inadequacies? The impact of positive psychological capital. *European Journal of Educational Sciences*, 9(1), 1–10. DOI: 10.19044/ejes.v9no1a1

Ford, T. G., Olsen, J., Khojasteh, J., Ware, J., & Urick, A. (2019). The effects of leader support for teacher psychological needs on teacher burnout, commitment, and intent to leave. *Journal of Educational Administration*, 57(6), 615–634. DOI: 10.1108/JEA-09-2018-0185

Fullan, M., Spillane, B., & Fullan, B. (2022). Editorial: Commentary: Connected autonomy. *Journal of Professional Capital and Community*, 7(4), 329–333. DOI: 10.1108/JPCC-10-2022-105

Furtună, R. (2024). *Educational implications of developing socio-emotional competence among teachers: An empirical research.* DOI: 10.26755/revped/2024.1/167

Galea, E. (2024). Advancing pedagogy through the science of teaching and learning: A vision for educational practitioners. *The Psychology of Education Review/Psychology of Education Review*, 48(1), 58–67. DOI: 10.53841/bpsper.2024.48.1.58

Gandzel, A. (2022). Being right or building relationships? Positive discipline in the school classroom. *Horyzonty Wychowania*, 21(60), 91–100. DOI: 10.35765/hw.2022.2160.10

Gaston, N. L. (2015). *Perceptions of discipline policy, practices, and student incivilities related to Senge's five disciplines.* https://scholarworks.waldenu.edu/cgi/viewcontent.cgi?article=1261&context=dissertations

Gilmour, A. F., & Sandilos, L. E. (2023). The crucial role of administrators in shaping the working conditions for teachers and students with EBD. *Journal of Emotional and Behavioral Disorders*, 31(2), 109–119. DOI: 10.1177/10634266221149933

Goh, Z., Eva, N., Kiazad, K., Jack, G. A., De Cieri, H., & Spreitzer, G. M. (2021). An integrative multilevel review of thriving at work: Assessing progress and promise. *Journal of Organizational Behavior*, 43, 197–213. DOI: 10.1002/job.2571

Gorghiu, G., Sherborne, T., Kowalski, R. P. G., Vives-Adrián, L., & Ribeiro, S. F. (2024). Enhancing teachers' self-efficacy supported by coaching in the content of open schooling for sustainability. *Sustainability*, 16(22), 10131. DOI: 10.3390/su162210131

Granziera, H., Collie, R. J., & Martin, A. J. (2019). Adaptability: An important capacity to cultivate among pre-service teachers in teacher education programmes. *Psychology Teaching Review*, 25(1), 60–66. https://eric.ed.gov/?id=EJ1216443

Granziera, H., Collie, R. J., & Martin, A. J. (2021). Understanding teacher wellbeing through job demands-resources theory. In Mansfield, C. F. (ed) *Cultivating Teacher Resilience*. Springer. DOI: 10.1007/978-981-15-5963-1_14

Gundlach, H. A. D., Slemp, G. R., & Hattie, J. (2024, May). A meta-analysis of the antecedents of teacher turnover and retention. *Educational Research Review*, 44. DOI: 10.1016/j.edurev.2024.100606

Hazan-Liran, B., & Karni-Vizer, N. (2023). Psychological capital as a mediator of job satisfaction and burnout among teachers in special and standard education. *European Journal of Special Needs Education*, 1–15. DOI: 10.1080/08856257.2023.2215009

Hernández Grande, A., Farr-Wharton, B., Sharafizad, F., Darcy, S., & Gavin, M. K. (2024). Catching on: Work stress, employee wellbeing, and the moderating role of team-level emotional contagion. *Journal of Management & Organization*, 1–14. DOI: 10.1017/jmo.2024.44

Hill, H. C. (2009). Fixing teacher professional development. *Phi Delta Kappan*, 90(7), 470–476. DOI: 10.1177/003172170909000705

Hill, H.C., Lynch, K., Gonzalez, K., & Pollard, C. (2020, January 27). Professional development that improves STEM outcomes. *Phi Delta Kappan*. https://kappanonline.org/professional-development-improves-stem-outcomes-hill-lynch-gonzalez-pollard/

Hill, H. C., & Papay, J. P. (2022). *Building better pl: How to strengthen teacher learning*. Research Partnership for Professional Learning. https://rpplpartnership.org/wp-content/uploads/2024/10/rppl-building-better-pl.pdf

Hu, B., Park, K. H., & Xu, Z. (2024). The mediating effect of teachers' collective innovativeness between school climate and job satisfaction. *European Journal of Educational Research*, 13(4), 1573–1585. DOI: 10.12973/eu-jer.13.4.1573

Humphrey, R. H., Burch, G. F., & Adams, L. L. (2016). The benefits of merging leadership research and emotions research. *Frontiers in Psychology*, 7, 1022. DOI: 10.3389/fpsyg.2016.01022

Ingersoll, R. M., & Tran, H. (2023). Teacher shortages in rural schools in the US: An organizational analysis. *Education Administration Quarterly*, 59(2), 396–431. DOI: 10.1177/0013161X231159922

Isidori, E., Leonova, I., Abele, A., Caione, G., Zakharova, L., & Sandor, I. (2023). Teacher well-being: Between counseling and resilience pedagogy. *Educaţia* 21. DOI: 10.24193/ed21.2023.25.37

Istiningtyas, L., Purba, D. E., Poerwandari, E. K., Takwin, B., & Milla, M. N. (2025). Systematic literature review on the theory of social embeddedness of thriving at work. *SA Journal of Industrial Psychology*. DOI: 10.4102/sajip.v51i0.2229

Johari, J., Tan, F. Y., & Zulkarnain, Z. I. T. (2018). Autonomy, workload, work-life balance, and job performance among teachers. *International Journal of Educational Management*, 32(1), 107–120. DOI: 10.1108/IJEM-10-2016-0226

Jugović, I., Marušić, I., & Matić, J. (2025). Early career teachers' social and emotional competencies, self-efficacy and burnout: A mediation model. *BMC Psychology*, 13(1). DOI: 10.1186/s40359-024-02323-2

Kaiser, F. J., & Thompson, R. (2021). Slowing the burn: Principal leadership supports to reduce attrition. *School Leadership Review*, 16(1). https://scholarworks.sfasu.edu/slr/vol16/iss1/6

Kleine, A. K., Rudolph, C. W., & Zacher, H. (2019). Thriving at work: A meta-analysis. *Journal of Organizational Behavior*, 40(9–10), 973–999. DOI: 10.1002/job.2375

Klijn, A. F. J., Tims, M., Lysova, E. I., & Khapova, S. N. (2021). Personal energy at work: A systematic review. *Sustainability*, 13(23), 13490. DOI: 10.3390/su132313490

Korisky, A., Davidesco, I., Ben-Abu, O., Levy, O., Abrahami, K., Geri, O., & Zion Golumbic, E. (2024). Me, My Brain, and I: A framework for neuroscience curriculum fostering research-practice partnership between scientists and educators. *Mind, Brain, and Education*. DOI: 10.1111/mbe.12432

Kraft, M. A., Blazar, D., & Hogan, D. (2018). The effect of teacher coaching on instruction and achievement: A meta-analysis of the causal evidence. *Review of Educational Research*, 88(4), 547–588. DOI: 10.3102/0034654318759268

Krummenacher, I., Hascher, T., Mansfield, C., Beltman, S., Morinaj, J., & Guidon, I. (2024). Understanding professional challenges and coping strategies within the resilience process that support teacher well-being. *Frontline Learning Research*, 12(4), 85–112. DOI: 10.14786/flr.v12i4.1211

Lagawid, E. L. (2024). Overloading in elementary school teachers: A review. *Cognizance Journal*, 4(11), 289–299. DOI: 10.47760/cognizance.2024.v04i11.016

Lazarides, R., & Warner, L. M. (2020). *Teacher Self-Efficacy*. DOI: 10.1093/ACREFORE/9780190264093.013.890

Leithwood, K., Anderson, S. F. Mascall, B., & Strauss, T. (n.d.) School leaders' influences on student learning: The four paths. https://www.leadershippartnerstx.com/files/1_school_leaders_influence_4_paths_to_learning.pdf

Leithwood, K., & Beatty, B. (2009). *Leading with teacher emotions in mind*. Corwin Press.

Liang, W., Song, H., & Sun, R. (2020). Can a professional learning community facilitate teacher well-being in China? The mediating role of teaching self-efficacy. *Educational Studies*, 48, 358–377. DOI: 10.1080/03055698.2020.1755953

Lochmiller, C. R., Perrone, F., & Finley, C. (2024). Understanding school leadership's influence on teacher retention in high-poverty settings: An exploratory study in the U.S. *Education Sciences*, 14, 545. DOI: 10.3390/educsci14050545

Lu, L., Cui-Ying, W., & Wang, Y. (2024). The contribution of teacher self-efficacy, resilience and emotion regulation to teachers' well-being: Technology-enhanced teaching context. *European Journal of Education*. DOI: 10.1111/ejed.12755

Makgato, M. (2023). Teachers' views on the application of educational technologies in the classroom: A case of selected Tshwane west secondary schools in Gauteng. *Journal of Curriculum Studies Research*, 5(2), 151–166. DOI: 10.46303/jcsr.2023.23

Mok, S. Y., Rupp, D., & Holzberger, D. (2023). What kind of individual support activities in interventions foster pre-service and beginning teachers' self-efficacy? A meta-analysis. *Educational Research and Reviews*. DOI: 10.1016/j.edurev.2023.100552

Mornar, M. (2024). Teachers' social and emotional competencies and their role in occupational well-being. *Psychological Topics*, 33(3), 503–526. DOI: 10.31820/pt.33.3.2

Mouza, C. (2022). Learning to teach with new technology. *Journal of Research on Computing in Education*, 35(2), 272–289. DOI: 10.1080/15391523.2002.10782386

Nguyen, D., Boeren, E., Maitra, S., & Cabus, S. (2024) A review of the empirical research literature on PLCs for teachers in the Global South: Evidence, implications, and directions. *Professional Development in Education*, 50(1), 91–107. DOI: 10.1080/19415257.2023.2238728

Nguyen, T. D. (2021). Linking school organizational characteristics and teacher retention: Evidence from repeated cross-sectional national data. *Teaching and Teacher Education*, 97, 103220. DOI: 10.1016/j.tate.2020.103220

Nwoko, J. C., Anderson, E., Adegboye, O. A., Malau-Aduli, A. E. O., & Malau-Aduli, B. S. (2024). "SHIELDing" our educators: Comprehensive coping strategies for teacher occupational well-being. *Behavioral Science*. DOI: 10.3390/bs14100918

O'Bryan, S. (2019). *Work-Related Stress and Coping Strategies for Elementary Teachers.* https://repository.stcloudstate.edu/edad_etds/62/

Okros, N., & Virga, D. (2025). From social support to thriving at work via psychological capital: the role of psychosocial safety climate in a weekly study. *Journal of Managerial Psychology*, 40(1), 52–66. DOI: 10.1108/JMP-07-2023-0409

Owen, S. M. (2016). Professional learning communities: Building skills, reinvigorating the passion, and nurturing teacher wellbeing and "flourishing" within significantly innovative schooling contexts. *Educational Review*, 68, 403–419. DOI: 10.1080/00131911.2015.1119101

Park, J. H., Cooc, N., & Lee, K. H. (2020). Relationships between teacher influence in managerial and instruction-related decision-making, job satisfaction, and professional commitment: A multivariate multilevel model. *Educational Management Administration & Leadership*, 51, 116–137. DOI: 10.1177/1741143220971287

Peterson, A., Dumont, H., Lafuente, M., & Law, N. (2018). Understanding innovative pedagogies: Key themes to analyse new approaches to teaching and learning. *Research Papers in Economics*. DOI: 10.1787/9F843A6E-EN

Pinheiro, G., & Alves, J. M. (2024). Educational teams: Building professional and organizational learning communities. *Frontiers in Education*, 9. DOI: 10.3389/feduc.2024.1446905

Porath, C. (2022). *Mastering community: The surprising ways that coming together moves us from surviving to thriving.* New York: Balance (Hachette).

Porath, C. L., Gibson, C. B., & Spreitzer, G. M. (2022). To thrive or not to thrive: Pathways for sustaining thriving at work. *Research in Organizational Behavior*, 42, 1–17. DOI: 10.1016/j.riob.2022.100176

Pozo-Rico, T., Poveda, R., Gutiérrez-Fresneda, R., Castejón, J. L., & Gilar-Corbi, R. (2022). Revamping teacher training for challenging times: Teachers' well-being, resilience, emotional intelligence, and innovative methodologies as key teaching competencies. *Psychology Research and Behavior Management*, 16, 1–18. DOI: 10.2147/PRBM.S382572

Price, H. (2021). Weathering fluctuations in teacher commitment: Leaders relational failures, with improvement prospects. *Journal of Educational Administration*, 59(4), 493–513. DOI: 10.1108/JEA-07-2020-0157

Quinn, R. W., Spreitzer, G. M., & Lam, C. F. (2012). Building a sustainable model of human energy in organizations: Exploring the critical role of resources. *The Academy of Management Annals*. DOI: 10.1080/19416520.2012.676762

Rahimi, M., & Arnold, B. (2024). Understanding Australia's teacher shortage: The importance of psychosocial working conditions to turnover intentions. *The Australian Educational Researcher*. DOI: 10.1007/s13384-024-00720-5

Sáez-Delgado, F., López-Angulo, Y., Mella-Norambuena, J., Hartley, K., & Sepúlveda, F. (2023). Mental health in school teachers: An explanatory model with emotional intelligence and coping strategies. *Electronic Journal of Research in Educational Psychology*, 21(61), 559–586. DOI: 10.25115/ejrep.v21i61.8322

Sartain, L., & Estrera, E. (2023). *Follow the leader: Principal characteristics and teachers' labor market decisions*. Annenberg Institute. DOI: 10.26300/8zpz-mr67

See, B. H., Gorard, S., El Soufi, N., Ledger, M., Morris, R., Maude, K., & Ivarsson-Keng, N. (2024). A structured review of the potential role of school leaders in making teaching more attractive. *Educational Review*. DOI: 10.1080/00131911.2024.2392565

Shell, D. L., Hurt, C. S., & White, H. (2023). Principal characteristics' effect on teacher retention: A systematic review. *Educational Research and Reviews*, 18(6), 104–113. DOI: 10.5897/ERR2023.4318

Simon, N., & Moore-Johnson, S. (2015). Teacher turnover in high-poverty schools: What we know and can do. *Teacher College Record*, 117, 030308. DOI:10.1177/016146811511700305

Somech, A., & Bogler, R. (2020) Antecedents and consequences of teacher organizational and professional commitment. *Educational Administration Quarterly*, 38(4), 555–577. DOI: 10.1177/001316102237672

Soykan, A., Gardner, D., & Edwards, T. (2019). Subjective Wellbeing in New Zealand teachers: An examination of the role of psychological capital. *Journal of Psychologists and Counsellors in Schools*, 29(2), 130–138. DOI: 10.1017/JGC.2019.14

Spreitzer, G., Sutcliffe, K., Dutton, J., Sonenshein, S., & Grant, A. M. (2005). A socially embedded model of thriving at work. *Organization Science*, 16(5), 537–549. DOI: 10.1287/orsc.1050.0153

Sugrue, E. P. (2019). Moral injury among professionals in K-12 education. *American Educational Research Journal*, 57(1). DOI: 10.3102/0002831219848690

Täschner, J., Dicke, T., Reinhold, S., & Holzberger, D. (2024). "Yes, I Can!" A systematic review and meta-analysis of intervention studies promoting teacher self-efficacy. *Review of Educational Research*. DOI: 10.3102/00346543231221499

Timotheou, S., Miliou, O., Dimitriadis, Y., Villagrá Sobrino, S., Giannoutsou, N., Cachia, R., Martínez-Monés, A., & Ioannou, A. (2022). Impacts of digital technologies on education and factors influencing schools' digital capacity and transformation: A literature review. *Education and Information Technologies*, 28(6), 6695–6726. DOI: 10.1007/s10639-022-11431-8

Tran, H., Cunningham, K., Yelverton, V., Osworth, D., & Hardie, S. (2023). How can school leaders retain teachers? The relative importance of different administrative supports for teacher retention in different types of schools. *NASSP Bulletin*, 107(3), 185–217. DOI: 10.1177/01926365231198858

Urick, A. (2016). The influence of typologies of school leaders on teacher retention: A multilevel latent class analysis. *Journal of Educational Administration*, 54(4), 434–468. DOI 10.1108/JEA-08-2014-0090

Vangrieken, K., Dochy, F., Raes, E., & Kyndt, E. (2015). Teacher collaboration: A systematic review. *Educational Research Review*, 15, 17–40. doi: 10.1016/j.edurev.2015.04.002

von der Embse, N. P., Sandilos, L. E., Pendergast, L. L., & Mankin, A. (2016). *Teacher Stress, Teaching-Efficacy, and Job Satisfaction in Response to Test-Based Educational Accountability Policies*. https://files.eric.ed.gov/fulltext/ED578430.pdf

Walsh, N., Ginger, K., & Akhavan, N. (2020). Benefits of instructional coaching for teacher efficacy: A mixed methods study with PreK-6 teachers in California. *Issues in Educational Research*, 30(3), 1143–1161. http://www.iier.org.au/iier30/walsh-abs.html

Walumbwa, F. O., Muchiri, M. K., Misati, E., Wu, C., & Meiliani, M. (2017). Inspired to perform: A multilevel investigation of antecedents and consequences for thriving at work. *Journal of Organizational Behavior*, 39(3), 249–261. DOI: 10.1002/job.2216

Wang, X., Gao, Y., Wang, Q., & Panpan, Z. (2024). Relationships between self-efficacy and teachers' well-being in middle school English teachers: The mediating role of teaching satisfaction and resilience. *Behavioral Sciences*, 14(8), 629. DOI: 10.3390/bs14080629

Waters, P. (2019, April 5). Relationships, resources, resilience: Professional learning communities to improve teacher retention. *2019 annual meeting of the American Educational Research Association*. DOI: 10.3102/1439078

Weddle, H. (2022). Approaches to studying teacher collaboration for instructional improvement: A review of literature. *Educational Research Review*, 35, 100415. DOI: 10.1016/j.edurev.2021.100415

Welsh, R. (2023). Administering discipline: An examination of the factors shaping school discipline practices. *Education and Urban Society*. DOI: 10.1177/00131245231208170

Wilkins, N., Verlenden, J. M., Szucs, L. E., & Johns, M. M. (2022). Classroom management and facilitation approaches that promote school connectedness. *Journal of School Health*. DOI: 10.1111/josh.13279

Williams, P. L., Kern, M. L., & Waters, L. (2015). A longitudinal examination of the association between psychological capital, perception of organizational virtues and work happiness in school staff. *Psychology of Well-Being*, 5(1), 5. DOI: 10.1186/S13612-015-0032-0

Woods, S., Sebastian, J., Herman, K. C., Huang, F. L., Reinke, W. M., & Thompson, A. M. (2023). The relationship between teacher stress and job satisfaction as moderated by coping. *Psychology in the Schools*, 60(7), 2237–2256. DOI: 10.1002/pits.22857

Yang, J., Bin Arshad, M. A., Zhao, M., & Cao, S. (2024). The relationship between high-performance work practices and employee turnover intention: An analysis based on a systematic literature review. *International Journal of Academic Research in Economics and Management Sciences*, 13(4). DOI: 10.6007/ijarems/v13-i4/24062

Zee, M., & Koomen, H. M. Y. (2016). Teacher self-efficacy and its effects on classroom processes, student academic adjustment, and teacher well-being: A synthesis of 40 years of research. *Review of Educational Research*. DOI: 10.3102/0034654315626801

Zhang, W., He, E., Mao, Y., Pang, S., & Tian, J. (2023). How teacher social-emotional competence affects job burnout: The chain mediation role of teacher-student relationship and well-being. *Sustainability*, 15(3), 2061. DOI: 10.3390/su15032061

Zhou, P.-L., Zhou, Y., Li, T., Zhao, R., & Sun, W. (2024). How do personal resources and homeroom teacher job demands influence teachers' professional identity? A perspective based on the job demands-resources model. *Psychology in the Schools*. DOI: 10.1002/pits.23308

The District's Role in Improving Teacher Retention

Principal Paul Bridges took his seat next to fellow principal Pauline Garcia at their administrative team meeting and released a heavy sigh. "Looking forward to this one, too?" Garcia asked with a knowing smile. Bridges chuckled. "I've got so much on my plate, and half of what's covered in these meetings could be handled by email. I want to move my school forward, but I'm stuck hearing about all these operational details." Garcia nodded in agreement as their superintendent called the meeting to order.

After an hour of budget planning and hiring discussions, the administrators took a break for coffee. Conversation drifted to recruiting and hiring practices: how to find better candidates beyond blanket job postings and a few job fairs. Garcia suggested treating recruitment more like professional sports, using data to gauge each candidate's strengths and how they might contribute to different school teams. Another principal argued that once teachers were hired, the district needed a better system for developing and retaining them; these hiring decisions were expensive, so investing in new hires was crucial. She added that some teachers left because of district pressures rather than school-based issues.

A separate group of principals began talking about visits from their central office evaluator. One said, "All I ever hear is 'You need to improve,' but I don't get practical strategies or real advice on how to do that. It's all words, no action."

> As the break ended, Bridges braced himself for the usual agenda—reports to fill out, a discussion about bus behavior, and yet another lecture on the district's vision. He noticed other principals seemed as stressed as he was and wondered if anyone at the district office could provide real guidance or coaching to help him retain more teachers. "It'd be nice," he thought, "to focus on that instead of loading us up with managerial tasks that don't really move the needle."

The preceding chapters have explored how a school's social-emotional climate, demands, resources, and leadership all influence teacher retention. Yet school districts and charter management organizations (CMOs) also bear a significant responsibility for supporting schools in retaining their educators. Historically, central offices have been seen and often operated as compliance-driven bodies, focusing on oversight, policy enforcement, and standardized accountability. This emphasis on compliance has inadvertently contributed to increased teacher stress, diminished autonomy, and higher turnover (Ingersoll & Tran, 2023; Matthews et al., 2022).

To tackle teacher retention and support school efforts successfully, districts and CMOs must deliberately shift from compliance-driven roles toward capacity-building roles using the three primary strategies explored previously as a guide. This new paradigm positions the district as a critical partner in reducing demands, enhancing resources, and fostering a positive social-emotional climate rather than merely enforcing regulations or reacting to issues. Since a school district or CMO is a system of schools, improving the inherent systemic relationships between the central office and schools is a critical interdependence to develop. This new paradigm also positions the role of central office administrators or principal supervisors as coaches who can help school leaders become better instructional leaders (Honig & Rainey, 2020) and leaders of the adult social-emotional climate as well as teacher retention.

This chapter extends the key concepts of the Teacher Retention Model (TRM), focusing on how districts and CMOs can further these principles.

The District's Role in Improving Teacher Retention

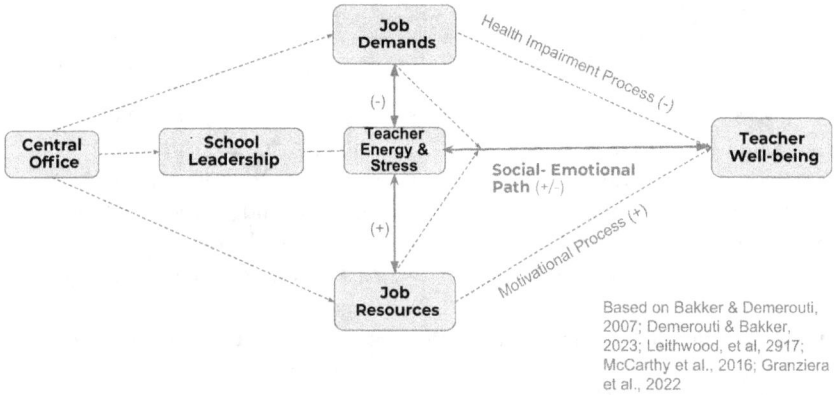

Figure 7.1 The district's role in the Teacher Retention Model.

While a district or CMO can influence all facets of the TRM, this chapter emphasizes the influence of the district or CMO on these key ideas (see Figure 7.1 below):

- **Key Idea #5**: Job demands drain energy.
- **Key Idea #6**: Excessive demands lead to health impairment through stress and burnout.
- **Key Idea #7**: Job resources replenish energy.
- **Key Idea #8**: Resources promote a motivational process and thriving.

And a special emphasis on the need for significant support of school leaders centered on

- **Key Idea #4**: Leaders' social-emotional leadership skills matter for teacher retention

Analyzing a District's Orientation Exercise

Review the two lists below: one portraying a compliance-oriented district approach and the other a capacity-building approach for teacher retention. Which of these descriptions better matches your district or CMO? What evidence leads you to that conclusion? (Table 7.1)

Table 7.1 Analyzing District Orientation Exercise

Compliance-Oriented District/CMO	Capacity-Building Oriented District/CMO
• Treats teacher retention as a school-level responsibility only. • Responds primarily to problems once they emerge. • Automatically removes a teacher from the district when released from a school • Uses traditional recruitment and hiring strategies • Enforces rules and regulations reactively • Creates oversight through excessive paperwork, checklists and bureaucracy • Emphasizes formal rules • Leaves principals on their own to figure things out on their own	• Recognizes teacher retention as a shared, systemic responsibility • Supports schools to proactively anticipate and prevent turnover • Tries to find the best fit for teachers, even if they are released from another school • Facilitates continuous improvement through inquiry cycles, coaching and mentoring • Reduces teacher stress through streamlined processes, good support, and reducing unnecessary demands • Uses data proactively to anticipate retention challenges and address root causes before they escalate • Prioritizes relational trust, collaborative teams, and teacher agency as the foundation for retention • Specifically focuses on supporting principals

A Different Role for Districts and CMOs

Many district-level initiatives for teacher retention currently focus on salaries and benefits, enforcing working conditions through policy, and active recruitment and hiring practices. While these measures are essential, they may not ensure long-term teacher retention. To better support schools and leaders in implementing the three key strategies described earlier, districts and CMOs must adopt a capacity-building approach (Honig & Rainey, 2023). Achieving this shift requires school districts or CMOs to move from telling to teaching, transforming the central office's role and providing differentiated support for principals.

To date, very little research has been conducted on how school districts support schools and school leaders in retaining teachers. However, Honig and Rainey's (2020, 2023) research on how central offices transform for equity-focused teaching and learning, as well as the development of principals as instructional leaders, provides a blueprint for district support.

First, learning through doing emerges as a critical element. Principals benefit from hands-on learning in their specific contexts rather than relying on directives or short-term professional development (PD) (Honig & Rainey, 2020). Grounded in socio-cultural learning theory (Collins et al., 1991), Honig and Rainey's research shows that principals develop more effectively when they have a clear task, a supportive mentor who uses a teaching-and-learning approach, and opportunities to collaborate, such as in communities of practice or an apprenticeship model. Applied to the TRM, principal supervisors might coach leaders in developing social-emotional competencies (Chapter 4) or facilitate plan-do-study-act (PDSA) cycles to strengthen school-level resources (Chapter 6).

Second, transforming central office roles is essential for transitioning from compliance-driven operations to capacity-building. As a blueprint for how districts or CMOs can support the TRM, Honig (2014) and Honig and Rainey (2014, 2020, 2023) show that as districts reorient their purpose toward meaningful support of teaching and learning, they move away from rigid organizational charts and focus on the "right work" (Honig & Rainey, 2023). Supported by external expertise, these districts reformed their core functions, human resources, principal supervision, operations, and cabinet-level leadership to better assist schools and principals. In the context of the TRM, this means that each central department could develop specific ways to reduce demands, enhance resources, and strengthen the adult social-emotional climate to promote teacher well-being and retention.

Last, differentiated support for principals acknowledges that schools vary in their needs, challenges, and the skill levels of their school leaders, particularly in terms of job demands, resources, and the adult social-emotional climate. Ford et al. (2020) applied social-cognitive theories of motivation to principal support, arguing that districts are the primary source of leaders' professional needs. As school leadership becomes increasingly complex, district leaders must invest in the learning and development of principals. Ford et al. (2020) suggest that district leaders and other critical personnel, through various structures, routines, and mindsets, can shape or ignore the support for principals and their schools. In their systematic review of 63 studies, Ford et al. (2020) found that the "motivational environment" a district creates directly influences the actions and learning of principals, which in turn shape outcomes within schools. Their review found that, overall, the motivational environment created by the district can have implications for what principals do and learn and how that influences what happens in schools (Ford et al., 2020).

In summary, emerging research has shown that principals attempting to address systemic problems, such as teacher retention, cannot do it alone. They require the support of the central office or CMOs through learning together, shifting the roles and functions of central office work, and differentiating the support needed for different schools and different principals to help build the necessary capacity to retain more teachers. Honig and Rainey (2023) suggest that, "when it comes to systemic change, the primary units of change are the premises that underlie the current work." Schools and principals will continue to struggle with the turnover issue if districts continue to operate under the premise that their current work is merely a matter of compliance.

Supporting the Three Strategies

Like the districts in Honig and Rainey's (2023) research on equitable teaching and learning, districts and CMOs looking to support schools and leaders in retaining more teachers should start by developing a theory of action. Too often, district offices jump into initiatives without fully examining the root of the problem or the assumptions that influence whether a particular approach will succeed or fail. By contrast, a theory of action functions as a clear roadmap, illustrating the cause-and-effect relationships between desired outcomes and the strategies presumed to produce those results. It offers a succinct explanation of how and why specific actions should lead to the intended goals.

A well-crafted theory of action works backward from your target outcomes, linking each necessary step and specifying the reasoning behind it. In the context of the TRM, the simplest version of a theory of action for district leaders, supervisors, and department heads starts with the school's strategy, and the district's role firmly oriented toward support. It sounds something like this:

> If we support the school's strategy of (1) improving the adult social-emotional climate or (2) removing demands or (3) adding resources) by (taking specific actions), this should improve teacher retention because (add in assumptions behind actions).

Of course, developing a theory of action is more complex than this simple outline, but it serves as a crucial starting point for districts striving to support schools and leaders. Superintendents and school boards must first acknowledge the problem of teacher turnover and recognize its impact on student learning. From there, collaboration among the superintendent's cabinet, human resources, teaching-and-learning teams, principal supervisors, and operations staff is essential for building the district's capacity to help schools retain more teachers (Honig & Rainey, 2023). Adopting a coherent theory of action unifies these diverse departments around a shared purpose, guiding their work with school teams and principals and ensuring that necessary services and resources are effectively brokered. Below, we explore specific steps that districts can take to advance each strategy.

Supporting the Development of Adult Social-Emotional Skills

As explored in Chapters 3 and 4, a poor social-emotional climate in a school can increase stress on teachers, decreasing their energy. Once diagnostic information is gathered and a clearer understanding of the adult social-emotional need emerges, district leaders and principals begin to develop a theory of action. Their beginning theory of action might include this:

> If we support the school's strategy of (1) improving the adult social-emotional climate by (taking or developing specific actions), this should improve teacher retention because (the adult social-emotional climate will improve, decreasing one cause of stress on teachers).

A more detailed process for developing a theory of action would include the following steps and questions (based on Center for Educational Leadership, 2014). The tools to use these steps are located in Appendix K.

1. Identify the adult social-emotional problem in the school or district.
2. Determine the general conditions affecting the problem.
3. Go deeper to find more specific problems of practice.

4. Develop a more complete theory of action.
5. Plan for action steps.

Supporting the Removal of Demands

As explored in Chapter 5, teaching and leading schools present specific risk factors associated with stress and energy depletion that differ from any other role in education. If demands become too extreme, they can hamper performance (Collie et al., 2020). The more demands placed on the educator, the more energy is required to meet those demands, leading to increased stress as teachers question if they have the personal and organizational resources to meet them. While many of these demands stem from differences in school processes, leadership, and climate, some originate directly from district leaders and departments. To support the removal of demands, the following process could be used by districts or CMOs. Specific tools to support this strategy are outlined in Appendix K.

1. Determine perceptions about excess demands at the principal and district levels.
2. Compare the results and consider how these may decrease the demands on schools, school leaders, and teachers.
3. Determine which demands may be most feasible to reduce.
4. Use short PDSA cycles to determine the impact of removing these demands, led by district leaders and department heads.

Supporting the Increase of Resources

As explored in Chapter 6, fostering teacher thriving requires structures, systems, and resources that support schools and school leaders in creating a positive work environment. Spreitzer et al. (2005) emphasize that teachers' broader social context significantly influences their well-being, highlighting a critical role for district leaders and departments in providing expertise, building capacity, and serving as key resources through collaborative approaches.

For instance, district leaders can offer greater autonomy at the school level while maintaining an autonomy-supportive stance, and principal supervisors can coach principals in delivering stronger instructional support. Technology departments can design more efficient and user-friendly tools for on-demand assistance, while teaching-and-learning teams can develop or source curriculum-aligned materials tailored to special populations. Human resources can tailor recruitment processes to meet specific team needs, and data or research departments can facilitate evidence-based improvement cycles, such as the PDSA method. In summary, by developing and brokering these types of resources, districts can enhance school and leadership capacity, thereby increasing teacher retention.

The following process could be used to support the increase of resources at schools. Specific tools to support this strategy are in Appendix K.

1. Determine perceptions around the resources most needed at the school level and the strengths of district leaders, departments, and principal supervisors.
2. Compare perceptions and ways to increase resources for schools, school leaders, and teachers.
3. Determine which resources may be most feasible to increase.
4. Utilize short PDSA cycles to assess the impact of increasing resources led by district leaders and department heads.

To illustrate what each of these processes might look like in practice, we use a case study below to demonstrate how a district implemented these processes to support the three TRM strategies.

Case Example of District Support

Year 1

Principal Bridges' Northwood School District was increasingly concerned about rising teacher turnover and sought to reverse the trend. In the spring, Superintendent Rich Kelly and the school board declared teacher retention a top district priority for the next three years. Once the school year ended, Superintendent Kelly and his cabinet convened all department heads and principals for a three-day work session to tackle the problem.

A Blueprint for Teacher Retention

On the first day, Superintendent Kelly, supported by external facilitators, presented his vision for teacher retention and outlined a plan to build both district- and school-level capacity. He declared that Northwood would become a district "where no teacher would ever want to leave." The rest of the day focused on strengthening the team's relationships and familiarizing everyone with the three strategies in the Teacher Retention Model. Recently collected teacher survey data revealed that adult social-emotional climate and teacher well-being needed improvement across all schools. Superintendent Kelly emphasized that school needs, rather than district mandates, should guide the support provided.

Over the following days, small groups of principals, district leaders, and department heads applied the five-step Theory of Action protocol described earlier. With open dialogue and ample modeling from the facilitators, the group spent considerable time discussing assumptions and goals. By the end of the third day, they reached a consensus on key elements for their theory of action (see Appendix K for relevant tools).

Go Deeper to Find More Specific Problems of Practice

	District Level	*Principal Level*	*(Start Here and Work to the Left) Teacher Level*
Specific changes needed	What specifically do district leaders, departments, and others need to do to support principals and schools? Why? What supports will they need?	What aspects of principal leadership do we need to support to support the adult social-emotional climate? What specifically do we need principals to do differently? Why? What supports will principals need to develop these skills or practices	Why are we prioritizing this level?

District Level	Principal Level	(Start Here and Work to the Left) Teacher Level
To better support principals, district leaders and departments need to 1. Model the same personal and interpersonal skills that principals need to develop. 2. Mentors will specifically coach principals on their development and how to develop teaching teams. 3. Cabinet-level leaders will also work on developing their interpersonal skills and work with their teams in the same way 4. Teaching & learning (T&L) will support coaches to use inquiry cycles to develop more teaching efficacy. 5. HR team will review their processes for hiring to include more adult social-emotional skills and develop support teams to help schools learn and develop personal/interpersonal skills.	To better support trust and efficacy, principals need to 1. Support personal skill development in their schools and teams. 2. Develop enhanced interpersonal skills. 3. Work with their instructional leadership teams to enhance efficacy. 4. Principals will need support from their mentors, T&L team and HR team.	Trust and efficacy Teacher data suggested that they perceived trust to be low between teachers and between teachers and principals. Other data suggested the need to develop better personal and interpersonal skill levels and feelings of efficacy in their work with students.

A Blueprint for Teacher Retention

Develop a More Complete Theory of Action

If district leadership and departments …	Then principals will be able to …	**So that** teachers develop more … and choose to stay
Develop similar personal and interpersonal skills and support principals and schools with coaching and services around adult social-emotional.	*Increase their personal and interpersonal skills and support the collective level to be more supportive of teachers and teacher teams.*	*Trust in each other, their leaders and the district leaders, and receive more support for their self-efficacy so they choose to stay in the district and never want to leave.*

Over the summer, Superintendent Kelly and his leadership team, including department heads and principal supervisors, developed concrete action steps and professional learning plans designed to strengthen each school's adult social-emotional climate. Their work centered on cultivating the same social-emotional competencies among district staff, both to model these skills and to build capacity for coaching school leaders. Throughout the process, they gathered ongoing data at both the school and department levels to inform adjustments and identify the next steps. Leadership meetings focused on sharing new skills and insights gained from working with schools, enabling district leaders to better understand emerging needs and refine their support accordingly.

Year 2

By the end of Year 1, data indicated that the adult social-emotional climate had improved, yet teachers continued to report high demands that impacted their well-being. In response, Superintendent Kelly and other central office leaders began strategizing how to reduce demands at both the school and district levels. To celebrate progress on their first strategy and plan further steps to strengthen the social-emotional climate, the leadership team convened another three-day retreat.

Before the summer break began, each principal administered the Job Demands Diagnostic for Schools (Appendix I) to gather teacher feedback. Guided by external facilitators, the team used the tools in Appendix K to address excessive demands. Principals collaborated to consolidate findings across their schools, while the Teaching & Learning department reviewed the demands they placed on schools and considered which could be modified or eliminated. The outcomes of these efforts are summarized below.

Determine Perceptions Around Excess Demands (Principal Version)

District or CMO Department	What requests, requirements, or processes do principals perceive as excessive?	Who does this perceived excessive demand most impact? (Principals, building staff, teachers?)	Might there be any unintended consequences if we remove this demand?
- **Teaching-and-learning department** - **Special education**	Intervention testing	Teachers, principals	Student needs?
	Intervention reporting	Teachers, principals	No
	Pull out training	Teachers	No
	Duplicate walk-throughs (Assistant Superintendent and Principal Supervisor)	Principals	Combine?
	Materials ordering	Teachers	Increased delivery
	Non-aligned professional development	Teachers	No

A Blueprint for Teacher Retention

Determine Perceptions Around Excess Demands (District Leadership and Department Version)

District or CMO Department	Of all requests, requirements, or processes required for schools, school leaders, teachers and other school personnel, which do you or your department perceive as taking the most time and effort?	Who does this perceived excessive demand most impact? (Principals, building staff, teachers?)	Could this demand be reduced or removed? Might there be any unintended consequences if we remove this demand?
- **Teaching-and-learning department**	*Intervention reporting*	*Teachers*	*Reduced*
	Pull out training	*Teachers*	*Removed*
		Teachers	*Modified*
- **Special education**	*Materials ordering*	*Teachers*	*Modified*
	Pacing guides		

1. Compare results and how this may decrease the demands on schools, school leaders and teachers.
2. Determine which demands may be most feasible to reduce.

District or CMO Department	Principal suggestions	District leadership and department suggestions	Which suggestions have most potential to remove demands on schools, school leaders, teachers, or other personnel? Is removal feasible?

- **Teaching-and-learning department** - **Special education**	*Intervention testing* *Intervention reporting* *Pull out training* *Duplicate walk-throughs (Assistant Superintendent and Principal Supervisor)* *Materials ordering* *Non-aligned professional development (PD)*	*Intervention reporting* *Pull out training* *Materials ordering* *Pacing guides*	*Intervention reporting (feasible- use tech tools)* *Training (feasible)* *Pacing guides (modified)* *Non-aligned PDs (move work to professional learning communities and coaching)*

Leaders in the Teaching-and-Learning Department teamed up with a small group of principals over the summer to devise strategies for alleviating some of the most pressing demands on schools and teachers. They then employed PDSA plans to assess the impact of these changes on the well-being of teachers and principals. Other departments employed a similar approach, generating solutions such as faster computer login processes (Technology), taking over notifications for overcharged meal accounts (Food Services), and securing waivers for certain annual state-mandated trainings (Human Resources).

Year 3

By the end of Year 2, the district's use of PDSA cycles fostered strong collaboration between departments and schools. Data tracking the effects of reduced demands revealed clear improvements in teacher well-being but also uncovered new insights into additional stressors. Specifically, the Job Demands-Resources Diagnostic for Schools (Appendix I) revealed that many teachers found meetings and teams to be lacking in effectiveness.

In response, principals and district leaders convened once again after the school year ended to determine how best to bolster these areas. Using the Increasing Resources tools, they identified strategies to enhance meeting quality, strengthen team dynamics, and further improve teacher *well-being in the upcoming year. The outcomes of these discussions are summarized below.*

Determine Perceptions Around Needed Resources (Principal Version)

1. Based on your diagnostic, which resource areas require the most support?	2. Beyond the diagnostic, what other evidence supports these resource needs?	3. What might this resource support look like if it came from the district?
Effective use of professional learning communities (PLCs) *More collaborative team skills*	*Observations of most teams reveal no clear goals or effective facilitation of the team's objectives.* *Teachers' complaints about excessive conflict on some teams* *Some requests about needing a more emotionally supportive environment*	*Facilitation modeling* *Assistance team for PLCs that need more support* *Team lead training and support*

Determine Perceptions Around Resource Availability (District Leadership and Department Version)

	What resource area do you believe schools(s) most need support?	What evidence supports these resource needs?	What skills, programs, tools, or practices do you have now that help support this resource need? What skills, tools, or practices might you need to develop to support this resource need?
You personally *District leadership consensus*	*Teams and professional learning communities (PLCs)*	*School diagnostics* *Principal meetings* *Grievances*	*Modeling meeting facilitation* *Help principals observe team dynamics*

The District's Role in Improving Teacher Retention

Your department and team (Human Resources and Teaching & Learning)	Teams and PLCs	School diagnostics Principal meetings Teacher discussions Transfer requests PLC survey data	Have now: PLC refresher Facilitation skills Coaching Need to Develop Team coaching skills Team leader coaching Conflict resolution skills

1. Compare perceptions and ways to increase resources for schools, school leaders, and teachers.
2. Determine which resources may be most feasible to increase.

Resource areas most in need of support	Principal ideas for resource support	District leadership and department ideas for resource support	Which suggestions have the most potential to increase resources for schools, school leaders, teachers, or other personnel? Is adding this resource feasible?
More effective use of professional learning communities (PLCs) Enhanced team skills	Facilitation modeling Assistance team for PLCs that need more support Team lead training and support	Have now: PLC refresher Facilitation skills Coaching Need to Develop Team coaching skills Team leader coaching Conflict resolution skills	Team lead training and support Ongoing team support through team coaching skills/conflict resolution Team observation support for principals

By utilizing these straightforward strategies and resource-building tools, leaders from the Teaching-and-Learning Department, along with coaches and Human Resources volunteers, spent the summer refining their skills to support school teams more effectively. They developed various support structures and coaching models designed to help teams thrive. Meanwhile, principal supervisors created a concise process for coaching principals on observing and intervening when conflicts or interpersonal challenges arose within their teams.

Supporting Principals Differently

Above, we discussed the role of principal motivation as an essential consideration for supporting principal learning and development, particularly in relation to acquiring new skills to enhance teacher retention. The systematic review by Ford et al. (2020) can be narrowed down to these important claims about the essential interactions between principal motivation and district support:

- **The support from the district for principal competence and self-efficacy is vital for motivation and effective leadership.** This support includes ongoing professional development, mentoring, and school-based supervision opportunities that offer vicarious learning and establishing clear models of leadership for coherence across the district. Learning structures, such as one-on-one coaching and learning communities, work together to address common problems with learning that is done primarily at school sites. Frameworks as tools for meaning-making and clarity also help bring coherence to school leadership. These models and learning structures build principals' belief in their capabilities to lead effectively. Some evidence suggests that interpersonal support from central office leaders can also enhance principal efficacy (Ford et al., 2020).
- **Districts that afford autonomy support to principals, balanced with a clear district vision ("defined autonomy"), improve job satisfaction and commitment.** When principals feel they have the autonomy to lead their schools effectively, supported by clear expectations and resources, their motivation increases. Conversely, controlling district

policies and a lack of involvement in decision-making can significantly undermine principals' sense of autonomy and motivation (Ford et al., 2020).

- **Districts that align district learning support with principals' values and goals cultivate autonomous motivation.** Principals are more motivated when professional development and district initiatives are relevant, show utility value to their needs, and help them achieve their school goals. Evidence also suggests that principals value mentoring and supervision over other forms of learning when the learning is focused on their specific skill needs. However, accountability policies that conflict with principals' values can lead to decreased motivation (Ford et al., 2020).

- **School district leaders can influence principals' motivation for learning and development by shaping their causal attributions and goal orientations.** Districts can foster a sense of control by focusing feedback on processes and controllable factors. Principal attributions for school success and failure can also be supported by school districts by giving principals more autonomy and removing unnecessary demands, allowing them to focus on essential problems of practice, such as teacher retention. Emphasizing continuous improvement and mastery over competitive performance goals can also be more conducive to sustained motivation and effort among principals (Ford et al., 2020).

- **Last, fostering strong relationships and a sense of relatedness between principals and district leaders is crucial for their motivation, learning, and professional development.** Collaborative activities, mentoring, and trust-building help principals feel connected and supported, which in turn positively impacts their motivation and effectiveness. Collaborative networks of experts, extending from the central office to the classroom, have also been shown to unite people around common goals (Ford et al., 2020).

To bolster principals' motivation for learning and development, particularly in the context of retaining more teachers, districts and CMOs may need a new paradigm for principal supervision that goes beyond traditional compliance practices. Honig and Rainey's (2020, 2023) work provides a blueprint for this shift by outlining how principal supervisors can transition from a compliance-oriented approach to one focused on capacity-building. In their study, principal supervisors engaged with school leaders as coaches and professional equals, helping them acquire essential skills and address school-specific challenges.

Although Honig and Rainey's (2020) research did not explicitly target principal motivation, many of Ford et al.'s (2020) findings about fostering competence, self-efficacy, and autonomy were evident. For instance, by coaching principals to develop new capabilities, supervisors built leaders' self-efficacy and shaped how they attributed school outcomes. Providing customized support to each school enhanced principals' sense of autonomy.

To guide this teaching-and-learning approach to supervision, Honig and Rainey (2020) developed a framework illustrating how supervisors can effectively work with principals. While originally intended for improving instructional leadership, it can also serve as a blueprint for boosting teacher retention. The framework identifies "teaching moves" that principal supervisors can employ when partnering with principals on retention-related challenges. Below, we explore those moves with examples of how they might be applied in practice.

- **Fostering leaders' agency**: These moves help school leaders develop their agency over time, enabling them to enhance their professional growth and learning. For example, at the beginning of a supervisor working on a goal with a principal, they may direct them toward resources but, over time, may have the principal create their own learning plan.

- **Joint work moves**: These moves help school leaders see practices as collectively valued through clear definitions and guides for the practices. For instance, a supervisor and school leader may collaborate on emotional regulation during meetings and create a shared guide to use together.

- **Modeling**: These moves allow the supervisor to demonstrate a practice for school leaders using metacognitive explanations of what is being modeled and why. For instance, using the emotional regulation guide, the supervisor might lead a meeting and model his thinking around emotional regulation throughout the meeting for the principal.

- **Talk moves**: These moves are employed by the supervisor to engage school leaders in making sense of new practices and how to use them.

For example, after observing a meeting where the principal is practicing their emotional regulation, the supervisor might use a talk move, such as challenging the principal about their interpretation of a part of the meeting or questioning them on the phrasing of certain responses.

- **Buffering and brokering**: Buffering is a strategy to protect a principal's learning, whereas brokering is a strategy that connects the school leader to other resources to enhance their learning. For instance, a supervisor might suggest online training on emotional regulation for the school leader or recommend discussing this skill with a colleague who displays it.

- **All learners as a resource**: This move enlists school leaders in learning from one another in a learning community, recognizing their learning and development as an ongoing process. To illustrate, in a principal's learning community meeting, a supervisor could use a structure where principals shift partners every 10 minutes to discuss their goals, progress, and learning plans.

- **Differentiation**: This move recognizes the importance of personalization for each school leader, acknowledging that each has unique strengths and needs and utilizes diagnostic tools and other forms of evidence to assess the needs of individual principals. For example, a supervisor might have school leaders use the Interpersonal Diagnostic (Appendix D) or the Collective Level Diagnostic (Appendix E) to identify specific areas for social-emotional growth, and then work with them to develop a plan to address those areas.

Adult learners, including principals, typically move from novice to expert through sustained support, appropriate mindsets, and strong motivation (Bohle-Carbonell & van Merrienboer, 2019). Many of the leadership skills presented in this book may be unfamiliar or differently positioned in relation to teacher retention, making it unrealistic for principals to master them after a single PD session. Indeed, long-term professional learning for school leaders requires ongoing support, feedback, and resources (Hill & Papay, 2022). These findings suggest that to grow and develop school leaders who will retain more teachers, they will need extensive learning opportunities supported by supervisors who share a teaching-and-learning perspective for their work and are willing to adopt a different approach to working with principals.

Conclusion

This chapter emphasized the importance of districts and CMOs in critically evaluating the demands they impose on schools, expanding available resources in various forms, and enhancing school leaders' capacity to retain teachers. Given the broadening scope of principals' responsibilities, they cannot do this work alone.

Connecting these insights to the TRM, we see how excessive demands placed on schools and principals drain energy (Key Idea #5), ultimately causing stress and burnout (Key Idea #6). Conversely, when districts or CMOs introduce multifaceted resources, they can boost energy (Key Idea #7), thereby encouraging motivation and fostering thriving environments. Finally, motivating and supporting school leaders to develop key social-emotional and retention-focused skills (Key Idea #4) require new district-level leadership structures. In short, both school and district leadership play a pivotal role in improving teacher retention.

 ## Leadership Considerations

- For district leaders, what is your stance toward supporting the skill development of school leaders?
- For school leaders, what is your stance toward receiving developmental support from district leaders?
- Why should the motivation of principals be considered when developing new skills?
- Which of the claims about supporting principal's motivation makes the most sense to you? Why?
- How does your district currently support schools and school leaders in addressing teacher retention?
- Of the three strategies, which one might be easiest for district leaders to support? Why?
- Why do you believe that principal supervisors need a different support perspective?
- What new skills might principal supervisors need to learn to use a teaching-and-learning perspective with principals?

References

Bohle-Carbonell, K., & van Merrienboer, J.J. (2019). Adaptive expertise. In P. Ward, J.M. Schraagen, J. Gore & E.M. Roth (Eds).*The oxford handbook of expertise* (pp. 262–286). Oxford Press. DOI: 10.1093/oxfordhb/9780198795872.013.12

Center for Educational Leadership (2014). *Creating a theory of action for improving teaching and learning.* University of Washington-College of Education. https://k-12leadership.org/tools/creating-a-theory-of-action/

Collie, R. J., Malmberg, L. E., Martin, A. J., Sammons, P., & Morin, A. J. S. (2020). A multilevel person-centered examination of teachers' workplace demands and resources: Links with work-related well-being. *Frontiers in Psychology*, 11, 1–19. DOI: 10.3389/fpsyg.2020.00626

Collins, A. M., Brown, J. S., & Holum, A. (1991). Cognitive apprenticeship: Making thinking visible. *American Educator*, 15(3). https://www.academia.edu/281205/Cognitive_Apprenticeship_Making_Thinking_Visible

Ford, T. G., Lavigne, A. L., Fiegener, A. M., & Si, S. (2020). Understanding district support for leader development and success in the accountability era: A review of the literature using social-cognitive theories of motivation. *Review of Educational Research*, 90(2), 264–307. DOI: 10.3102/0034654319899723

Hill, H. C., & Papay, J. P. (2022). *Building better PL: How to strengthen teacher learning.* Research Partnership for Professional Learning. Brown University. https://annenberg.brown.edu/sites/default/files/rppl-building-better-pl.pdf

Honig, M. I. (2014). District central office leadership as teaching: How central office administrators support principals' development as instructional leaders. *Educational Administration Quarterly*, 48(4), 733–744. DOI: 10.1177/0013161X12443258

Honig, M. I., & Rainey, L. R. (2014). Central office leadership in principal professional learning communities: The practice beneath the policy. *Teachers College Record*, 116(4). https://eric.ed.gov/?id=EJ1020221

Honig, M. I., & Rainey, L. R. (2020). *Supervising principals for instructional leadership: A teaching and learning approach.* Harvard Education Press.

Honig, M. I., & Rainey, L. R. (2023). *From tinkering to transformation: How school district central offices drive equitable teaching and learning.* Harvard Education Press.

Ingersoll, R. M., & Tran, H. (2023). Teacher shortages and turnover in rural schools in the US: An organizational analysis. *Educational Administration Quarterly*, 59, 396–431. DOI: 10.1177/0013161X231159922

Matthews, R. A., Wayne, J. H., Smith, C. E., Casper, W. J., Wang, Y., & Streit, J. (2022). Resign or carry-on? District and principal leadership as drivers of change in teacher turnover intentions during the COVID-19 crisis: A latent growth model examination. *Journal of Occupational and Organizational Psychology*, 95(3), 687–717. DOI: 10.1111/joop.12397

Spreitzer, G., Sutcliffe, K., Dutton, J., Sonenshein, S., & Grant, A. M. (2005). A socially embedded model of thriving at work. *Organization Science*, 16(5), 537–549. DOI: 10.1287/orsc.1050.0153

Solving the Retention and Attrition Crisis

After three years of intentionally focusing on retaining teachers in the Northwood District and at his school, Principal Bridges felt optimistic about the next school year, as he had to replace only one teacher, whose wife had received a job offer they couldn't refuse in a nearby city. Principal Bridges realized that people make decisions based on various factors, but at least the teacher's decision to leave was based on something positive rather than being impacted by something the school or district was doing to create excess stress or burnout. Over the three years since he first heard about and learned the Teacher Retention Model (TRM), Principal Bridges and his leadership team had substantial data revealing increases in their teachers' well-being and the adult social-emotional climate. Using leading indicators, such as flash surveys on stress and energy, provided Principal Bridges with actionable data to determine when he needed to lower demands and increase his emotional support for his teachers. While not perfect, he and his team believed they had created an environment where staff and leadership could openly communicate and strive to increase resources when problems arose. Even when new initiatives had started to meet the needs of their students, the staff knew they would have a voice in deciding how they were learned and implemented.

As Principal Bridges walked out of his office to leave for the day at the end of the school year, he reflected on the days when he had wondered if he could be a principal for the rest of his career or if he

DOI: 10.4324/9781003628767-8

> needed to pursue something less stressful and healthier. He remembered how his new supervisor, three years ago, had coached him on increasing his self-awareness and emotional regulation as well as how to give more autonomy and trust back to his teachers. It wasn't easy at first, but he had grown in those areas, along with learning how to remove demands that interfered with the essentials of teaching and learning, and increasing support for his teachers. As he reached his car, he smiled as he knew that tomorrow at the next three-day retreat, he had lots to celebrate. He was actually looking forward to it.

Over the past seven chapters, we have explored the issue of teacher retention, examining how schools in the United States and other countries have reached this point. We also explored a large-scale strategy that could help solve this problem: creating an intentional retention system in every school designed to enhance teacher well-being and reestablish purpose and meaning in the teaching profession. Without some intentional strategy, however, the number of teachers leaving the classroom yearly will continue to increase. As a quick reminder of the staggering size of the problem, the teacher turnover rate was already a troubling 16% (Sutcher et al., 2016) prior to Covid, with the rate increasing to around 18%–19%, equating to around 760,000 teachers need to be replaced yearly (Bleiberg & Kraft, 2022). If the demands of the educational system continue without intentional action to address teacher retention, the costs to our students and their futures will be dramatic. This cost will be especially true for students of color and those from low-SES (socioeconomic status) backgrounds, who already face the highest rates of teacher turnover in their schools and the least prepared teachers.

As this final chapter is being written, thousands of educators are quietly deciding whether they should stay in education next year or seek something less stressful and more fulfilling. Whether we like it or not, over the past two decades, we have inadvertently created an intentional turnover system, largely due to what Fullan (2021) labels as the wrong drivers for improving our educational system. Our teachers have been caught between their ideals of helping students and the misguided drivers for improving education, such as test-focused accountability, which have created substantial unintended consequences, including teacher turnover.

Unfortunately, as this problem has worsened, educational leaders and policymakers have often misinterpreted cause and effect in their attempts to address the issue of teacher turnover but with limited success. *The Burnout Challenge* (Maslach & Leiter, 2022) uses an apt analogy to show how cause and effect have become distorted. The book examines how individuals interact with their jobs and the prevalence of stress and burnout in various industries, including education. In this book, the analogy of the canary and the coal mine is used to help explain stress and burnout. In the early days of mining, miners would take a canary down into the mines to check the air quality. If the canary died, the air was unsafe, and people took action to fix the air so that workers would not die. The canary was neither blamed nor threatened or incentivized to do better. Nor did people try to evaluate the canary, build a more robust and resilient one, or buy the canary a gym membership so it would breathe better. The miners tried none of these after-the-fact solutions. If the canary died, the work was stopped until the environment was fixed. Workers blamed the environment or work conditions, not the canary.

What is most interesting about this early method of gauging air quality is that it serves as an interesting analogy for not only stress and burnout but also educator retention and attrition today. Every day, our educators, the canaries, go to work facing not bad air quality (in most cases) but workplace demands that can lead to excess stress, burnout, decreased well-being, and eventual turnover. To extend the metaphor, we place almost the entirety of the blame for school issues on the educator or the canary in the coal mine. In the US today, we believe that if we build a stronger, more resilient educator, we will never have to worry about or question the work environment. However, DeNeve and Ward (2025) suggest that leaders often confuse employee wellness with overall well-being, which encompasses not only physical health but also a person's psychological, emotional, cognitive, and social well-being.

Many policymakers and leaders believe that offering a higher salary as the sole consideration for educator retention is sufficient, regardless of the impact of the coal mine. They believe that by offering a gym membership or telling teachers to develop more resilience or practice self-care, the coal mine does not matter. Not that any of these ideas are bad or cannot help the issue of retention. However, even if you were offered a huge salary to teach but you knew the coal mine was poisonous, you would likely not accept it. The safety of coal mines is crucial and matters greatly; the same applies to schools. The mental, emotional, and physical well-being of our educators matters, and it matters a great deal.

In this final chapter, we will provide a brief review of the TRM and the Eight Key Ideas, discuss why the well-being of teachers should become our primary outcome measure in teacher retention, and explore what the TRM means for the future of schools and education moving forward.

The TRM and Eight Key Ideas

The TRM, along with its three strategies for retaining teachers, offers school and district leaders, as well as policymakers, an opportunity to rethink and enhance the working conditions for teachers. The TRM offers a lens through which to view educator dissatisfaction and well-being. As a result, the TRM can help leaders understand, interpret, explain, and change those factors that affect teacher well-being in the workplace (Granziera et al., 2021; Mazzetti et al., 2021). The central idea in this model is that human energy is necessary for productive work, and workers require balance to avoid exhaustion, much like the canary needs clean air to breathe. To develop your blueprint for retaining more of your teachers, the key ideas help you understand the causes of decreasing teacher well-being and attrition as well as the consequences of not addressing these issues systematically. Below, we recap the Eight Key Ideas that build the TRM.

> With **Key Idea #1**, we examined the nature of teaching as an **energy-intensive** profession. We examined the nature of energy and the different forms that teachers need daily to teach students, including psychological and emotional, social, cognitive, and physical modes. The leadership takeaway: When creating your retention blueprint, consider the concept of energy by measuring it continuously and observing signs of declining energy in your teachers.
>
> With **Key Idea #2**, we analyzed the role of stress as a **biopsychosocial process** and how stress can have the largest impact on teacher energy. Stress, as a biopsychosocial process, helps us understand that how our teachers interact with and interpret what is happening in the classroom, school, or district can have long-term physical impacts on their health. The leadership takeaway: When creating your retention blueprint, work to understand the social stressors impacting teachers at the

personal, team, and collective levels and how teachers are reacting to those stressors.

With **Key Idea #3**, we also analyzed how a teacher's **emotions** can either increase or decrease energy and how strengthening social-emotional skills within oneself, with others, and across the school shapes that energy day after day. Similarly, how other people and the organization work to support the emotions of teachers can influence these energy levels. It is a reciprocal relationship that needs constant attention. The leadership takeaway: When creating your retention blueprint, acknowledge that your teachers grapple with their emotions every day in their roles and that the emotional path and its various levels affect teachers in different ways.

With **Key Idea #4**, understanding how leaders develop and utilize their **social-emotional leadership skills** is central to retaining teachers. School leaders who intentionally act to support their teachers' energy levels and emotions in encouraging ways have a higher likelihood of retaining their teachers. Similarly, district leaders who develop and use their social-emotional leadership skills have a higher likelihood of supporting and keeping their principals in place. The leadership takeaway: When creating your retention blueprint, understand that you, as the principal, must lead the emotional path in your school as a primary support for teachers and that these skills can be learned through intentional practice.

Key Idea #5 reveals that any **job demand** will drain energy, incurring specific costs to the well-being of teachers, and excessive demands over time accumulate greater costs for teachers. The costs of these excess demands that accumulate over time can be reduced with proper attention and management. The leadership takeaway: When creating your retention blueprint, recognize the numerous demands placed on your teachers and utilize both quantitative and qualitative data to determine when these demands exceed your teachers' resources.

Key Idea #6 continues with the concept of job demands, illustrating that these excessive demands can lead to **health impairment** through stress, burnout, and decreased well-being among teachers. While teachers can, for a time, handle the excess demands placed upon them, the long-term consequences for their well-being can create other problems. The leadership takeaway: When creating your retention blueprint, pay more attention to the health and well-being of your teachers, not just when they are sick, but constantly.

Key Idea #7 acknowledges that **job resources** in their various forms can replenish energy. Job resources, as we explored, primarily manifest as the personal and professional relationships that teachers crave in their work, along with the supportive leadership of principals. The leadership takeaway: When creating your retention blueprint, determine if your resources exceed the demands. If not, decide with your teachers what resources need developing.

Last, **Key Idea # 8** demonstrates that these job resources promote **motivational processes** that lead to thriving in teachers' work. Job resources are the hidden secret of teacher well-being, and when they are developed and used properly, a natural energy source materializes. The leadership takeaway: When creating your retention blueprint, collect data to identify which teachers are thriving and which are not, so you can work with them to enhance their well-being.

In short, these Eight Key Ideas are the starting point for you to begin creating a more intentional retention system for your school. By recognizing how these ideas interact to influence teacher well-being for the better or worse, you can begin to pay more attention to fixing the coal mine while supporting the canary.

The Benefits of Well-Being

A quick review of the TRM (see Figure 8.1 below) suggests that the Eight Key Ideas will ultimately impact teacher well-being, for better or worse. In the TRM, teacher well-being is the ultimate adult outcome of a successful and well-functioning school. As we explored in Chapter 3, well-being can be defined as "the capacity for teachers to respond to the cognitive, emotional, health, and social conditions pertaining to their work and their profession" (Viac & Fraser, 2020, p. 18). In the TRM, well-being consists of four distinct but interrelated forms:

- **Psychological and emotional well-being** involves cultivating both positive and negative emotions in a healthy balance, developing a clear sense of purpose and meaning in one's professional and personal life, and maintaining a sense of optimism.

Solving the Retention and Attrition Crisis

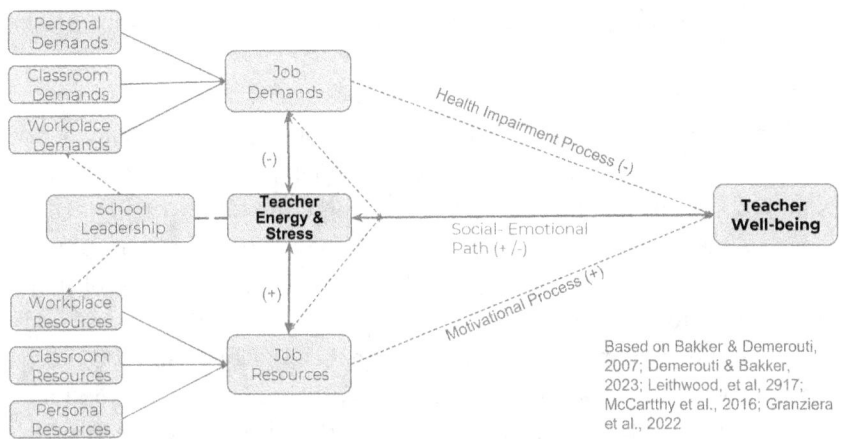

Figure 8.1 The Teacher Retention Model.

- **Social well-being** is characterized by meaningful and supportive relationships within and beyond the school context, a sense of belonging to a community, and effective collaboration with peers, families, and students.
- **Cognitive well-being** involves sustaining intellectual engagement and curiosity, maintaining mental agility and focus, and continuously developing professional competencies.
- **Physical well-being** encompasses maintaining overall physical health, vitality, and energy through sufficient rest, healthy nutrition, and active stress management.

So, why is well-being the primary outcome in the TRM? Why not something different, such as classroom instruction or improved interaction with students, as that is the ultimate role of a teacher? In much of the research on organizations, well-being is viewed as an enabler of other important outcomes rather than an end in itself (Ahmed & Malik, 2019; Ward, 2024). In the TRM, teacher well-being acts as a catalyst for the complex functions of teaching. Consider this: the fewer positive emotions, the less sense of belonging, the less focus, the less vitality felt, and the lower well-being a teacher experiences are all bound to influence their classroom instruction and relationships with students. In contrast, the more well-being a teacher feels, such as more positive emotions and a sense of purpose, a purposeful community, constant intellectual stimulation, and an overall feeling of energy and vitality, the more energy a teacher will have for their classroom instruction and student interactions.

It goes without saying that a happy employee is a more productive and better employee in the long run. Many leaders understand this claim at one level, but before spending critical resources on improving well-being, they want proof to make a business case for using these resources. Thankfully, these claims about the relationship between well-being and critical work outcomes, such as performance, retention, and costs, have been substantiated by numerous research findings across various fields over many decades.

Concerning well-being and job performance, Judge et al. (2001) used job satisfaction as a proxy for well-being (psychological and emotional) and found through their meta-analysis that the overall effect size of job satisfaction on performance was a moderate 0.30. Bellet et al. (2023) used a weekly pulse check with call center workers assessing their happiness (psychological and emotional; social well-being) and found that those who were very happy had over 13% more sales.

While these two studies showed relationships between well-being and performance in the business world, is there evidence in the education field? Ahmed and Malik (2019) found that psychological empowerment and well-being were significantly and positively related to job performance. Similarly, Klusmann et al. (2008) found that teachers' occupational well-being, as measured by their levels of emotional exhaustion and job satisfaction, predicted the quality of instruction in mathematics classrooms. Finally, Dreer (2023) conducted a systematic review of well-being research from numerous countries, finding that higher levels of well-being are strongly associated with teachers' self-efficacy, teaching behavior, quality of instruction, and improved teacher–student relationships. Simply put, teachers with higher levels of well-being perform better and are more productive in their instruction.

In terms of retention and well-being, other research indicates that employees with higher levels of well-being, including teachers, tend to stay in their roles longer. This finding shows up in numerous and diverse contexts. For example, Kaiser and Oswald (2022) find that job satisfaction, even as a single rating, has high predictive value for staying in a job or changing to another. Further research using large-sample online surveys shows that unhappy employees tend to search for more jobs and that employee ratings of their companies have high correlations with turnover percentages, meaning the higher a company's overall rating on satisfaction, purpose, happiness, and lower stress ratings, the less likely it is for employees to leave. Specific to education, Wang and Hall (2021) found that teacher well-being is significantly related to teacher retention, and Collie (2023) found that well-being, specifically vitality (physical well-being) and relatedness to colleagues (social well-being), is associated with teachers' desire to stay in their roles.

Third, well-being costs less than its counterpart, illness. As medical and insurance costs continue to rise, leaders who can recognize the relationship between work stressors and employee health costs can work to reduce these costs. The costs to employers for treating work-related illnesses and injuries are typically reflected in health insurance premiums, which have increased by 87% since 2000 (Jauregui & Schnall, 2009). At the same time, healthcare costs have increased by 14% more than general prices in the US since 2000 (Papanicolas et al., 2024). Six of the top 10 conditions financially affecting health care and insurance costs have been connected to psychosocial stressors, including hypertension, diabetes, and low back pain, and mental health issues such as anxiety, depression, and alcoholism have also been associated with workplace stressors.

Other research finds that people who experience job strain have a 1.82 times greater chance of developing common mental health issues (Dobson & Schnall, 2009). Specific to education, Singh and Gautman (2024), in their review of research on the relationship between job satisfaction and teacher mental health, found that lower levels of job satisfaction have a significant impact on teachers' well-being and mental health. These findings suggest that when workplace demands and stressors are not addressed, schools and districts will ultimately incur increased costs through higher insurance premiums.

In short, well-being as a primary outcome of an intentional retention system is a goal worthy of time and resources. In numerous studies across diverse industries, including education, well-being has been linked to higher performance and productivity levels, increased retention rates, and improved physical and mental health. These findings suggest that investing resources in improving working conditions for teachers not only saves money in the long run but also may be a worthy school improvement goal that does not increase the demands on teachers. Simply stated, teachers with higher levels of well-being tend to teach more effectively.

Future of Educational Change, Work, and Retention in Schools

So far, we have examined how school or district actions either drive or prevent teacher turnover. However, other societal forces also impact districts and schools, contributing to the retention problem, including a narrow focus on the purpose of education. As Fullan (2025) argues, "The reforms and models we have used for the last 6 decades are obsolete. World society is crumbling. Education at best is a bystander." In this brief section, we will examine the relationship between the future of educational change, the role of teachers, and its potential impact on teacher retention.

First, the current drivers for improving education have had unintended consequences, including increased teacher disengagement and turnover. Fullan (2021, 2025) explains a driver as a societal force that attracts power and generates motion within the educational system. These drivers aim to reform education for a specific purpose and influence all aspects of the educational system, including teacher retention. In his writings on the drivers influencing educational reform (Fullan, 2021), Fullan discusses what he considers the wrong drivers, including academic obsession, machine intelligence, austerity, and fragmentation, and how these create a "single, integrated model" that has shaped a paradigm about schools. For example, the focus on test scores, such as academic obsession instead of other important outcomes, has driven districts and schools in a certain direction. So far this century, this set of misguided drivers, implemented through policy and other methods, has regrettably been done to teachers and students rather than alongside them, resulting in disengagement among students and excessive stress and burnout among teachers and school leaders to meet these demands. In essence, this loss of autonomy and intensification of work in pursuit of test scores have been external contributors to teacher turnover.

Second, a new purpose and a new set of drivers for education may help increase teacher retention, as they better align with teacher values and purpose. Fullan (2025) again turns to the notion that, moving forward, the educational system as a whole (schools, districts, states, and federal) needs to engage a set of new or "right" drivers to better improve schools toward meeting the changing needs of society. The right drivers, or what he refers to as the "Human Paradigm" and the next model, are more focused on developing individuals who work to influence and address societal problems (Fullan, 2025). Shunning the current model of academic obsession and test-based accountability, he describes the right drivers:

- A focus on well-being and deeper learning can help students become more balanced, focus on a broader set of important outcomes, and be more intrinsically engaged and motivated. Notice how this aligns with the focus on teacher well-being that we discussed earlier.
- A focus on social intelligence helps students understand themselves better and work effectively with others to tackle challenges.
- A focus on equality through strategic, equity-driven investments can expand resources and capacity for every student (see Chapter 6).

In short, if the educational system begins to recognize the shortcomings of the academic obsession and the need for a new and more meaningful purpose and set of drivers, teacher retention may increase as student engagement increases and teachers begin to see the increasing value match between the new role of education and why they wanted to teach in the first place.

Third, returning to our initial discussion of an intentional retention system, Fullan (2021, 2025) introduces systemness, his fourth driver, which involves reversing top-down mandates and focusing more on the local context first. He discusses systemness as a "subjective sense of being in a system" and the ownership in improving the system in which you work, starting in the local context. Fullan (2025) suggests that the primary driver of change going forward must originate from the bottom, with students, teachers, parents, and principals instead of waiting for the state or federal government to mandate changes,, so that necessary changes are implemented with teachers rather than imposed upon them. With this argument, the TRM becomes even more important, as school leaders and teams must work to create a social-emotional environment that fosters change, increases resources, and reduces unnecessary demands.

Moving Forward

Teacher turnover has been increasing for decades, eroding continuity in schools and districts, straining budgets, and, most critically, diminishing students' learning experiences and opportunities for a better tomorrow. This book set out to meet that challenge by introducing the TRM and equipping you with a practical blueprint for an **intentional retention system** (see Appendix A). Three pillars anchor that system:

1. **A clear model of teacher well-being**. By naming the physical, emotional, cognitive, and social energies that fuel great teaching, you gain a shared language for diagnosing stressors and celebrating strengths.
2. **Tools to collect useful data**. Flash surveys, interviews, energy audits, and data on working conditions transform perceptions into evidence, revealing where demands outstrip resources and where quick wins can be achieved.
3. **Processes for small-scale changes**. Improvement cycles of plan-do-study-act let you prototype solutions in weeks and not years, learn from your actions, and build momentum through visible results.

When these three elements work in concert, they create what Fullan (2025) calls *systemness*: a culture in which every adult, teacher, administrator, support staff, and central-office partner shares ownership in making the school a place where educators *choose* to stay. Your next step is to integrate the model, data tools, and rapid-change routines into everyday practice. Do that consistently, and teacher retention shifts from a chronic headache to a competitive advantage: a protective and energizing ecosystem so supportive that great teachers will not just arrive, they'll remain, thrive, and drive student success for years to come. It's time to start!

Leadership Considerations

- What is your biggest takeaway about well-being from this chapter?
- Which of the arguments about the importance of well-being most resonates with you? Why?
- After finishing the book, how do you now see the interaction of the Eight Key Ideas?

- Which drivers are most apparent in your school or district?
- How might you begin to shift away from the wrong drives and more toward the right drivers?
- How might the right drivers help retain more of your teachers?
- What is your plan to design your teacher retention blueprint?

References

Ahmed, N. U., & Malik, B. (2019). Impact of psychological empowerment on job performance of teachers: Mediating role of psychological well-being. *Review of Economics and Development Studies*. DOI: 10.26710/READS.V5I3.693

Bellet, C., De Neve, J. E., & Ward, G. (2023). Does employee happiness have an impact on productivity? *Management Science*, 70(3), 1656–1679. https://wellbeing.hmc.ox.ac.uk/publications/does-employee-happiness-have-an-impact-on-productivity-2/

Bleiberg, J., & Kraft, M. (2022). *What happened to the K-12 education labor market during COVID? The acute need for better data systems.* (EdWorkingPaper: 22-544). Annenberg Institute at Brown University: DOI: 10.26300/2xw0-v642

Collie, R. J. (2023). Teacher well-being and turnover intentions: Investigating the roles of job resources and job demands. *British Journal of Educational Psychology*, 93, 712–726. DOI: 10.1111/bjep.12587

DeNeve, J. E., & Ward, G. (2025). *Why workplace well-being matters: The science behind employee happiness and organizational performance.* Harvard Business Review Press.

Dobson, M. & Schnall, P. L. (2009). From stress to distress: The impact of work on mental health. In P.S. Schnall, M. Dobson & E. Rosskom (Eds.), *Unhealthy work: Causes, consequences, cures* (pp. 113–132). Baywood Publishing Company.

Dreer, B. (2023). On the outcomes of teacher well-being: A systematic review of research. *Frontiers in Psychology*, 14, 1205179. DOI: 10.1037/0022-0663.100.3.702

Fullan, M. (2021). The right drivers for whole system success. East Milbourne, Victoria: Centre for Strategic Education. https://www.cse.edu.au/leading-edu.ation-series-01/

Fullan, M. (2025). *The new meaning of educational change: Sixth edition.* Teachers College Press.

Granziera, H., Collie, R., & Martin, A. (2021). Understanding teacher well-being through job demands-resources theory. In Mansfield, C.F. (Ed.), *Cultivating teacher resilience*. Springer.

Jauregui, M., & Schnall, P. L. (2009). Work, psychosocial stressors, and the bottom line. In P.S. Schnall, M. Dobson & E. Rosskom (Eds.), *Unhealthy work: Causes, consequences, cures* (pp. 153–172). Baywood Publishing Company.

Judge, T. A., Thoresen, C. J., Bono, J. E., & Patton, G. K. (2001). The job satisfaction performance relationship: A qualitative and quantitative review. *Psychological Bulletin*, 127(3), 376–407. DOI: 10.1037/0033-2909.127.3.376

Kaiser, C., & Oswald, A. J. (2022). The scientific value of numerical measures of human feelings. *Proceedings of the National Academy of Sciences*, 119(42). DOI: 10.1073/pnas.2210412119

Klusmann, U., Kunter, M., Trautwein, U., Lüdtke, O., & Baumert, J. (2008). Teachers' occupational well-being and quality of instruction: The important role of self-regulatory patterns. *Journal of Educational Psychology*, 100, 702–715. DOI: 10.1037/0022-0663.100.3.702

Maslach, C., & Leiter, M. P. (2022). *The burnout challenge: Managing people's relationship with their job*. Harvard University Press.

Mazzetti, G., Robledo, E., Vignoli, M., & Topa, G. (2021). Work engagement: A meta-analysis using the job demands-resources model. *Psychological Reports*, 126(2), 1–38. DOI:10.1177/00332941211051988

Papanicolas, I., Cylus, J., & Lorenzoni, L. (2024). Cross-country comparisons in health price growth over time. *Health Services Research*, 1–10. DOI: 10.1111/1475-6773.14295

Singh, Y. K., & Gautman, D. (2024). The impact of job satisfaction of teacher mental health: A call to action for educational policymakers. *Open Education Studies*, 6, 20240008. DOI: 10.1515/edu-2024-0008

Sutcher, L., Darling-Hammond, L., & Carver-Thomas, D. (2016). *A coming crisis in teaching? Teacher supply, demand, and shortages in the U.S.* Palo Alto, CA: Learning Policy Institute. https://learningpolicyinstitute.org/product/coming-crisis-teaching

Viac, C., & Fraser, P. (2020). Teachers' well-being: A framework for data collection and analysis for PISA and TALIS. OECD Working Papers No. 213. www.oecd.org/content/dam/oecd/en.publications/reports/2020/01/teachers-well-being_bdafdeaf/c36fc9d3-en.pdf

Wang, H., & Hall, N. C. (2021). Exploring relations between teacher emotions, coping strategies, and intentions to quit: A longitudinal analysis. *Journal of School Psychology*, 86, 64–77. DOI: 10.1016/j.jsp.2021.03.005

Ward, G. (2024). *Workplace well-being and employee turnover*. Wellbeing Research Centre. University of Oxford Working Paper. https://wellbeing.hmc.ox.ac.uk/wp-content/uploads/2023/11/2304-WP-Workplace-Wellbeing-and-Firm-Performance-DOI-2024.pdf

Appendix A
Your Blueprint for Teacher Retention

School Name:	School Year:
Background data: How many teachers have resigned or are considering resigning this year? (Do not include retirees.)	What percentage of your entire teaching staff is that? # resigned/total # of teachers = turnover rate
3-year goal: By XXXX, we will have retained X% of our non-retiring teachers.	1-year goal: By the end of the XXXX school year, we will have retained X% of our non-retiring teachers.

Analysis Plan: Which diagnostic tool(s) do I want to use to understand possible root causes of turnover?

Use: Yes or No	Diagnostic Tool	When and How Administered
	Teacher well-being diagnostic	
	Personal-level diagnostic	
	Interpersonal-level diagnostic	
	Collective-level diagnostic	
	Collective skill diagnostic	
	Job demands and resources diagnostic	
	Stress diagnostic	

Data analysis: What does your data show? List three insights from the diagnostic(s) you used.

- <u>Insight 1</u>:
- <u>Insight 2</u>:
- <u>Insight 3</u>:

Appendix A

Strategies for Retention: Based on your data, which strategy do you want to focus on? Remember to start small to be more intentional. You can add more as you see an impact. After choosing, fill in your plan in the aligned strategy below.

- ☐ 1. Improve the adult social-emotional path.
- ☐ 2. Decrease demands.
- ☐ 3. Increase resources.

Strategy 1: Improve the Adult Social-Emotional Path.

Which level and skill do you want to improve?	What is your theory of action? We want to improve ————
☐ Personal level ————	———— to ————
☐ Interpersonal level ————	———— and retain more of our
☐ Collective level ————	teachers.
What is your plan to develop these skills as habits? Plan Do Study Act	

Strategy 2. Decrease Demands

Which area and demand(s) do you want to decrease?	What is your theory of action? We want to decrease ————
☐ Personal ————	———— to ————
☐ Classroom ————	———— and retain more of
☐ Workplace ————	our teachers.
What is your plan to remove this demand (or these demands)? Plan Do Study Act	

Appendix A

Strategy 3. Increase Resources

Which area and resources do you want to increase?	**What is your theory of action?**
❏ Personal ———————	We want to increase ———————
❏ Classroom ———————	——————— to ———————
❏ Workplace ———————	——————— and retain more of our teachers.
What is your plan to increase this resource (or these resources)? Plan Do Study Act	

Appendix B
Well-Being Diagnostic

Directions: Please rate the following questions about your personal well-being on a scale of 1 (strongly disagree) to 5 (strongly agree). When you finish, average each area and list the averages below to get a well-being profile.

	Strongly disagree	Disagree	Neutral	Agree	Strongly agree
1. Psychological and emotional well-being					
a. I have a clear sense of purpose in my role as an educator.	1	2	3	4	5
b. I can effectively manage my emotions in challenging classroom situations.	1	2	3	4	5
c. I recover quickly from stressful or discouraging situations at school.	1	2	3	4	5
d. I maintain a hopeful and positive outlook about my teaching career.	1	2	3	4	5
e. I rarely feel emotionally drained by my teaching responsibilities.	1	2	3	4	5
Average	Total/5=				

Appendix B

	Strongly disagree	Disagree	Neutral	Agree	Strongly agree
2. Social well-being					
a. I have supportive colleagues or mentors I can turn to for help or advice.	1	2	3	4	5
b. I feel a genuine sense of belonging in my school community.	1	2	3	4	5
c. I regularly engage in productive collaboration with my colleagues, school leaders, and students.	1	2	3	4	5
d. My contributions to the school environment are valued and acknowledged.	1	2	3	4	5
e. I rarely feel isolated or disconnected from others at work.	1	2	3	4	5
Average	Total/5=				
3. Cognitive well-being					
a. My teaching role provides me with sufficient intellectual challenge and growth.	1	2	3	4	5
b. I can maintain focus and clarity of thought when working with students.	1	2	3	4	5
c. I can easily handle the growing complexity of teaching tasks.	1	2	3	4	5
d. I actively seek out professional development opportunities to enhance my skills.	1	2	3	4	5

Appendix B

		Strongly disagree	Disagree	Neutral	Agree	Strongly agree
e.	I have no problem keeping up with new pedagogical methods, technologies, or curricula.	1	2	3	4	5

Average — Total/5=

4. Physical well-being

		Strongly disagree	Disagree	Neutral	Agree	Strongly agree
a.	I rarely experience physical symptoms (headaches, muscle tension, etc.) due to stress at work.	1	2	3	4	5
b.	I typically get sufficient rest to feel refreshed for my teaching duties.	1	2	3	4	5
c.	I can maintain healthy habits (e.g., balanced meals, short breaks, and exercise) throughout my workweek.	1	2	3	4	5
d.	My workload and physical environment at school support my overall physical health.	1	2	3	4	5
e.	I usually feel energetic when I am teaching.	1	2	3	4	5

Average — Total/5=

5. Overall energy levels

		Strongly disagree	Disagree	Neutral	Agree	Strongly agree
a.	I have enough mental energy to keep up with the cognitive requirements that I face as a teacher.	1	2	3	4	5

Appendix B

	Strongly disagree	Disagree	Neutral	Agree	Strongly agree
b. I feel I can maintain meaningful, supportive interactions with colleagues and students without feeling drained.	1	2	3	4	5
c. I can concentrate and remain mentally sharp throughout most of my teaching responsibilities.	1	2	3	4	5
d. I have sufficient physical energy to handle the demands of my teaching schedule.	1	2	3	4	5
e. I have enough emotional energy to cope with the daily challenges I face as a teacher.	1	2	3	4	5
Average	Total/5=				

My Well-Being Profile

1. Psychological and emotional well-being _____
2. Social well-being _____
3. Cognitive well-being _____
4. Physical well-being _____
5. Overall energy level _____

Appendix C
Personal-Level Diagnostic

Diagnostic directions: Please rate the following questions about your interpersonal skills on a scale of 1 (strongly disagree) to 5 (strongly agree). When you finish, average each area and list the averages below to get a profile of your personal strengths and needs.

Personal skill area	Strongly disagree	Disagree	Neutral	Agree	Strongly agree
1. Understanding my personality					
a. I have a clear understanding of my personal strengths.	1	2	3	4	5
b. I am aware of my personal areas for growth.	1	2	3	4	5
c. I actively reflect on how my personality traits affect my interactions with others.	1	2	3	4	5
d. I feel comfortable explaining my personality traits to others if asked.	1	2	3	4	5
e. I can adapt my behavior in different situations without losing my sense of self.	1	2	3	4	5
Average	Total/5=				

Appendix C

Personal skill area	Strongly disagree	Disagree	Neutral	Agree	Strongly agree
2. Breathing to reduce stress					
a. When I feel stressed, I consciously practice slow, deep breathing.	1	2	3	4	5
b. I notice a positive change in my stress level after engaging in mindful breathing.	1	2	3	4	5
c. I use breathing exercises to refocus when I am distracted or overwhelmed.	1	2	3	4	5
d. I believe that intentional breathing helps me remain calm in challenging situations.	1	2	3	4	5
e. I regularly include breathing techniques in my daily routine to maintain focus.	1	2	3	4	5
Average	Total/5=				
3. Acknowledging and labeling emotions					
a. I can identify what I am feeling in the moment without confusion.	1	2	3	4	5
b. I can accurately label my emotions (e.g., anger, excitement, and sadness).	1	2	3	4	5
c. I recognize when my emotions shift, and I can pinpoint the cause.	1	2	3	4	5
d. I understand how my emotions influence my thoughts and behaviors.	1	2	3	4	5

Appendix C

Personal skill area	Strongly disagree	Disagree	Neutral	Agree	Strongly agree
e. I communicate my emotions openly and appropriately.	1	2	3	4	5
Average	Total/5=				

4. Reflecting on social-emotional skills and events

	Strongly disagree	Disagree	Neutral	Agree	Strongly agree
a. I often review past interactions to understand my emotional responses.	1	2	3	4	5
b. I consider how others might have felt during emotional or social conflicts.	1	2	3	4	5
c. I try to learn from each emotional situation to improve my future reactions.	1	2	3	4	5
d. I seek feedback from trusted individuals about how I handled emotional events.	1	2	3	4	5
e. I apply lessons from past social-emotional challenges to new challenges.	1	2	3	4	5
Average	Total/5=				

5. Expressing gratitude

	Strongly disagree	Disagree	Neutral	Agree	Strongly agree
a. I regularly think about things I am grateful for.	1	2	3	4	5
b. I make an effort to thank people who have helped or supported me.	1	2	3	4	5
c. I pay attention to the positive aspects of my day, even if they are small.	1	2	3	4	5

Appendix C

Personal skill area	Strongly disagree	Disagree	Neutral	Agree	Strongly agree
d. I feel comfortable sharing my appreciation with others.	1	2	3	4	5
e. I believe that expressing gratitude strengthens my relationships and personal well-being.	1	2	3	4	5
Average	Total/5=				

My Personal-Level Profile

1. **Understanding my personality** _____
2. **Breathing to reduce stress** _____
3. **Acknowledging and labeling emotions** _____
4. **Reflecting on social-emotional skills and events** _____
5. **Expressing gratitude** _____

Appendix D
Interpersonal-Level Diagnostic

Diagnostic directions: Please rate the following questions about your interpersonal skills on a scale of 1 (strongly disagree) to 5 (strongly agree). When you finish, average each area and list the averages below to get a profile of your interpersonal strengths and needs.

Interpersonal skill area	Strongly Disagree	Disagree	Neutral	Agree	Strongly Agree
1. Self-awareness- mindfulness					
a. I intentionally pause to notice my thoughts and feelings throughout the school day.	1	2	3	4	5
b. I find myself focusing on what is happening in the present moment rather than worrying about past or future events.	1	2	3	4	5
c. I practice mindfulness techniques (e.g., deep breathing and grounding exercises) to calm myself when feeling stressed.	1	2	3	4	5

Appendix D

Interpersonal skill area	Strongly Disagree	Disagree	Neutral	Agree	Strongly Agree
d. I am aware of how my emotional state affects my interactions with students and colleagues.	1	2	3	4	5
e. I consciously direct my attention to the "here and now" during class activities.	1	2	3	4	5
Average	Total/5=				

2. Self-management- emotional regulation

	Strongly Disagree	Disagree	Neutral	Agree	Strongly Agree
a. I usually remain calm and composed during challenging class or work situations without letting my emotions take over.	1	2	3	4	5
b. I take a moment to pause before reacting when I experience strong emotions at work.	1	2	3	4	5
c. I recover quickly after feeling upset or frustrated, returning to a productive mindset.	1	2	3	4	5
d. I usually maintain patience and composure, even when colleagues or students exhibit challenging behaviors.	1	2	3	4	5
e. I use coping strategies (such as reframing or deep breathing) to manage stress throughout the day.	1	2	3	4	5

Appendix D

Interpersonal skill area	Strongly Disagree	Disagree	Neutral	Agree	Strongly Agree
Average	Total/5=				

3. Social awareness- positive communication

a. I make a point to greet my colleagues and students individually each day in a warm and welcoming manner.	1	2	3	4	5
b. I regularly ask open-ended questions that encourage others to share their thoughts.	1	2	3	4	5
c. I offer specific, sincere compliments to recognize students' or colleagues' efforts and achievements.	1	2	3	4	5
d. I frequently use positive, supportive language to motivate and inspire students and colleagues to keep trying.	1	2	3	4	5
e. I share struggles or lessons learned from my own experience to support others.	1	2	3	4	5
Average	Total/5=				

4. Relationship skills- relational energy

a. I typically convey enthusiasm and positivity in my interactions with colleagues and students.	1	2	3	4	5

Appendix D

Interpersonal skill area	Strongly Disagree	Disagree	Neutral	Agree	Strongly Agree
b. I listen attentively when others share their perspectives or concerns.	1	2	3	4	5
c. I actively seek to understand others' emotional needs and backgrounds.	1	2	3	4	5
d. My presence and attitude help others feel energized and inspired.	1	2	3	4	5
e. I make an effort to support the social and emotional well-being of those around me.	1	2	3	4	5
Average	Total/5=				

5. Responsible decision-making- psychological flexibility

	Strongly Disagree	Disagree	Neutral	Agree	Strongly Agree
a. I am willing to adapt when new information or data suggests it is necessary.	1	2	3	4	5
b. I am comfortable acknowledging my mistakes and adjusting my approach accordingly.	1	2	3	4	5
c. I consider multiple perspectives before making important decisions.	1	2	3	4	5
d. I can hold conflicting viewpoints or emotions at the same time without feeling overwhelmed.	1	2	3	4	5

Interpersonal skill area	Strongly Disagree	Disagree	Neutral	Agree	Strongly Agree
e. I view mistakes as opportunities for growth and use them to inform my future choices.	1	2	3	4	5
Average	Total/5=				

Interpersonal Profile (enter your average scores below)

Self-awareness- mindfulness _____
Self-management- emotional regulation _____
Social-awareness- positive communication _____
Relationship skills- relational energy _____
Responsible decision-making- psychological flexibility _____

Appendix E
Collective-Level Diagnostic

Below are two different diagnostic tools. The first is for school and team leaders to rate their specific skill level on the advanced skills at the collective level. Individuals should review their results to identify their strengths and areas for growth. The school faculty and staff can use the second diagnostic to assess the collective affective states influencing them. These results should be aggregated to find common and agreed-upon areas of strength and opportunities for improvement.

Advanced Collective Skill Diagnostic

Diagnostic Directions: Please rate the following questions about your skills in developing and supporting collective affective states on a scale of 1 (strongly disagree) to 5 (strongly agree). When you finish, average each area and list the averages below to get a profile of your advanced skill strengths and needs.

Collective Skill Area	Strongly Disagree	Disagree	Neutral	Agree	Strongly Agree
1. Empowerment					
a. I actively include team members in decisions that affect their work or students.	1	2	3	4	5
b. I encourage team members to take initiative and explore creative solutions independently.	1	2	3	4	5

Collective Skill Area	Strongly Disagree	Disagree	Neutral	Agree	Strongly Agree
c. I ensure that staff have the necessary resources (e.g., time, materials, and professional support) to carry out their responsibilities effectively.	1	2	3	4	5
d. I communicate trust in staff members' judgment and allow them latitude in how they meet goals.	1	2	3	4	5
e. I regularly acknowledge and celebrate individuals' and teams' successes and contributions.	1	2	3	4	5
Average	Total/5=				
2. Creating mastery experiences					
a. I provide regular, targeted feedback to help staff and teams reflect on and refine their skills.	1	2	3	4	5
b. I create opportunities for staff to experience small wins that build confidence.	1	2	3	4	5
c. I advocate for team processes that allow for learning from their efforts.	1	2	3	4	5
d. I encourage staff to reflect on their progress, identify successes, and plan next steps for improvement.	1	2	3	4	5
e. I deliberately assign tasks and responsibilities that stretch staff members' abilities without overwhelming them.	1	2	3	4	5
Average	Total/5=				

Appendix E

Collective Skill Area	Strongly Disagree	Disagree	Neutral	Agree	Strongly Agree
3. Reinforcing meaning					
a. I regularly communicate how our daily work connects to our school's vision and mission.	1	2	3	4	5
b. I help staff see the positive impact that their work has on students' academic and personal growth.	1	2	3	4	5
c. I encourage staff to share moments or stories that highlight the significance of their work.	1	2	3	4	5
d. I explicitly link routine tasks to broader school goals and values.	1	2	3	4	5
e. I acknowledge and celebrate the way that staff contributions serve the greater good of our school community and education as a whole.	1	2	3	4	5
Average	Total/5=				
4. Reframing & reappraising					
a. When setbacks occur, I guide individuals or teams to view them as learning opportunities rather than failures.	1	2	3	4	5
b. I encourage staff to see unexpected changes as chances for professional and personal growth.	1	2	3	4	5

Collective Skill Area	Strongly Disagree	Disagree	Neutral	Agree	Strongly Agree
c. I help staff reframe stressful situations by focusing on potential solutions and positive outcomes.	1	2	3	4	5
d. I openly address challenges, facilitating a supportive environment for collective problem-solving.	1	2	3	4	5
e. I model calm, constructive responses to difficulties, demonstrating healthy reappraisal strategies.	1	2	3	4	5
Average	Total/5=				

Advanced Skill Profile

1. **Empowerment** _____
2. **Creating mastery experiences** _____
3. **Reinforcing meaning** _____
4. **Reframing & reappraising** _____

Collective Affective State Diagnostic

Diagnostic directions: Please rate the following questions about your perceptions of our school's important collective affective states on a scale of 1 (strongly disagree) to 5 (strongly agree). When you finish, average each area to create a profile of the collective affective states in your school, highlighting their strengths and needs.

Appendix E

Collective Affective State Areas	Strongly Disagree	Disagree	Neutral	Agree	Strongly Agree
1. Trust					
a. I feel my colleagues consistently follow through on their commitments at this school.	1	2	3	4	5
b. My colleagues and I share information openly and honestly.	1	2	3	4	5
c. If I face a challenge, I can count on my colleagues to offer help without judgment.	1	2	3	4	5
d. I believe my colleagues have the skills and knowledge to do their jobs effectively.	1	2	3	4	5
e. I trust my colleagues' actions align with our school's values and mission.	1	2	3	4	5
Average	Total/5=				
2. Collective efficacy					
a. Teachers in this school feel confident that together we can overcome most instructional challenges.	1	2	3	4	5
b. We work as a team to find effective solutions for student learning or behavior issues.	1	2	3	4	5

Appendix E

Collective Affective State Areas	Strongly Disagree	Disagree	Neutral	Agree	Strongly Agree
c. There is a shared belief here that our teaching can make a real difference in student outcomes.	1	2	3	4	5
d. Teachers in this school take collective responsibility for each student's success.	1	2	3	4	5
e. When facing new challenges, we believe we can find or develop the resources needed to succeed.	1	2	3	4	5
Average	Total/5=				

3. Job satisfaction

	Strongly Disagree	Disagree	Neutral	Agree	Strongly Agree
a. Overall, I find my work at this school to be personally fulfilling.	1	2	3	4	5
b. I am satisfied with the resources and support provided for my teaching.	1	2	3	4	5
c. I have access to meaningful professional development and feel encouraged to grow.	1	2	3	4	5
d. I feel recognized and appreciated for my contributions.	1	2	3	4	5
e. I would recommend this school as a good place to work to other educators.	1	2	3	4	5
Average	Total/5=				

Appendix E

Collective Affective State Areas	Strongly Disagree	Disagree	Neutral	Agree	Strongly Agree
4. Recovering from stress (resilience)					
a. Our staff openly discusses healthy ways to manage stress and supports each other in doing so.	1	2	3	4	5
b. When unexpected challenges arise, we adapt quickly and effectively as a team.	1	2	3	4	5
c. Staff here generally maintain a sense of hope and optimism, even during difficult times.	1	2	3	4	5
d. In this school, people look out for one another's well-being and mental health.	1	2	3	4	5
e. We regularly reflect on challenging experiences to improve our practices and grow stronger.	1	2	3	4	5
Average	Total/5=				

Collective Affective States Profile

1. **Trust** _____
2. **Collective efficacy** _____
3. **Job satisfaction** _____
4. **Recovering from stress** _____

Appendix F
The Habit Formation Guide

Fogg (2019) describes how many of our attempts to change our behaviors stem from having a flawed approach to developing behavioral changes. Information alone does not change behaviors, but having a solid process to try and practice these new behaviors over time does. The following is a brief guide based on the science of habit formation, utilizing three simple steps.

A Simple Model for Creating Habits (based on Fogg, 2019 and Clear, 2018)

1. **Cues**: Choose a simple way to remind yourself to engage in the action you want to take.
   - Use an existing routine to act as a reminder, like the start of a meeting.
   - Choose a typical space where the routine occurs, like staff or professional learning community (PLC) meetings.
   - Use physical reminders, such as notes placed in a visible location, like the Habit Development Plan (Appendix G).

2. **Action**: Execute the new behavior you want to establish.
   - Choose a skill and its associated practice based on your diagnostics.
   - Focus on one or two steps to master at a time.
   - Follow the practice steps specifically and adjust them as they feel more comfortable.

3. **Reward**: Celebrate to create a positive emotion to reinforce the new behavior.
   - Choose a small action to celebrate after the behavior.
   - Combine a physical and verbal action to complement each other.

Example Habit Formula
1. **Cue**
   - Before the start of our PLC meeting, as part of the opening
   - Refer to my Habit Plan.

2. **Action**
   - Personal skill: Breathing
   - Use box breathing for 1 minute.

3. **Reward**
   - Pump my fist and say "Yes".

Appendix G
Habit Development Plan

(Based on Fogg, 2019 & Clear, 2018)

Habit level:	Specific skill/Practice to develop:
☐ Personal ☐ Interpersonal ☐ Collective	

Fill in this small table to design your behavior change.

Start date	Cue: What routine and space will I hook the practice to?	Action: Skill: Practice:	Reward: What will I do to celebrate my use of the behavior?
	1.	1.	
	2.	2.	
	3.	3.	
	4.	4.	
		5.	

Appendix G

Fill in this chart as you practice the behavior.

Date	Did I use the anchor moment? (Yes or No)	What step of the practice will I focus on today?	Did I celebrate my use of the practice?

Appendix H
Social-Emotional Walk-Through Protocol

To gain a clear understanding of the emotional climate in your school, you or a team can adopt an anthropological approach, gathering observations about adult interactions using the familiar walk-through structure outlined here, which incorporates PDSA (plan, do, study, act) cycles. Instead of focusing on classroom instruction, you'll watch for emotional cues, such as tone of voice, body language, or how people support each other. This process helps everyone become more aware of emotional dynamics and share responsibility for creating a supportive environment.

Purpose
1. Observe and reflect on how emotions are expressed and managed in adult spaces, such as staff meetings, professional learning communities (PLCs), the staff lounge, or classrooms.
2. Identify patterns or areas where stress or tension appears to be highest.
3. Reveal details about your school's climate that might not appear in surveys.

Plan: Preparing for the walk-through
1. **Define a focus**.
    - Decide which social-emotional elements you want to observe (e.g., in interpersonal interactions, the tone of voice, facial expressions, or types of supportive language).
    - Clarify what each element might look or sound like, so everyone is on the same page.

Appendix H

2. **Create an observation tool**.
   - Develop a simple checklist or notes form to track what you see.
   - For instance, you might list categories such as "emotions displayed," "words used," "body language," and "how conflicts are handled."

3. **Form a team**.
   - Invite a small group of teachers and staff to join you.
   - Different perspectives help capture a broader picture.

Do: Process for the walk-through

1. **Set norms and expectations**.
   - Begin with a short meeting to explain the purpose: You're gathering information, not judging anyone's performance.

2. **Set a schedule**.
   - Plan your observations at different times of the day and in various spaces (e.g., classrooms, meeting rooms, staff lounge, or office).

3. **Document observations**.
   - Use your observation tool to write down specific examples of emotional interactions.
   - Note details like who was involved, what happened, and how people responded.
   - Example notes: "Teacher appeared visibly frustrated during a correction" or "During a PLC meeting, teachers used paraphrasing to understand each other."

Study: Reflection and analysis of the data

1. **Debrief the observations**.
   - Bring the observers together to share what they have noted without judgment or analysis.

2. **Analyze the findings**.
   - Ask guiding questions.
     - What common emotions and stressors did you see?
     - What patterns emerged?
     - Were there certain times or spaces more positive or stressful?
     - What social-emotional skills stood out?
     - Which areas need more attention?
3. **Map the findings**.
   - Organize your observations into categories such as strengths, challenges, noticeable skills, or places needing improvement.
4. **Share the findings**.
   - Present the results to the school community and invite ideas for how to address any concerns.

Act: Follow-up actions

1. **Create an action plan**.
   - Use your observational data to decide next steps, such as training staff in specific emotional skills or providing extra support in high-stress areas.
2. **Track progress**.
   - Repeat the walk-throughs after a month or two to assess whether the changes are effective and make adjustments as needed.
3. **Celebrate successes**.
   - Recognize and acknowledge the positive changes in your school's social-emotional climate.

Appendix I
The Job Demands and Resources Diagnostic for Schools

Part 1: Demands

Diagnostic directions: Demands refer to the factors that require the teacher's energy and time. Please rate the following questions in the three categories of demands on a scale of 1 (very low) to 5 (very high). When you finish, average each category to get a profile of your perceived demands and add any thoughts in the open-ended questions.

Personal demands: In general, how demanding on your time and energy is each of the following currently:	Very low 1	Low 2	Neutral 3	High 4	Very high 5
a. Managing my time to get everything done at work and home	1	2	3	4	5
b. Caring for my personal health	1	2	3	4	5
c. Trying to balance my work, family, and personal life	1	2	3	4	5
d. Doing all of the household chores	1	2	3	4	5

Personal demands: *In general, how demanding on your time and energy is each of the following currently:*	Very low 1	Low 2	Neutral 3	High 4	Very high 5
e. Conflicts over work and family	1	2	3	4	5
f. Childcare issues	1	2	3	4	5
g. Taking care of older parents	1	2	3	4	5
Average	Total/ 6=				
Which areas did you mark as the highest demands on your time and energy? Do you have other personal demands that significantly impact your time and energy?					

Classroom demands: *In general, how demanding on your time and energy is each of the following currently:*	Very low 1	Low 2	Neutral 3	High 4	Very high 5
a. Following required pacing guides or assessment schedules	1	2	3	4	5
b. The requirements to use a specific curriculum or instructional model	1	2	3	4	5
c. Pressure to have my students do well on state or district tests	1	2	3	4	5
d. Student behavior in my classroom	1	2	3	4	5
e. Student motivation and engagement in my classroom	1	2	3	4	5
f. The diversity of student learning needs in my classroom	1	2	3	4	5

Appendix I

Classroom demands: In general, how demanding on your time and energy is each of the following currently:	Very low	Low	Neutral	High	Very high
	1	2	3	4	5
g. The emotional aspects of teaching	1	2	3	4	5
h. All of the thinking and cognitive demands that go with teaching	1	2	3	4	5
i. The number of digital tools and platforms I am required to use	1	2	3	4	5
j. The need to find or create materials for students	1	2	3	4	5
Average	Total/ 10=				

Which areas did you mark as the highest demands on your time and energy?

Do you have other classroom demands that significantly impact your time and energy?

Workplace demands: In general, how demanding on your time and energy is each of the following currently:	Very low	Low	Neutral	High	Very high
	1	2	3	4	5
a. The overall workload and time required for my job	1	2	3	4	5
b. The number of changes we are trying to implement	1	2	3	4	5
c. The pace of the changes we are going through	1	2	3	4	5
d. Parental demands or conflicts	1	2	3	4	5

Workplace demands: In general, how demanding on your time and energy is each of the following currently:	Very low 1	Low 2	Neutral 3	High 4	Very high 5
e. Demands put on me by school leadership	1	2	3	4	5
f. The number and frequency of meetings	1	2	3	4	5
g. Interpersonal conflicts with colleagues	1	2	3	4	5
h. Schoolwide behavior issues	1	2	3	4	5
i. Other duties assigned to me (committees, clubs, lunch, etc.)	1	2	3	4	5
j. Required forms and paperwork	1	2	3	4	5
k. Professional development time	1	2	3	4	5
Average	Total/10=				

Which areas did you mark as the highest demands on your time and energy? Do you have other workplace demands that significantly impact your time and energy?	

Summary: Which demands were the highest in each category?

Personal:
Classroom:
Workplace:
What other demand ideas should be considered?

Appendix I

Part 2: Resources

Diagnostic directions: Resources are the tools, supports, or working conditions that can help you perform your job more effectively or provide extra energy and time. Please rate the following questions about the perceived need for resources in the three categories on a scale of 1 (very low) to 5 (very high). When you finish, average each category to get a profile of the perceived need for resources and add any thoughts in the open-ended questions.

Personal resources: In general, how much need is there to increase this resource to help your time and energy?	Very low 1	Low 2	Neutral 3	High 4	Very high 5
a. Health prevention routines	1	2	3	4	5
b. Social and emotional coping skills	1	2	3	4	5
c. A better balance between work and home	1	2	3	4	5
d. My own agency and self-efficacy	1	2	3	4	5
e. A better balance of childcare or household chores	1	2	3	4	5
f. An ability to reappraise situations for the positive	1	2	3	4	5
Average	Total/ 6=				

Which areas did you mark as the highest resource needs to enhance your time and energy?

Do you have other personal resource ideas that could significantly enhance your time and energy?

Appendix I

Classroom resources: In general, how much need is there to increase this resource to help your time and energy?	Very low 1	Low 2	Neutral 3	High 4	Very high 5
a. Better relationships with students	1	2	3	4	5
b. My own social-emotional skills in the classroom	1	2	3	4	5
c. Engaging instruction	1	2	3	4	5
d. Specialized resources and materials that address different learning needs	1	2	3	4	5
e. More in-class help	1	2	3	4	5
f. More support for classroom discipline	1	2	3	4	5
g. Responsive technology support and training	1	2	3	4	5
h. Responsive instructional support	1	2	3	4	5
i. Increased autonomy	1	2	3	4	5
Average	Total/ 10=				

Which areas did you mark as the highest resource needs to enhance your time and energy?

Do you have other classroom resource ideas that could significantly enhance your time and energy?

Workplace resources: In general, how much need is there to increase this resource to help your time and energy?	Very low 1	Low 2	Neutral 3	High 4	Very high 5
a. Supportive and engaged leadership	1	2	3	4	5
b. An effective team to help solve problems and improve learning	1	2	3	4	5

229

Appendix I

Workplace resources: In general, how much need is there to increase this resource to help your time and energy?	Very low 1	Low 2	Neutral 3	High 4	Very high 5
c. Control of my classroom teaching and time	1	2	3	4	5
d. The ability to participate in decisions that affect me and my classrooms	1	2	3	4	5
e. Colleagues who are willing to discuss not only student behavior but teaching and learning	1	2	3	4	5
f. Continual reminders of our purpose and goals as a school	1	2	3	4	5
g. More teacher-led professional development based on our needs	1	2	3	4	5
h. More performance feedback	1	2	3	4	5
i. A consistent and multi-year focus	1	2	3	4	5
j. Trust between all stakeholders	1	2	3	4	5
Average	Total/10=				

Which areas did you mark as the highest resource needs to enhance your time and energy?

Do you have other workplace resource ideas that could significantly enhance your time and energy?

Appendix I

Summary: Which resources were the highest in each category?

Personal:
Classroom:
Workplace:
What other resource ideas have potential?

Appendix J
PDSA Planning Template

Directions: Use this template to create cycles of inquiry for reducing demand or increasing resources.

Our **overall aim**: Our overall aim is to increase/decrease teachers' _____

by _____

by (date) _____
_____.

The **purpose** of this cycle of inquiry is to
☐ Reduce a demand: _____

☐ Increase a resource: _____

☐ Cycle 1
☐ Cycle 2
☐ Cycle 3
☐ Cycle 4
☐ Cycle 5

Our **theory of action** is that if we reduce/increase _____, then we can improve teachers' _____

because _____
_____

Cycle timing: This cycle will run between _____ _____ and _____ _____.

PDSA

Plan

1. Which demand/resource will we focus on for this cycle? What will we actually do?
2. What type of reduction/increase is needed? Why?
3. What is our prediction about what will happen if we reduce/increase this?
4. Do we predict any impact on student outcomes if we make this reduction/increase? Why?
5. What data should we collect to determine if the reduction/increase is impacting stress and energy?
6. What steps must we take to make this reduction/increase happen? Consider
   - Communication to staff
   - Exact expectations for reduction/increase
   - Timeline
   - Data collection
   - Identifying other impacts
   - Other?

Do

1. What will the execution of the plan look like in practice?
2. How will we communicate the plan and expectations to staff?
3. How will we know the plan and expectations for reduction/increase are being followed?

Appendix J

4. How will we collect and store the data we are collecting?
5. How can we attune ourselves to any unexpected impacts?

Study

1. What is the best way to analyze and display these data? Average, by week?
2. Was our prediction correct or not? Why?
3. What did we learn from our change idea?
4. Were there any unintended consequences because of the reduction? How do you know?

Act

1. What should we decide (adopt, adapt, abandon) about our idea?
2. What is our next step toward reducing/increasing?

Appendix K
Developing a Theory of Action for District Support

Supporting the Development of Adult Social-Emotional Skills

1. **Identify the Adult Social-Emotional Problem in the School/District.**

a. Describe a situation that embodies core concerns about the social-emotional climate.	b. Review the evidence and diagnostic data from the schools.	c. Define the specific problem (e.g., most schools show that stress is too high or that trust is too low).	d. Explain the logic between the problem and teacher turnover (e.g., teachers tend to leave when they don't feel trust).

2. **Determine the Conditions Affecting the Problem.**

	District level	Principal level	(Start here and work to the left) Teacher level
The experiences, policies, or practices that may be affecting the problem	How might district leadership or departments be contributing to the problem for leaders or teachers?	How might principals be contributing to the problem for teachers?	How might teachers be perceiving the problem?

Appendix K

	District level	Principal level	(Start here and work to the left) Teacher level
Changes needed	What needs to change in district leadership and departmental roles and functions to support principals and teachers?	What needs to change in principal practice to better support teacher social-emotional climate?	What needs to change for teachers?

3. Go deeper to Find More Specific Problems of Practice.

	District level	Principal level	(Start here and work to the left) Teacher level
Specific changes needed	What specifically do district leaders, departments, and others need to do to support principals and schools? Why? What supports will they need?	What aspects of principal leadership do we need to support to support the adult social-emotional climate? What specifically do we need principals to do differently? Why? What supports will principals need to develop these skills or practices?	Why are we prioritizing this level?

236

4. Develop a More Complete Theory of Action.

If district leadership and departments ...	Then principals will be able to ...	So that teachers develop more ... and choose to stay.

5. Plan for Action Steps.

	District level	Principal level	Teacher level
Necessary supports and resources needed at each level			
Evidence needed to collect to determine success or adjustments			

Supporting the Removal of Demands

1. Determine perceptions around excess demands (principal version).

	What requests, requirements, or processes do principals perceive as excessive?	Who does this perceived excessive demand most impact? (Principals, building staff, teachers?)	Might there be any unintended consequences if we remove this demand?
District or charter management organization (CMO) department			
Superintendent **Human resources department** **Teaching and learning department** - **Special education**			

Appendix K

District or charter management organization (CMO) department	What requests, requirements, or processes do principals perceive as excessive?	Who does this perceived excessive demand most impact? (Principals, building staff, teachers?)	Might there be any unintended consequences if we remove this demand?

Technology department
Principal supervisor
Operations
  - **Business**
  - **Facilities**
  - **Food service**
  - **Transportation**
  - **Other?**			

1a. Determine perceptions around excess demands (district leadership and department version).

District or CMO Department	Of all requests, requirements, or processes required for schools, school leaders, teachers and other school personnel, which do you or your department perceive as taking the most time and effort?	Who does this perceived excessive demand most impact? (Principals, building staff, teachers?)	Could this demand be reduced or removed? Might there be any unintended consequences if we remove this demand?

2. **Compare results and how this may decrease the demands on schools, school leaders, and teachers.**
3. **Determine which demands may be most feasible to reduce.**

District or CMO Department	Principal suggestions	District leadership and department suggestions	Which suggestions have most potential to remove demands on schools, school leaders, teachers, or other personnel? Is removal feasible?

4. **Use short PDSA (plan-do-study-act) cycles to determine the impact of removing these demands.**

The Plan phase of reducing demands for schools

Steps	Questions to consider
1. Prepare your department to reduce demands	1. How might I explain what reducing demands may do for schools, leaders and teachers?
2. Predict the impact of reducing the demand	2. What is our prediction about what will happen if we reduce that demand?
3. Decide on the type of reduction-remove, reduce, re-engineer, or replace (Hamilton et al., 2023).	3. What type of reduction is needed for this demand? Why?
4. Determine if there may be any impact on other important outcomes or legal requirements when the reduction happens.	4. Do we predict any impact on student outcomes if we make this reduction? Why?
5. Determine how you will measure the impact on schools, school leaders, and teachers	5. How will we know the impact on school, school leaders and teacher stress and energy if we make the reduction?

Appendix K

Steps	Questions to consider
6. Create an action plan for communication of reduction and what this will look for staff	6. What steps must we take to make this reduction happen? Consider • Communication to staff • Exact expectations for reduction • Timeline • Data collection • Identifying other impacts • Other?

The Do phase of reducing demands for schools

Steps	Questions to consider
1. Communicate the plan and expectations to your staff and schools on the reduction.	1. How will we communicate the plan and expectations to staff and schools?
2. Carry out the plan.	2. How will we know the plan and expectations for reduction are being done?
3. Collect the practical measurement data.	3. How will we collect and store the data we are collecting?
4. Observe and note anything unexpected.	4. How can we attune ourselves to any unexpected impacts?

The Study phase of reducing demands for schools

Steps	Questions to consider
1. Collate and analyze the data collected.	1. What is the best way to analyze and display these data? Average, by week?
2. Compare the results to your predictions.	2. Was our prediction correct or not? Why?
3. Determine what was learned from your change idea.	3. What did we learn from our change idea?
4. Determine if there were any unintended consequences because of the reduction.	4. Were there any unintended consequences because of the reduction? How do you know?

Appendix K

The Act phase of reducing demands for schools

Steps	Questions to consider
1. Discuss if you want to adopt the reduction in full and move to another reduction idea, adapt or modify the reduction idea, or abandon the reduction and focus somewhere else.	1. What should we decide?
2. Begin the plan phase again.	2. What is our next step?

 ## Supporting the Increase of Resources

1. Determine Perceptions Around Needed Resources (Principal Version).

1. Based on your diagnostic, which resource areas require the most support?	2. Beyond the diagnostic, what other evidence supports these resource needs?	3. What might this resource support look like if it were provided by the district?

1a. Determine perceptions around resource availability (district leadership and department version).

	What resource area do you believe schools (s) most need support in?	What evidence supports these resource needs?	What skills, programs, tools, or practices do you have now that help support this resource need?
			What skills, tools, or practices might you need to develop to support this resource need?
You personally			
Your department and team			

241

Appendix K

2. **Compare perceptions and ways to increase resources for schools, school leaders, and teachers**.
3. **Determine which resources may be most feasible to increase**.

Resource areas most in need of support	Principal ideas for resource support	District leadership and department ideas for resource support	Which suggestions have the most potential to increase resources for schools, school leaders, teachers, or other personnel? Is adding this resource feasible?

4. **Utilize short PDSA cycles to assess the impact of increasing resources, led by district leaders and department heads**.

The Plan phase of increasing resources for schools

Steps	Questions to consider
1. Prepare your department to increase resources.	1. How might I explain what increasing resources may do for schools, leaders and teachers?
2. Predict the impact of increasing resources.	2. What is our prediction about what will happen if we increase that resource?
3. Decide on the type of resource increase: refine, reconstruct, reculture, or reconnect (Hamilton et al., 2023).	3. What type of increase is needed for this resource? Why?
4. Determine if there may be any impact on other important outcomes or legal requirements when the increase happens.	4. Do we predict any impact on student outcomes if we make this increase? Why?
5. Determine how you will measure the impact on schools, school leaders, and teachers.	5. How will we know the impact on school, school leaders and teacher stress and energy if we make the increase?

Appendix K

Steps	Questions to consider
6. Create an action plan for the communication of resource increase and what this will look like for staff.	6. What steps must we take to make this increase happen? Consider • Communication to staff • Exact expectations for reduction • Timeline • Data collection • Identifying other impacts • Other?

The Do phase of increasing resources for schools

Steps	Questions to consider
1. Communicate the plan and expectations to your staff and schools on the reduction.	1. How will we communicate the plan and expectations to staff and schools?
2. Carry out the plan.	2. How will we know the plan and expectations for the increase are being done?
3. Collect the practical measurement data.	3. How will we collect and store the data we are collecting?
4. Observe and note anything unexpected.	4. How can we attune ourselves to any unexpected impacts?

The Study phase of increasing resources for schools

Steps	Questions to consider
1. Collate and analyze the data collected.	1. What is the best way to analyze and display these data? Average, by week?
2. Compare the results to your predictions.	2. Was our prediction correct or not? Why?
3. Determine what was learned from your change idea.	3. What did we learn from our change idea?
4. Determine if there were any unintended consequences because of the reduction.	4. Were there any unintended consequences because of the increase? How do you know?

The Act phase of increasing resources for schools

Steps	Questions to consider
1. Discuss if you want to adopt the increase in full and move to another idea, adapt or modify the increase idea, or abandon the increase and focus somewhere else.	1. What should we decide?
2. Begin the plan phase again.	2. What is our next step?

For Product Safety Concerns and Information please contact our EU
representative GPSR@taylorandfrancis.com
Taylor & Francis Verlag GmbH, Kaufingerstraße 24, 80331 München, Germany

www.ingramcontent.com/pod-product-compliance
Lightning Source LLC
Chambersburg PA
CBHW070245230426
43664CB00014B/2411